Safeguarding Babies and Very Young Children from Abuse and Neglect

Safeguarding Children Across Services
Series editors: Carolyn Davies and Harriet Ward

Safeguarding children from abuse is of paramount importance. This series communicates messages for practice from an extensive government-funded research programme designed to improve early recognition of child abuse as well as service responses and interventions. The series addresses a range of forms of abuse, including emotional and physical abuse and neglect, and outlines strategies for effective interagency collaboration, successful intervention and best practice. Titles in the series will be essential reading for practitioners with responsibility for safeguarding children.

Carolyn Davies is Research Advisor at the Thomas Coram Research Unit at the Institute of Education, University of London.

Harriet Ward is Director of the Centre for Child and Family Research and Research Professor at Loughborough University.

Safeguarding Babies and Very Young Children from Abuse and Neglect

*Harriet Ward, Rebecca Brown
and David Westlake*

Jessica Kingsley *Publishers*
London and Philadelphia

First published in 2012
by Jessica Kingsley Publishers
116 Pentonville Road
London N1 9JB, UK
and
400 Market Street, Suite 400
Philadelphia, PA 19106, USA

www.jkp.com

Library of Congress Cataloging in Publication Data
A CIP catalog record for this book is available from the Library of Congress

British Library Cataloguing in Publication Data
A CIP catalogue record for this book is available from the British Library

ISBN 978 1 84905 237 5
eISBN 978 0 85700 481 9

Printed and bound in Great Britain

Contents

List of Tables and Figures

Acknowledgements

This book is based on the findings from a study funded by the Department for Children, Schools and Families (now Department for Education). The project has greatly benefited by the wise counsel and expertise of our advisory group: Richard Bartholomew, Sarah Byford, Helen Chambers, Isabella Craig, Carolyn Davies, Elaine Dibben, Jenny Gray, Helen Jones, David Quinton, Marjorie Smith, Caroline Thomas, Matt Walker and Julie Wilkinson. We are very grateful for the time and effort they put into this.

We would also like to thank Emily Munro, who led the early stages of the study, Jenny Blackmore and Doug Lawson for their invaluable work on data collection, and Sharon Slater for her continuing help and support. We would also like to acknowledge the advice and assistance of our colleagues at the Centre for Child and Family Research, in particular Suzanne Dexter and Harriet Lowe for their input to format and produce the final version of the book.

The authors are particularly grateful to the ten local authorities that took part in the study, and all the professionals who found time to participate, despite heavy workloads. We would especially like to thank the birth parents, relatives and carers who allowed us access to information and agreed to be interviewed. We recognize that recounting often difficult and emotional experiences was not easy, and we greatly appreciate their involvement, which has substantially enhanced the value of the research.

Note on Initial Assessments, Core Assessments and Section 47 Enquiries

The procedures to be followed by practitioners and front-line managers who have particular responsibilities for safeguarding and promoting the welfare of children in England and Wales are set out in two volumes of guidance: the *Framework for the Assessment of Children in Need and their Families* (Department of Health, Department for Education and Employment and the Home Office 2000) and *Working Together to Safeguard Children* (HM Government 2010).

Following a referral to children's social care, the local authority is required to consider 'whether there are concerns about impairment to the child's health and development or the child suffering harm which justifies an *initial assessment* to establish whether this child is a child in need' (HM Government 2010, para 5.34).

An *initial assessment* should be completed by local authority children's social care, working with colleagues, within a maximum of ten working days of the date of referral, to determine whether: the child is in need; there is reasonable cause to suspect the child is suffering, or is likely to suffer, significant harm; the services and types of services required, and whether a further, more detailed core assessment should be undertaken (HM Government 2010, para 5.38).

Section 47 of the Children Act 1989 places on local authorities a duty to make enquiries when they have 'reasonable cause' to suspect that a child who lives, or is found, in their area is suffering, or likely to suffer, significant harm. The *core assessment* is the means by which a section 47 enquiry is carried out and should be completed within 35 working days. In these circumstances the objective of the local authority's involvement is to determine whether and what type of action is required to safeguard and promote the welfare of the child (HM Government 2010, para 5.38).

A core assessment is defined as an in-depth assessment which addresses the central or most important aspects of the child's needs. There are several junctures at which a core assessment may start, depending on the child's circumstances, and the existence of child protection concerns is not a pre-requisite. Over a third (40%) of core assessments are not related to section 47 enquiries (Department for Education 2011a).

Both initial and core assessments should be undertaken in accordance with the *Framework for the Assessment of Children in Need and their Families* (Department of Health *et al.* 2000), and information should be gathered and analysed within the three domains of: the child's developmental needs; the parents' or caregivers' capacity to respond appropriately to those needs; and the wider family and environmental factors (HM Government 2010, paras 5.39, 5.62).

At the time of writing, the Munro Review (Munro 2011) has recommended that the government should revise the statutory guidance that sets out these requirements. Specifically, there is a recommendation 'to remove the distinction between initial and core assessments and associated timescales in respect of these assessments' and to replace nationally designed assessment forms and performance indicators with local innovation and professional judgement (p.10). We do not know at present how far this will impact on the processes discussed in this book, and particularly in Chapter 4. However, it seems probable that, regardless of whatever changes are to come, locally based, less formal assessments will still need to explore the inter-relationship between parenting capacity, wider familial and environmental factors and children's developmental needs that has proved so central to this book.

1

Introduction

Decisions made by practitioners to safeguard and promote the welfare of very young children suffering, or likely to suffer, significant harm are undoubtedly complex and have become more problematic in the wake of intense public interest engendered by high-profile tragedies such as the deaths of Victoria Climbié and Peter Connelly (see Brandon *et al.* 2009; Laming 2003, 2009; Parton 2006) and campaigns that claim that local authorities remove babies unnecessarily from birth parents, sometimes 'stealing' them in order to meet adoption targets (see Alderson, Leapman and Harper 2008; Hemming 2007; Hilpern 2008; Lloyd-Selby 2008). Ill-considered decisions will have long-term consequences for children's life chances. Those who are perceived as having made the wrong decision, whether it be to separate children unnecessarily from their families or to leave them in dangerous situations, can find themselves vilified by the media. It is therefore important to know how such decisions are made, and whether they can be improved. This book presents the findings from a study which explored the decision-making process that influenced the life pathways and developmental progress of a sample of very young children who were identified as suffering, or likely to suffer, significant harm before their first birthdays and were then followed until they were three.

Two major English studies have recently shown that in this country children are left in damaging situations for too long before being placed away from home, and/or are returned from care or accommodation to neglectful families who continue to abuse them (see Farmer and Lutman forthcoming; Wade *et al.* 2011). However, it is also clear that some parents do overcome entrenched problems to provide a nurturing home for a child (see Cleaver *et al.* 2007; Jones, Hindley and Ramchandani 2006). Professionals need to be able to distinguish between those children who can safely remain with their parents and those who cannot. The issue is complicated further by the matter of timing. The window of opportunity for decisive action for very young children is narrow; if decisions are not made in a timely manner the long-term consequences for their future life chances can be severe (see, for example, Currie and Widom 2010; Farmer and Lutman forthcoming; Gerhardt 2004).

Decisions to intervene when children are suffering, or likely to suffer, significant harm are made by a wide range of people. Referrals to children's social care come from professionals, such as those working in health, education, the police and probation, and also from neighbours and relatives. Decisions concerning what action to take are then made in a range of different forums, including child protection conferences, adoption panels and the courts. They are influenced by both the understanding and knowledge of those who make them and also by their values and assumptions. Where very young children are concerned, parents play a particularly fundamental role in the decision-making process. The principle of partnership introduced by the Children Act 1989 is intended to ensure that parents' views are heard and taken into account in all decisions concerning their children (Department of Health 1989), although the evidence suggests that many continue to feel intimidated or excluded from the process (see Morgan 2008). Perhaps more significantly, as this book shows, the actions of parents, particularly those that demonstrate a capacity for change, have a major impact on the decisions that are made. The study attempted to trace the key decisions that were made by the professionals involved and the rationale behind them; the part played by parents and their perceptions of professional decisions; and the consequences for the children.

Issues to be balanced in the decision-making process

A wide range of issues needs to be balanced in making decisions when children are suffering, or likely to suffer, significant harm. Professionals have to make use of evidence concerning those factors within parents, children and the environment that render maltreatment and its recurrence more, or less, likely; what is known about effective interventions to address parental problems; the consequences of abuse and neglect in terms of their likely short and long-term impact on children; and the outcomes of decisions to separate children, through adoption, special guardianship or placement in the care of the local authority. Such decisions are not value free, and are also informed by views on the appropriate role of the state in family life, by consideration of parental rights and by concerns about empowering families with multiple disadvantages. They are also influenced by limitations of time and resources.

Issues affecting parenting capacity

A range of different adversities can impair parents' capacity to meet the needs of their children: these include mental ill-health, substance misuse, learning disability and intimate partner violence (see among others Cleaver *et al.* 2007;

Cleaver, Unell and Aldgate 2011; Ward, Munro and Dearden 2006). Children growing up in families affected by these issues are at greater risk of being maltreated (see among others Barnard 2007; Cleaver *et al.* 2007; Kroll and Taylor 2003; Tunnard 2002). When these adversities cluster together, their inter-reaction may increase still further the likelihood that children's long-term wellbeing will be compromised (Rutter 2000).

Cleaver and colleagues (2011) have provided a comprehensive analysis of the manner in which such adversities can impact on parenting capacity and trigger abuse and neglect. To summarize: *intimate partner violence* may undermine parents' self-esteem and confidence in their parenting skills; their attention may be focused on the necessity to placate the perpetrator rather than on their children's needs; and they may not be able to protect children from physical abuse and emotional trauma if they get caught up in or witness an attack. *Alcohol and drug-misusing parents* may be subject to unpredictable mood swings; they may steal or prostitute themselves to obtain drugs and become absorbed in a criminal culture; and they may be emotionally unavailable, unable to provide basic care, and at times unable to keep children safe. *Mental health problems* may inhibit parents' capacity to respond to children's needs and provide consistent care; they can result in delusional thinking and a lack of predictability, both of which can be a source of anxiety and worry to children. However, mental health problems often fluctuate over time and may have a sporadic impact on parenting capacity. Parents with *learning disabilities* may provide a nurturing home for their children if they are given adequate, long-term support; however, the extent and nature of other coexisting adversities, such as intimate partner violence and substance misuse, has a major impact on their ability to parent (see Cleaver *et al.* 2011; Stanley, Cleaver and Hart 2009).

The existence of parental problems such as those noted above does not necessarily mean that children will be abused or neglected, but unless mitigating factors such as a non-abusive partner, or a supportive extended family, are available, they render maltreatment more likely.

Research evidence concerning maltreatment and its consequences

The national statistics on safeguarding children in England suggest that either maltreatment is increasing or, more probably, that it is becoming better recognized and more likely to elicit a response. The data indicate that in the year ending 31 March 2011, 111,700 children became the subject of an enquiry under section 47 of the Children Act 1989[1], and just under

---

1   Section 47 of the Children Act 1989 places on local authorities a duty to make enquiries when they have 'reasonable cause to suspect that a child who lives, or is found, in their area is suffering, or likely to suffer, significant harm'.

half that number (49,000) were made the subject of child protection plans (Department for Education 2011a). The number of children for whom child protection plans are made, and who therefore have been considered to be suffering, or likely to suffer, significant harm, has been increasing year-on-year since 2005; they rose by 30 per cent in the two years following the national outcry engendered by the tragic death of Peter Connelly, whose case attracted intense media interest in 2008–9 and significantly raised public awareness of the problem (Department for Education 2010a, 2010b).

National statistics on safeguarding children show that very young children are over-represented: 13 per cent (5420) of children subject to a child protection plan on 31 March 2011 were infants aged under one, including those who were unborn (Department for Education 2011a). Neglect was the most common form of maltreatment for all children, accounting for 43.9 per cent of child protection plans, with emotional abuse accounting for 28.2 per cent, physical abuse 10.6 per cent, sexual abuse 5.4 per cent, and multiple forms of abuse 11.8 per cent (Department for Education 2011a).

However, the statistics in themselves reflect responses to concerns about maltreatment, and not its prevalence. Prevalence studies conducted in a number of countries, including the UK and the USA, suggest that abuse is substantially under-reported, and that many more children are maltreated than come to the attention of services (Gilbert *et al.* 2009). The most recent prevalence study of child maltreatment in the UK, undertaken in 2009, found that about 8.9 per cent of children aged under 11, 21.2 per cent of 11–17-year-olds and 24.5 per cent of 18–24-year-olds had experienced maltreatment or direct victimization by a parent or caregiver at some point during their childhoods; and that 2.5 per cent of under-11-year-olds and 6 per cent of 11–17-year-olds had had such experiences in the previous year (Radford *et al.* 2011). These figures are far higher than the approximately 0.3 per cent[2] of children who became the subjects of child protection plans in the same year (Department for Children, Schools and Families 2009b; Hughes, Church and Zealey 2009).

Both prevalence studies and national statistics on service responses need careful interpretation, for child maltreatment can be understood in very different ways, and definitions vary. This is a particular issue where attempts are made to compare international statistics (see Hearn *et al.* 2004; Munro *et al.* 2011). The problem is that maltreatment is exceptionally difficult to define, and definitions can vary over time and between cultures. In the UK, for instance, physical abuse was not identified as a form of maltreatment until the 1880s; witnessing intimate partner violence did not become a cause for

---

2   Figure calculated from data on child population, 2008, and children subject to child protection plans, 2009.

concern until at least a century later (see Ward forthcoming); and bullying by peers and siblings is only now becoming recognized as a form of abuse (see Radford *et al.* 2011). In some cultures physical abuse of children or intimate partner violence are regarded as normative behaviours; neglect tends to be disregarded in populations that are living in poverty; and the Pitcairn Islanders have argued, with varying degrees of success, that the sexual abuse of young girls is acceptable because it is a traditional norm in Polynesian culture (see Marks 2009). It is therefore unsurprising that, in a multicultural society, the identification of abuse and neglect and the response of public agencies are controversial issues.

Outcomes of abuse

The long-term consequences of child abuse and neglect have been reviewed by Jones (2008). Maltreatment is known to have a negative impact across all areas of child development, and is linked with conduct disorder, eating disorders, attempted and actual suicide and substance misuse, aggression and violent behaviour. The consequences are also known to extend to physical and mental health and to persist into adult life (Irish, Kobayashi and Delahanty 2009; Jones 2008; Malinosky-Rummell and Hansen 1993; Waylen, Stallard and Stewart-Brown 2008). Adverse outcomes also reach into the sphere of economic wellbeing: a recent study showed lower levels of education, employment and earnings during adulthood to be some of the 'large and enduring economic consequences' of physical abuse, sexual abuse and neglect during childhood (Currie and Widom 2010).

Neglect and emotional abuse have been evidenced as the most difficult types of maltreatment for professionals to identify, the most likely to occur alongside other types of abuse, and the most likely to recur (Farmer and Lutman forthcoming). They are also associated with the most damaging long-term consequences (see Barlow and Schrader McMillan 2010; Daniel, Taylor and Scott 2010; Gerhardt 2004).

For those making decisions, both neglect and emotional abuse can be particularly problematic as they seldom involve a specific crisis or incident. Such events, or 'triggers', which are more characteristic of physical or sexual abuse, often prompt specific interventions such as the deployment of services and support or the removal of a child. Without these 'triggers' to escalate matters to a more intensive level of intervention, children can be left in abusive situations for too long (Farmer and Lutman forthcoming; Laming 2003; Wade *et al.* 2011).

Why babies?

There is now an extensive body of research which shows conclusively that the early environment, and the first three years of life in particular, play a major role in shaping children's cognitive, socio-emotional and behavioural development (see Barlow and Underdown 2008). Recent research has focused on the role that early environment, and specifically infants' and toddlers' relationships with caregivers, has on the way in which the brain and the central nervous system develops, and the impact this has on the young child's ability to negotiate the key developmental tasks of impulse control, trust and attachment; it also shows how abuse and neglect during this period can be particularly damaging (see Gerhardt 2004; Schore 2003).

Developing the brain, regulating the emotions and establishing attachments

Unlike other animals, human infants are born with very immature brains, which then develop rapidly in the first two years of life. In the first year the brain more than doubles in weight. During this time there is a rapid proliferation and over-production of nerve pathways that increases in response to inter-personal and intra-personal experiences. Positive experiences, particularly in the first year of life, produce more richly networked brains. More neuronal connections produce better performance and more ability to use particular areas of the brain (Barlow and Underdown 2008; Gerhardt 2004).

Because so much of human brain development takes place after birth, it is particularly shaped by the social environment, and because the baby is so dependent on adults for survival, the intense bond formed with the primary caregiver (usually the mother) shapes the way in which the brain develops. Research on Romanian orphans, who were left in their cots all day with virtually no opportunities to develop relationships with adult caregivers, shows that, without such relationships, parts of the brain fail to develop, potentially permanently (see Chugani *et al.* 2001; Gerhardt 2004). In a less extreme context, O'Hagan identifies the perceptual deprivation which accompanies a lack of opportunities for interaction as one of the most common, and poorly recognized, forms of psychological abuse:

> The attack upon perceptual development is most serious in the sustained long-term sensory deprivations inflicted on babies and infants who are made to spend long hours in their cots and prams, in smoke-filled rooms, starved of natural light and human interaction…[which] has a profound, adverse impact upon the development of other crucially important mental faculties, as well

as on children's social, educational and psychological development.
(O'Hagan 2006, p.56)

The early interactions between mother and baby also play a significant role in establishing the normal range of emotional arousal and in setting the thermostat for later control of the stress response when this has been exceeded. Very small babies can express feelings of distress or discomfort but are dependent on adults to notice their signals and regulate their emotional states.

> Early regulation is…about responding to the baby's feelings in a non-verbal way. The mother does this mainly with her face, her tone of voice and her touch. She soothes her baby's loud crying and over-arousal by entering the baby's state with him, engaging him with a loud mirroring voice, gradually leading the way towards calm by toning her voice down and taking him with her to a calmer state. Or she soothes a tense baby by holding him and rocking him. Or she stimulates a lacklustre baby back into a happier state with her smiling face and dilated sparkly eyes. By all sorts of non-verbal means she gets the baby back to his set points where he feels comfortable again. (Gerhardt 2004, p.23)

Infants experience stress when adults do not respond to cries that indicate their need for food, warmth, comfort or protection – factors that relate to their physical survival and emphasize their dependency on caregivers to ensure it. When these needs are ignored, the stress response is activated: 'the adrenal glands generate extra cortisol to generate extra energy to focus on the stress and to put other bodily systems "on hold" while this is being dealt with' (Gerhardt 2004, p.59). Persistent and unrelieved chronic stress in infancy results in the baby's brain being flooded by cortisol for prolonged periods and an eventual lowering of the threshold for arousal (Barlow and Underdown 2008). There is some evidence that an over-reactive stress response can start to develop before birth amongst babies whose mothers abuse alcohol during the pregnancy (Wand *et al.* 2001).

There are well-established links between high cortisol levels and a range of psychological problems in adulthood, including depression, anxiety and suicidal tendencies, eating disorders, and alcoholism. There is also evidence that high cortisol levels are damaging to the body's physiological systems: they can affect the brain's ability to think and manage behaviour; they can compromise the immune system and make the body more vulnerable to infection; and they may be related to increases in blood glucose and insulin levels, rendering the body more vulnerable to diabetes and hypertension (see Gerhardt 2004 for further information).

In some children, however, prolonged exposure to stress may be linked to abnormally low levels of cortisol. This is particularly evident in those who have experienced low-grade, frequent emotional (and sometimes physical) abuse and neglect in very early childhood; it is thought that these children suppress the impact of painful or stressful experiences by switching off the stress response. These suppressed emotions tend to emerge in relatively safe settings, such as the playground:

> ...the most aggressive boys at school are not those who are high in stress hormones but low in them. Their anger simmers beneath the surface, probably outside their awareness. It also probably arose from very early experiences of neglect or chronic hostility, which has affected their stress response. (Gerhardt 2004, p.81)

McBurnett and colleagues (2000) found that the earlier anti-social behaviour develops in boys, the more likely it is to be associated with low cortisol. Low levels of cortisol are also associated with numerous disorders in later life, including post-traumatic stress disorder, a range of psychosomatic conditions and a lack of positive good feeling (Gerhardt 2004).

It therefore appears that abnormal levels of cortisol (either very high or very low), engendered by chronic exposure to stress in infancy, cause long-term physiological and psychological damage.

It is evident that the relationship with the caregiver plays a central role in the infant's neurophysiological development and that this is inextricably bound up with his or her emerging capacity to experience and regulate emotions. It is through the emotional bond or attachment which develops between infant and caregiver that emotions of distress or fear are regulated, the stress response is controlled and the infant develops an internal working model of what to expect from relationships. Babies who experience sensitive, emotionally responsive care during their first year are more likely to become securely attached and to develop the confidence to use the main caregiver as a secure base from which to explore the world. Those who experience insensitive, inconsistent or unresponsive care are more likely to become insecurely attached to caregivers upon whom they cannot depend; without a secure base, they may lack the confidence to explore the world, and they may develop defensive strategies to cope with poorly regulated emotions.

Abuse and neglect in infancy

The emerging research on infant mental health discussed above makes it clear that popular misconceptions that infants and toddlers are too young to be affected by abuse and neglect are false. A number of authorities argue that emotional abuse is the most damaging of all forms of maltreatment in early childhood because the perpetrator is almost invariably the primary carer, whose abusive behaviour represents a direct negation of the child's 'need for safety, love, belonging and self-esteem' (Barlow and Schrader McMillan 2010; Glaser 2002; Iwaniec 1995). However, it is also evident that parents who persistently neglect or respond in a hostile manner to children's signals of fear or discomfort are also likely to damage the child's ability to develop secure attachments.

Up to 80 per cent of children brought up in abusive environments where parenting is unpredictable, hostile and/or chaotic have disorganized attachments (Van IJzendoorn, Schuengel and Bakermans-Kranenburg 1999); they are acutely and chronically dysregulated and develop highly negative and inconsistent internal working models. These are consistently linked with a range of poor outcomes associated with a dysfunctional stress response and abnormal levels of cortisol; such outcomes include violence, aggression and serious psychological problems (see Barlow with Scott 2010).

One further reason why long-term outcomes are so poor is that infants who are abused or neglected in early childhood are denied the high-quality early experiences that might help them build up a degree of resilience to enable them to cope with later adversity:

> The impact of not receiving adequate caregiving for a child or young person should be seen against a backdrop of their developmental needs. From a developmental perspective deficits in early life would be expected to be more pervasive and severe in their effects than later parenting problems. The reason for this is because, from this perspective, developmental competencies build up over time, each one dependent and reliant upon successful negotiation of previous stages. (Jones 2009, p.289)

Timing

The research concerning the development of the brain and early affect regulation, together with our understanding of infants' psychological development, all indicate that timing is of critical significance in the early years, because there are windows of opportunity when interventions can be particularly effective. For instance:

- The quality and sensitivity of mother–child interaction at 6–15 weeks is correlated with secure attachments at 18 months (Lewis *et al.* 1984).

- The stress response system appears to stabilize by about the age of six months. Babies from Romanian orphanages who were adopted *before* the age of four months seemed able to regain a normal stress response, while those who were adopted *after* four months continued to have high levels of cortisol, even after adoption (Chisholm *et al.* 1995; Gerhardt 2004; Gunnar *et al.* 2001).

- Research on Romanian orphans and other grossly neglected children also shows that when social relationships are denied during the period in which the social part of the brain is developing (up to the age of three) there is little hope of gaining social abilities or developing this part of the brain adequately (Chugani *et al.* 2001; Gerhardt 2004).

- Babies who are placed for adoption before their first birthdays are more likely to become securely attached to adoptive carers than those placed at a later age (Van den Dries *et al.* 2009).

Such factors demonstrate the importance of identifying and responding decisively to evidence of maltreatment in very young children because, if ignored, there can be long-term, adverse consequences that are difficult, and sometimes impossible, to overcome (see Barlow with Scott 2010).

A number of specialist interventions are now available to help parents, children and families overcome both the causes and consequences of maltreatment (Barlow and Schrader McMillan 2010; Davies and Ward 2011; MacMillan *et al.* 2009; Montgomery, Gardner and Bjornstad 2009). However, these are not universally available, and parents need to be willing to engage with services within a timescale that meets the needs of the child. Moreover, there is considerable evidence that prevention is more effective than interventions designed to prevent the recurrence of maltreatment or to help children overcome its consequences. Like all habits, dysfunctional emotional responses can be hard to change, and later, reactive interventions can be:

> …like pouring money into the maintenance of a badly built house. The persistent damp problems, poor heat or sound insulation, subsidence due to poor foundations, may be temporarily alleviated – but nothing can change the fact that the house is not well built and will continue to be high maintenance. Likewise with human beings whose foundations have not been well built. Although expensive repairs may be undertaken later in life, the building stage – when adjustments can be made – is largely over. For prevention to be effective, it needs to be targeted at the point when it can make the most difference. (Gerhardt 2004, pp.2–3)

Infants are therefore of particular concern because the evidence shows them to be most vulnerable to adverse outcomes in all areas of development. Moreover, Brandon and colleagues' analyses of serious case reviews suggest that it is these very young children who are most likely to die or be seriously injured when left in abusive situations; almost half of those children who were the subject of a serious case review between April 2003 and March 2007 were under one year old and the youngest child in the family had 'a heightened level of vulnerability and risk of harm' (Brandon *et al.* 2008, 2009).

Separation

Where parental problems are deep-seated and intractable, separation may be necessary. Such decisions need to be made swiftly and lead to prompt and decisive action. Very young children need to be separated from abusive parents before their long-term wellbeing has been compromised by maltreatment. It is now clear that the longer young children remain in abusive families, the greater the likelihood of their suffering significant harm. There is also evidence to suggest that babies who are placed early for adoption are most likely to form secure attachments to new carers: Van den Dries and colleagues (2009) studied children who were adopted before 12 months of age. They found them to be as securely attached to adoptive parents as their non-adopted peers, whereas those adopted after their first birthday showed less attachment security than non-adopted children.

There are also strong practical arguments for early separation in that babies and very young children are more likely than older children to find secure adoptive placements (Selwyn *et al.* 2010). Where relatives and friends are not available for special guardianship, for both resource and child wellbeing reasons these are likely to be the optimal choice for permanency. Recent national statistics reveal how the chances of adoption diminish as children grow older: 91 per cent of children who were placed for adoption in 2010–11 entered their final period of care before the age of four, 63 per cent before their first birthday (Department for Education 2011b). Another body of evidence shows that as children grow older they may benefit less both from specialist interventions to address the consequences of abuse and from separation to prevent its recurrence (Montgomery *et al.* 2009; Ward, Holmes and Soper 2008).

Outcomes of care and adoption

Decisions about whether or not to separate children from their birth families will also be influenced by evidence concerning the outcomes of being looked after by the local authority – and for these very young children, the outcomes of adoption. There are long-standing and well-documented concerns about the poor outcomes of care and accommodation (see for instance House of Commons Children, Schools and Families Committee 2009; Sergeant 2006) and there are some difficult issues that need to be confronted. Instability of placements, low aspirations and insufficient support for young people making the transition to independence are particular concerns (Sinclair *et al.* 2007; Skuse and Ward 2003; Stein and Munro 2008; Stein, Ward and Courtney 2011; Ward 2009). There is also evidence that, in spite of numerous attempts to eradicate such problems, some children are still subject to abuse in both residential and foster care (Biehal and Parry 2010; Farmer and Pollock 1998; Sinclair and Gibbs 1998; Wade *et al.* 1998), and that some carers are indifferent to their wellbeing (Skuse and Ward 2003).

Nevertheless an increasing body of research demonstrates that the majority of children who become looked after benefit from care. Forrester's (2008) review of research on the welfare of children looked after over time found no study that showed a deterioration in children's welfare while they were in substitute care:

> In all but one study there were improvements (and in that one study there was no change) and in a number of studies the improvements were very substantial. Furthermore, the limited British research and more extensive American and Australian evidence suggested that when children returned home from care they tended to do less well than they did in care…when children were removed (from abusive birth families) to permanent alternative homes they tended to improve on a range of outcome measures, such as educational performance and behavioural adjustment. (Forrester 2008, p.208)

Hannon and colleagues' recent analysis of research into the English care system found that 'care can be a positive intervention for many groups of children' and that:

> The mistaken belief that care consigns all looked after children to a lifetime of underachievement and poor outcomes creates a culture of uncertainty, increasing delay and leading to instability later on. (Hannon, Wood and Bazalgette 2010, p.11)

A number of studies have demonstrated that, although in some circumstances the care system can compound and exacerbate children's difficulties, the major problem is its inability to compensate for earlier disadvantage. For instance, Darker, Ward and Caulfield (2008) found that those looked after children and young people who commit offences had usually begun to do so prior to entry, and that 70 per cent of children and young people in care or accommodation never offend. Similarly, Murphy and Ingram (2008) found that young people in residential care were no more likely to misuse drugs than if they had remained in their birth homes, despite reporting using drugs to escape the problems of being in care.

Moreover, evidence from self-report surveys and interviews with children who have experience of being looked after generally corroborates these positive findings (Forrester 2008). Written surveys tend to reach disproportionate numbers of young people in residential units, who have the most challenging needs, yet nevertheless show that at least 50 per cent of respondents view their care experiences in a positive light (Ward, Skuse and Munro 2005). Skuse and Ward (2003) interviewed 47 children and young people a year after they had ceased to be looked after, and found that 75 per cent felt they had benefited by the experience.

Recent evidence reveals that those maltreated children who remain looked after or move to adoptive families often fare better than do those who are reunited with birth families (see Biehal *et al.* 2010; Farmer and Lutman forthcoming; MacMillan *et al.* 2009; Ward *et al.* 2006). Wade and colleagues recently studied a sample of children who had become looked after by English local authorities for reasons of abuse or neglect, and compared the progress and outcomes of those who had remained looked after with those who had returned home, about four years after the key decision to retain or to reunite them had been made. They found that maltreated children who remained in substitute care did significantly better than those who returned to their birth families: they were more likely to be settled in a 'permanent' home than those who had been reunited; they were less likely to be involved in offending and alcohol or drug misuse; they had significantly better mean scores for health; and they were more likely to have close adult ties and to be considered to have a range of special skills, interests and hobbies. They were less likely to be habitual truants, to be in pupil referral units, or to have dropped out of school, although significant differences in school performance were not found (see Wade *et al.* 2011, pp.193–206). Children who had been neglected and/or emotionally abused by their birth families benefited the most by remaining looked after.

Such findings do, however, demand careful interpretation as they are not universally applicable. The nature and quality of relationships with birth families and their own wishes are important factors in determining whether or not long-term separation is in the child's best interests (see Sinclair *et al.* 2007).

Where very young children are concerned, the greatest problems arise from delays in decision-making which mean that they are exposed to lengthy periods of maltreatment, or that they continually move between birth families and foster carers, or from one temporary placement to another, before a permanence plan has been made or realized. Delays in social work decision-making are compounded by the courts which may postpone decisions while further assessments are made or expert witnesses are called; children may also wait for lengthy periods before a child's guardian can be appointed or a case can be heard in a particular court. There is a complex relationship between delay and instability, so that the longer children wait for a permanent placement, the greater their chances of changing carers, and the greater the likelihood that their opportunities for developing secure attachments or overcoming the consequences of maltreatment will be reduced (Ward *et al.* 2006).

Outcomes of kinship care

Where children cannot remain with their birth families, both legislation and policy indicate that kinship care should be the placement of choice. The Children Act 1989 states that local authorities should make arrangements for a looked after child to live with 'a relative, friend or other person connected with him, unless that would not be reasonably practicable or consistent with his welfare' (s.23.6b). Kinship care has since been further promoted by the introduction of Special Guardianship Orders in the Adoption and Children Act 2002, and through the Care Matters initiative (Department for Education and Skills 2007).

However, while the evidence suggests that abused and neglected children often fare better than those who remain with their birth families, it is unclear whether outcomes are better for those who are placed with relatives or friends than for those who are placed with unrelated carers. Some earlier studies indicated that children in kinship care are less likely to be maltreated and have fewer placement changes than those placed with strangers (Berridge and Cleaver 1987; Courtney and Needell 1997; Newton, Litrownik and Landsverk 2000). More recently, kinship carers have been found to be better able to promote stronger ties with birth families (Farmer and Moyers 2008). Hunt, Waterhouse and Lutman (2008) highlight the ability of extended families to 'rally round' and care for a child, and found that kin placements may achieve better outcomes in terms of meeting a child's emotional needs.

However, MacMillan and colleagues' recent international review of interventions to prevent child maltreatment and associated impairment found much evidence that did not favour kinship care. The studies reviewed showed that, on average, kinship carers were 'older, less well educated, less likely to be married, report more problematic parenting attitudes, receive fewer non-child welfare services and have less caseworker oversight than unrelated carers' (MacMillan *et al.* 2009, p.260). These factors relate to issues raised by a number of British studies, concerning low thresholds of approval for kinship carers, and inadequate remuneration, despite the Munby judgement (*R v. Manchester City Council* 2001) which clearly advocated parity with unrelated carers (Farmer and Moyers 2008; Ward *et al.* 2006). In view of this, it is perhaps unsurprising to find that some relatives and friends provide poor standards of care: Hunt and colleagues (2008) found concerns about kinship placements meeting the basic needs of nearly a quarter of children in their study (see also Peters 2005; Sinclair *et al.* 2007). Sinclair and colleagues (2007) found that placements with relatives are more likely to be seen as 'successful' by social workers, possibly because other advantages such as the maintenance of family ties are often thought to compensate for these disadvantages.

When child wellbeing outcomes of kinship care are compared with those for foster care outside the extended family, the results are again inconclusive, with some studies indicating that children in these placements do better in terms of behavioural, educational, mental health and social functioning, others indicating little or no difference, and some showing more negative outcomes in terms of delinquent behaviour and IQ (MacMillan *et al.* 2009). A recent study of children who are the subjects of Special Guardianship Orders found that, overall, wellbeing was lower for those living with unrelated foster carers who had previously fostered them than for those placed within their extended families (Wade, Dixon and Richards 2010). However, accurate comparisons are difficult to make because it seems likely that children who enter kinship care come from less dysfunctional families and have fewer behavioural or emotional problems than those placed with unrelated carers.

Outcomes of adoption

Studies of the long-term outcomes of infant adoptions are necessarily based on children who were placed several decades ago at a time when there were still powerful economic and social pressures on unmarried women to relinquish their children. Adoptions of these children, who are now in late middle age, show favourable psychosocial outcomes and low disruption rates (see Selwyn *et al.* 2006 for further details). It is unlikely that these children would have experienced abuse before placement.

However, the majority of children placed for adoption currently in the UK have experienced maltreatment prior to entry to care or accommodation, and many will have experienced lengthy delays, insecurity and instability before permanence decisions are made and adoptive placements found. On average, children are looked after for 2.7 years before the adoption is finalized (Department for Education 2011b), though they reach their permanent placement in a shorter period (Ward *et al.* 2006).

Given their previous experiences it is not surprising that some children who are adopted also experience emotional difficulties, depression and confusion over identity (Neil 2000; Smith and Brodzinsky 2002). Biehal and colleagues (2010) found that adopted children in England were more likely to experience mental health problems than the wider population.

Not all adoption placements last (Farmer *et al.* 2010; Selwyn *et al.* 2006; Thoburn 2005). Moreover, research using the self-reported feelings of adopted children suggests that statistics on placement breakdown hide an underlying unhappiness for some children in placements that do persist (Thoburn 2002). Disruptions are closely associated with emotional and behavioural difficulties, and especially 'aggressive, acting out behaviours including cruelty to others, getting into fights, threatening others, over activity, restlessness, hanging out with bad friends and overt sexualised behaviour' (see Selwyn *et al.* 2006 for further details). There are greater risks in adoption for sibling groups and children with additional needs (Rushton 2003).

Nevertheless, adoption has generally been associated with lower rates of disruption than long-term foster care (see Biehal *et al.* 2010), and the majority of adoptions last until adulthood. Howe's (1998) review of outcome studies found that, on a measure that combined disruption rates, developmental rates and adopter satisfaction rates, 50–60 per cent of late adoptions[3] were successful.

There are strong indications that the younger the child is when placed for adoption, the better the chances of both a stable placement and successful psychosocial outcomes. The older children are at placement, the more likely they are to display behavioural problems, including problems with peer relationships, attachment, conduct disorder and poor concentration (Biehal *et al.* 2010; Haugaard, Wojslawowicz and Palmer 1999), and therefore the greater the risk of disruption. As with local authority care, it appears that adoption can provide a nurturing environment from which most children will benefit, but the security of an adoptive home cannot always overcome the consequences of extensive maltreatment and neglect.

Policy context

Those who are responsible for identifying maltreatment and deciding how far and to what extent they should intervene thus have a substantial body of evidence upon which to draw. However, such decisions are also informed by the policy context in which they are made.

Since the implementation of the Children Act 1989, policy concerning the protection of children suffering, or likely to suffer, significant harm has been based on the fundamental principle that children are generally best looked after within their birth families; wherever possible initiatives have been aimed at preserving and strengthening families, with separation very much a last resort. Policy has also been driven by another principle, also embodied in the Act, that parents have enduring responsibilities towards their children, and that the state

---

3   Opinions vary as to when an adoption should be regarded as late. Howe's analysis of late adoptions covers studies of children placed after they were six months old.

should therefore work in partnership with them and that coercive interventions should be avoided unless absolutely necessary.

However, national policy has also been shaped by the need to respond to growing public awareness of the prevalence of abuse and neglect, magnified by intense media interest in high-profile child protection tragedies. In the early 1990s a major research initiative found that an over-concentration of social work effort went into investigating whether maltreatment was taking place, rather than in supporting families to overcome the difficulties that made it more likely (see Department of Health 1995). As Hardiker, Exton and Barker (1991) pointed out: '…the question asked at initial inquiry should be reframed from "has this child been abused?" to "what are the needs of this child (including child protection) which cannot be met without the provision of services?"' Attempts were therefore made to refocus children's social care, with a greater emphasis on strengthening families and protecting children through concentrating on early intervention and family support. This meant that more attention was given to improving preventative services, designed to promote children's welfare, on the hypothesis that there would then be less need for more intrusive services required to protect them from harm.

However, preventative services are delivered by a range of agencies; social care, which focuses on the more intrusive elements of child protection intervention, plays only a minor role in their delivery. It became increasingly evident that, if children's needs were to be properly addressed at an early stage, agencies would need to work together to support the family as a whole. The initiative to integrate children's services gained particular impetus following the tragic death of Victoria Climbié, when it became apparent that poor communication between agencies, a failure to acknowledge joint responsibilities, and concerns about sharing information had all contributed to the tragedy (Laming 2003). The Children Act 2004 provided the legislative framework for integrating children's services. It also underpinned the Every Child Matters policy initiative (Department for Education and Skills 2003) which established five outcome areas that were necessary to children's wellbeing and which all agencies should work together to support. 'Staying safe', including being protected from harm, was one of these areas.

Following the public furore in 2008–9 over the death of Peter Connelly, urgent enquiries were made as to what progress had been made in safeguarding children from harm following these initiatives. Lord Laming, who led the enquiry, confirmed that there had been an encouraging start, but he also found that 'there are real challenges still to address in safeguarding and child protection if children are to have services they can rely on when their own lives are in crisis' (Laming 2009, p.10, para 1.4). Areas that particularly needed attention were leadership and accountability, support for children, inter-agency working, children's workforce development, organization and finance and the legal framework.

The thrust of policy over the last 15 years or so has been largely towards ensuring that children can be safeguarded within their birth families: improving inter-agency working, setting outcome objectives and refocusing services towards offering stronger early interventions have all been aimed at providing better support to families to help them do this. The expectation is that the vast majority of children can be adequately supported at home, and only a very small minority, whose parents are not able to address the problems that endanger their safety and compromise their welfare within an appropriate timescale, will need to be placed away from home. The Adoption and Children Act 2002 was introduced with the aim of increasing opportunities for achieving permanence for those children who cannot remain at home. Measures to speed up the process of achieving permanency so that children did not remain unprotected in unviable family situations or languish in temporary placements were introduced in 2003 through the protocol on Judicial Case Management in Public Law (Lord Chancellor's Department 2002) and later through the Public Law Outlines, issued in 2008 and subsequently revised (Masson *et al.* 2008; President of the Family Division 2008); however, at the time of writing, further attention is again being given to this question, this time through the Family Justice Review (Norgrove 2011), once more demonstrating the difficulties in ensuring that permanency can be reached sufficiently swiftly to meet a child's needs. Findings from the study that forms the focus of this book emphasize the importance of this issue.

Recent policy developments, following the change of government in 2010, continue to follow these themes. The Munro Review of Child Protection (2011) was set up to answer the central question: 'What helps professionals to make the best judgements they can to protect a vulnerable child?' Although much of the review focuses on the need to move from a system that is widely perceived to have become over-bureaucratized and preoccupied with compliance rather than on meeting the needs of children and families, many of the recommendations reinforce already established themes. These include a renewed emphasis on early intervention, entailing strong multi-agency collaboration (see Munro 2011, Chapter 5 and Recommendations 2, 6 and 10, pp.11–12). The need for effective, early interventions is further evidenced by a major semi-official report, produced within a similar time period and currently laid before parliament (see Allen 2011). The Munro Review also calls for radical changes in social work training, 'to improve the knowledge and skills of social workers, from initial training through to continuing professional development' (see Munro 2011, Chapter 6, Recommendations 11 and 12 and pp.84 and 97), an issue of particular relevance to the study discussed in this book.

The study

Decisions made where children are suffering, or likely to suffer, significant harm are therefore shaped by policy and legislation that aim to improve early identification and strengthen the co-ordination of services designed to support their parents in helping them achieve satisfactory outcomes. They should also be informed by the wealth of evidence concerning risk and protective factors within families and the outcomes of abuse and neglect. Professionals' decisions will also be influenced by their own position on debates concerning parents' rights, the extent to which the family should be preserved at all costs, and the legitimacy of state intervention in family life. The study which forms the focus of this book traced the decisions made on behalf of a sample of infants who were suffering, or likely to suffer, significant harm, the reasons and assumptions upon which these decisions were based, and the consequences for both the children and their families.

The purpose of the study is to shed some light on these complex processes. In doing so, it aims to add to the evidence base upon which professionals can draw in deciding which children require permanent out-of-home placement and which can safely remain with their birth parents. It also offers further evidence that contributes to the debate on why decision-making is so often delayed, and provides some indicators as to how more proactive action can be taken more speedily. It does not stand alone, for it forms part of two major government-funded research programmes: the Adoption Research Initiative (Thomas forthcoming) and the Safeguarding Children Research Initiative (Davies and Ward 2011). Studies in these initiatives each focus on a specific topic within a broader research agenda, and their findings complement one another. Findings from studies in the Safeguarding Children Research Initiative on identifying and responding to neglect (Daniel, Taylor and Scott 2011), on neglected children returned to their parents (Farmer and Lutman forthcoming) and on the consequences for maltreated children of remaining looked after or returning home (Wade *et al.* 2011) are of particular relevance to the study discussed in this book. The study is also complemented by research that compares outcomes for children who are adopted with those who remain in foster care (Biehal *et al.* 2010); that explores the impact of special guardianship (Wade *et al.* 2010), the experiences of birth parents (Neil *et al.* 2010), and how children are placed with adoptive families (Farmer *et al.* 2010); and that examines specific issues in the adoption of black and ethnic minority children (Selwyn *et al.* 2010). All of these studies form part of the Adoption Research Initiative (Thomas forthcoming).

The rationale for *Safeguarding Babies and Very Young Children from Abuse and Neglect* stems from both a lack of evidence about how decisions are made when very young children are suffering, or likely to suffer, significant harm, and concerns about the apparently arbitrary manner in which some children are placed for adoption while others remain with their birth parents. An earlier study undertaken by the research team had also found that a number of infants who were looked after by local authorities before their first birthdays had experienced frequent changes of domicile and carer both before they entered care or accommodation and during the care episode and that, for some children, delays in achieving permanence had compromised their life chances (Ward *et al.* 2006). However, that study was not able to compare the experiences and progress of very young children, who perhaps show similar levels of need, but remain at home with family support services. Nor could it compare why different decisions are made and how these lead to different pathways.

This prospective longitudinal study was intended to explore these issues. The aim was to trace the decision-making process that influenced the life pathways of a sample of very young children who had been identified as suffering, or likely to suffer, significant harm in order to: improve understanding of how such decisions are reached and their consequences; consider the weight given to risk and protective factors in making such decisions; and explore the role participants, including birth parents, play in the decision-making process. Full information about the detailed aims and objectives, the study design and methodology, and the difficulties associated with recruiting and retaining the sample are given in Appendix 1. The following paragraphs provide summary information necessary for the reader to understand the conduct of the study and the nature of the data concerning the experiences of the children and families, the decisions that were made and their implications, discussed in later chapters.

Methodology

The study took place in ten local authorities and focused on a sample of children who were subject to a core assessment or a section 47 enquiry before their first birthdays; as many as possible were followed until they were three. It used a mixed methods design: quantitative data concerning children's life experiences, evidence of need, reasons for referral and changes of circumstances were collected from case files; in-depth, case-specific interviews were held at regular intervals with birth parents, carers, social workers and team leaders and, where appropriate, with children's guardians. Non-case-specific interviews were held with senior managers, judges, magistrates and local authority solicitors, and focus groups were held with health visitors.

The Home Observation for the Measurement of the Environment for Infants and Toddlers (IT-HOME Inventory) (Caldwell and Bradley 2003) was completed in interviews with birth parents, foster carers and adoptive carers, but did not prove to be a reliable means of distinguishing between satisfactory and unsatisfactory home situations, and the results are not included in the analysis of findings. We do not know why these scores proved unreliable in this study:

it may be that the researchers were inadequately trained in the use of the IT-HOME, that they scored it inaccurately or that for some reason it was not an appropriate measure for this particular sample. However, this problem has been encountered by other research teams (see Barlow *et al.* 2007).

Totsika and Sylva's (2004) review of research using the IT-HOME Inventory found that the instrument can detect differences in the home environments of children growing up in families with a number of risk factors, including: poverty; parental mental illness and psychopathology; and parental learning disability. However, there was some evidence that the IT-HOME Inventory was not sufficiently sensitive to the impact of parental substance misuse on children's home environments (Howard *et al.* 1995) or the impact of multiple risk factors on measures of maternal warmth (Brooks-Gunn, Klebanov and Liaw 1995); moreover the review did not cover the use of the IT-HOME with families where intimate partner violence was a concern. Subsequent chapters will show that the majority of children in this study came from families displaying these risk factors, and this may be a further reason for the unreliability of findings from the IT-HOME. Further details of the issues raised by the scores from the IT-HOME in this study and the reasons why they have not been utilized in the following chapters are given in Appendix 2. The IT-HOME data from this study is currently being further explored to ascertain whether these findings have implications for practitioners undertaking assessments (see Brown and Ward forthcoming (a)).

Sample

There were 57 babies in the sample; some data were available on all of them, and 43 were followed until they were three.

Attrition in a sample of this nature is inevitable, but it has meant that not all infants could be included in all the analyses: for instance, we could only discuss the decisions made between first and third birthdays for the 43 who could be traced to the end of the study. In order to make it clear to the reader which children are included in different parts of the discussion, the chapters which follow refer to three overlapping sample groups:

- **Full sample** – all 57 infants, including six whose parents withdrew after the initial interview.

- **Intermediate follow-up group** – eight infants whose parents gave initial consent to view files and speak to professionals, but who could not be followed for the full three years.

- **Full follow-up group** – 43 infants for whom case file information was available from birth (or pre-birth) to age three/case closure alongside interview data from professionals and birth parents (and carers where applicable).

The study was dependent to a large extent on the active participation of birth parents and other primary carers, 33 of whom continued to be interviewed at regular intervals until their child was three. All but two of these birth parents are, at the time of writing, still in contact with the research team who are continuing to follow the children until their fourth (and in some cases fifth) birthdays, in order to monitor their progress and explore their experiences at entry to school and pre-school (Ward, Brown and Maskell-Graham forthcoming).

LIMITATIONS OF THE SAMPLE

For ethical reasons babies could only be recruited to the study if their birth parents gave prior agreement to participate. The difficulties in accessing this very hard to reach population with a largely transient lifestyle were often compounded by professionals' concerns about the limits of confidentiality and by authorities' gate-keeping processes.

The babies were, coincidentally, all born in the same year as Peter Connelly, and professional concerns about access intensified following the extensive media coverage surrounding his death. A number of professionals refused to be interviewed and some case files proved inaccessible in spite of parents' written permission for the research team to view them.

For the reasons discussed above, only about 4 per cent of those children who met the study criteria were recruited, and information about some of them is incomplete. The small size of the sample means that it would be advisable to verify the findings with a larger group of children in similar circumstances. The size of the sample and the researchers' experiences in gaining access raise wider questions concerning the tensions between the protection of vulnerable service users, their rights to have their views heard and the extent to which their views, as expressed in their consent for researchers to access personal data, are respected. They also indicate a lack of clarity and a range of misperceptions concerning the purpose of research in children's social care; public organizations are clearly concerned to protect themselves from any backlash from negative findings about their practice, but these concerns can at times make it impossible for researchers to undertake their task and gather the information necessary for the future development of services (see Munro 2008).

Issues concerning access not only restricted the size of the sample and the completeness of the dataset, but also increased the possibility of bias. However, it was possible to compare summary data with those from the much larger group of children who were eligible for selection, in order to identify the extent to which the experiences of the sample children were likely to be representative of other babies in similar circumstances. This revealed that the final sample was skewed towards those infants who had definitely suffered, or were very likely to suffer, significant harm: sample children were statistically more likely to be referred before birth, to continue to receive services following a core assessment, and to become looked after before their first birthdays than other children who met the study criteria.

The sample is comprised of children fitting the selection criteria *whose parents gave their informed consent* for access to case records and to participate in an interview. Only certain parents will have volunteered to participate – judging from the interview data these were most likely to be parents who either had a very good or a very bad experience of social care interventions – with those whose experience was less polarized less likely to come forward.

These three factors therefore need to be taken into account in assessing the implications of the evidence discussed in the following chapters: the sample was very small and so the study needs to be replicated on a larger basis; there is some bias towards those infants who are most likely to suffer significant harm; and families whose experience of social care was neither particularly good nor particularly bad are probably under-represented.

Conclusion

The decisions traced in this study raise a number of questions. What are the consequences of social work interventions for children and their parents? Which children are adequately safeguarded, and which are not? Where children remain with potentially abusive birth families, what are the factors that precipitate change and safeguard them from significant harm, and what are the factors that fail to do so? What roles do social work support and specialist interventions, such as substance-misuse and parenting programmes, play in this dynamic? Furthermore, how effective are formal processes in ensuring children are safeguarded, and what impact do these have on parents' decisions to change? And finally, is it possible to identify clusters of factors that social workers, their managers and the courts might look for in making timely decisions as to which children would benefit by remaining with birth parents and which would not? The research team analysed the data collected from case files and interviews with parents and professionals in order to explore these issues in the following chapters, as indicated below.

Outline of chapters

- Chapter 2 examines the infants in the sample, their needs, characteristics, how far they were likely to suffer significant harm and the extent to which this risk was actuated.

- Chapter 3 looks at their parents. It explores the prevalence of the risk and protective factors that made it more – or less – likely that they would abuse, or continue to maltreat, their children. Building upon this evidence it classifies the infants into four groups: those where the likelihood of significant harm was severe, high, medium or low at entry to the study.

- Chapter 4 examines the decision-making process, starting with the referral stage, initial decisions and events leading up to and immediately following the core assessment. It explores the considerations that lay behind referrals from different agencies, and the issues these raised for smooth inter-agency working.

- Chapter 5 follows the children over the next three years. It identifies how some infants were permanently separated while others remained at home, and explores how children's pathways related to information concerning parental risk and protective factors.

- Chapter 6 explores three groups of children: those who were safeguarded through separation; those safeguarded while remaining with birth parents; and those who remained with birth parents at continuing risk of being harmed. It considers why some parents were able to overcome their difficulties while others were not, and it examines the consequences of decisions in terms of children's emotional and behavioural development.

- Chapter 7 takes a closer look at the decisions and the reasons behind them. It explores how concepts of parental rights, empowerment and concerns about dependency influenced decisions and discusses why neglect was so frequently overlooked.

- Chapter 8 examines parents' understanding of professional decision-making.

- Chapter 9 draws conclusions from the study, with recommendations for policy, practice and further research.

- Appendix 1 gives further details of the study design, methodology and issues concerning recruitment and retention of the sample.

- Appendix 2 gives further details of the reasons why scores from the IT-HOME Inventory were not included in the analysis.

2

The Children

Introduction

The purpose of this chapter is to introduce the reader to the children in the sample, and establish the type and extent of maltreatment they experienced. As the previous chapter has shown, the sample is to a certain extent skewed: there are significantly more infants referred to children's social care before birth and looked after before their first birthdays than the summative data on children eligible for selection would lead us to expect. There are also significantly fewer babies whose core assessment or section 47 enquiries led to no further action from children's social care. All these indicators would suggest that the infants in the study sample were living in families where they were more likely to suffer significant harm and therefore were more likely to receive extensive interventions from children's social care than the majority of very young children who reach the core assessment stage.

Readers will need to bear this point in mind when considering the implications of the findings from the study; they will also need to remember that we were only able to follow up 43 of the original 57 infants until they reached their third birthdays. Tantalizingly we do not know what happened to the 14 children who dropped out of the study or who could not be traced for the full three years. In order to make the findings as transparent as possible we have indicated whether they refer to the full sample (57 infants); the group who were followed up for a period but lost before they were three (eight infants: intermediate follow-up); and those who were followed until their third birthdays (43 infants: full follow-up group). The majority of the discussion in this and the following chapter focuses on the 57 babies in the full sample. The names of all the children and some minor identifying details have been changed in what follows, in order to ensure confidentiality.

The children

Thirty six (63%) of the children in the full sample were boys and 20 (35%) were girls. The gender of one baby is unknown as his/her parents took part in the study before this child was born and withdrew after the initial round of data collection. In their systematic review of abuse and its recurrence, Hindley, Ramchandani and Jones (2006) found no significant difference between girls and boys, and we do not know why there was such a heavy preponderance of boys in this sample. However, the proportion is not significantly different from that found in the population of infants eligible for selection in four participating authorities (see Appendix 1, Table A1.3).

As Table 2.1 shows, the majority (35/51: 69%) of the children were White British, although 16 (32%) were from Black and Minority Ethnic (BME) groups. Of the children from BME groups, 11 (69%) were of mixed heritage. The high proportion of BME infants of mixed heritage is similar to that found in other studies of very vulnerable young children (see Selwyn *et al.* 2010; Ward *et al.* 2006).

Table 2.1 Ethnicity of children (full sample: n=57)

Ethnicity	Number	Per cent
African – Black/Black British	3	6
Any other Black – Black/Black British	1	2
Any other mixed – Mixed	3	6
British – White	35	69
Not stated – Other ethnic groups	1	2
White and Asian – Mixed	5	10
White and Black African – Mixed	3	6
Total	**51**	**100***
Unknown	6	

* Percentages are rounded figures.

The diversity of the children's heritage added to the complexity of the social worker's task. Interpreters were needed – and not always trusted – by some parents. A number also came from cultures where, for instance, physical punishment and intimate partner violence were not recognized as abusive behaviours. This issue and its impact on decision-making is discussed in greater detail in Chapter 8.

Siblings

As Table 2.2 shows, 30 (64%) of the children in the full sample had older siblings; all of these were known to children's social care. In 20 (67%) cases these older children had already been permanently removed from their mother's care by the time of the birth/identification of the index baby; in the remaining ten (33%) cases siblings were receiving support from children's social care, but remained living with their birth parent.

Table 2.2 Older sibling groups: involvement with children's social care (full sample: n=57)

Older sibling groups	Number	Per cent
Removed from mother	20	67
Open case alongside index child	10	33
Total	**30**	**100***
1st child of mother (i.e. no older siblings)	17	
Data unavailable	10	

* Percentages are rounded figures.

During the course of the study 12 mothers gave birth to another baby. Three of these new siblings were also deemed to be suffering or likely to suffer significant harm and have been included in the full sample in order to allow us to explore more fully the issues that arise when concerns cover more than one child in a family. In addition, one set of twins is included; therefore the full sample comprises 49 lone children, and four sibling pairs.

Age at identification

Many of the parents were already known to children's social care because older siblings had previously been referred, with the result that concerns that the index child would be maltreated had often been raised before he or she was born. Thirty two (65%) of the infants in the follow-up groups were identified before birth as being likely to suffer significant harm, and 17 (35%) after they were born but before their first birthdays. As noted in Chapter 1, the preponderance of babies identified before birth suggests that the sample is skewed towards the more high risk families.

Health, disabilities and developmental needs

Information concerning the infants' developmental needs was only infrequently recorded on core assessments. Overall, in the current study, core assessments and section 47 enquiries contained less information on these young children's developmental needs than on parenting capacity or wider family and environmental factors that might impact on caregiving. This counters findings from other studies which have tended to find that practitioners are less able to identify key issues concerning parenting capacity than children's development (see Cleaver *et al.* 2011).

One reason for the paucity of information about them was the young age of the sample. Over half (28/49: 57%) of these assessments were undertaken before the baby's birth. In some cases social workers identified concerns that certain needs might remain unmet, based upon past involvement with the family, while in others they simply noted that it was not possible to provide information in the child development domain at this stage. This is an issue that needs to be brought to the attention of practitioners, given the potentially adverse consequences for infants who are exposed to alcohol and substance misuse or intimate partner violence *in utero*.

In cases where the assessment was undertaken *after* the baby's birth, only three identified specific concerns in relation to the child's developmental needs. In the first case, the possibility of future health difficulties associated with a non-accidental injury was identified as an issue. In the second, it was noted that although the infant's development appeared age appropriate, concerns had been expressed by family members that cannabis was being smoked in the baby's presence and that the mother lacked interest in her son and did not adequately feed him. In the third case a 'happy and good bond' between the child and mother was noted, but there were concerns regarding the baby's weight and 'grubbiness'. The limited attention given to children's development is consistent with findings from other studies, which have identified a tendency for practitioners to focus on parenting issues without analysing the impact these may have on the child (see Cleaver *et al.* 2008).

Nevertheless, we were able to piece together the following information concerning children's health, disabilities and developmental needs from case files and interviews. Eight infants in the full sample (8/57: 14%) were identified as having disabilities or special health care needs. These included microcephaly (two infants, siblings), epilepsy (one infant), cerebral palsy (one infant), Stickler syndrome (one infant), visual impairment (one infant), hearing impairment (one infant), and an unspecified disability (one infant). Three of the babies were also born prematurely and had related health difficulties. Children with disabilities and special health care needs are known to be at increased risk of being maltreated (see Hibbard and Desch 2007). Indeed, Sullivan and Knutson (2000) found that they are 3.4 times more likely than others to suffer abuse or neglect. Certainly disabled children are over-represented in this sample (see Department of Health 2000).

As we shall see in Chapter 3, the babies were born into families that were already vulnerable, with high rates of alcohol and substance misuse, mental health problems and intimate partner violence. Drug and alcohol use during pregnancy were significant risk factors. Sixteen (16/51: 31%) infants in the follow-up groups were at risk of foetal alcohol spectrum disorders (FASD) and/or neonatal abstinence syndrome (NAS). Although there is little recorded evidence of their showing any symptoms, carers described them as having difficulty sleeping and feeding, and generally being hard to manage. Edward's mother, for instance, had misused heroin and alcohol throughout her pregnancy. He was placed with foster carers who were aware that he might show symptoms of withdrawal. They found that he could not suckle properly and that he was 'a bit erratic to start with, very erratic feeding and, you know, sleeping and everything, but he settled down'.

Long-term effects of alcohol and drug use during pregnancy are difficult to detect, and more research is needed in this area. *In utero* exposure to substances can be a feature of children with developmental, behavioural and social delay, as well as attachment problems, although these can all also be attributed to poor parenting (Advisory Council on the Misuse of Drugs 2003). We also know that children with special health care needs and/or disabilities place higher emotional, physical, economic and social demands on their families, increasing the likelihood of abuse, and this is likely to have been the case with some of the sample children (Hibbard and Desch 2007).

As the study progressed it became evident that the infants' vulnerability was intertwined with their parents' own difficulties, so that incipient health and developmental risk factors were compounded by ongoing exposure to neglect and abuse, and combined to jeopardize some of these very young children's chances of achieving wellbeing.

Evidence of maltreatment

All but one of the 43 infants in the full follow-up group were assessed as suffering or likely to suffer significant harm; 23 (53%) of them were maltreated at some stage before their third birthdays. Sixteen (37%) infants were maltreated *in utero*, either through their mother's continuing misuse of alcohol or drugs and/or through her or her partner's violent behaviour; 12 (28%) of these babies continued to be maltreated after birth, as did a further 11 (26%) children who did not experience abuse or neglect until after they were born. Altogether 16 (37%) of these very young children continued to experience maltreatment while their cases were open to children's social care; for 12 (28%), these concerns were still present at the end of the study, and had been ongoing for at least the first three years of their lives.

There was a wide range of different types of maltreatment; some, such as physical abuse, were easily definable, particularly in such a young and vulnerable population, although the indicators were not always swiftly identified. Witnessing intimate partner violence (classified as emotional abuse) was relatively easy to identify, at least where the instance had been so severe as to involve the police, who routinely notified children's social care when this happened.

However, the commonest form of maltreatment, neglect, was also the most difficult to identify, a point that has been amply demonstrated by other studies (see for instance Daniel *et al.* 2011; Ward *et al.* 2004). This is partly because neglect is a chronic rather than an acute condition, and does not always produce a crisis that can precipitate action. It is also hard to identify because it takes many different forms. Some babies in the sample who were neglected were left on their own in the home; others were looked after by adults who were too much under the influence of drugs or alcohol to meet their needs; others were left dirty and unkempt and important appointments to address health conditions were overlooked. Many infants experienced more than one form of neglect, and indeed chronic neglect was often accompanied by other types of abuse.

Emotional abuse is also notoriously difficult to define and identify (see Ward *et al.* 2004). However, the contention that it is an underlying factor in all types of maltreatment (see Barlow and Schrader McMillan 2010; Howe 2005) was amply illustrated by some of the case histories where, again, the age of the sample brought into sharp focus the evidence of parents' failure to appreciate how their actions impacted on their children's wellbeing.

Table 2.3 (see facing page) shows how the evidence of maltreatment in this study has been classified, following the descriptions of abuse and neglect given in government guidance on safeguarding children (see HM Government 2010, pp.38–39).

The following paragraphs give illustrative examples from the infants' case histories of the maltreatment they experienced and the circumstances under which it occurred.

Physical abuse

Four children in the full follow-up group experienced physical abuse; for two of them this was part of a complex pattern of different forms of maltreatment, but for two there was evidence of physical abuse alone. Both these latter infants sustained severe non-accidental injuries prior to referral to children's social care, and before they were six months old; one had a subdural haematoma most likely caused by 'shaking', and the other a fractured arm most likely

Table 2.3 Defining maltreatment

Event/situation	Type of maltreatment
Physical assault	Physical abuse
In utero intimate partner violence	Physical abuse
Witness to intimate partner violence	Emotional abuse
Threats of abandonment	Emotional abuse
Presence in household of convicted paedophile	Risk of sexual abuse
Left alone	Neglect
In utero drugs	Neglect
Instability (frequent changes of primary carer and/or domicile)	Neglect
Drug use in household	Neglect
Unkempt	Neglect
Unsafe situations	Neglect
Chaotic lifestyle of parent	Neglect
Not meeting health needs	Neglect

caused by a 'snapping' action as well as old fractures that became evident after a full skeletal survey.

A further six infants were living in households where high levels of violence were evident, both between the adults and also between adults and other children in the home. Although there was no evidence that these babies had experienced physical abuse when the study began, it was thought likely that this might happen in the future, and most of the intimate partner violence cases were classified as carrying a risk of physical as well as emotional abuse.

The physical abuse cases demonstrate the need for close collaboration and information-sharing between agencies, the need for a historical understanding of children's long-term experiences and the need for prompt and decisive actions in response to evidence of maltreatment. Dabir is an example of one such infant:

Dabir was living with both his parents in somewhat cramped accommodation. His parents were both aged 19 when he was born; they had financial difficulties and his father was unemployed. His mother had suffered from post-natal depression after his birth. At four and a half months, Dabir was made the subject of a child protection plan after a number of concerns had been raised about his parents' rough handling and apparently poor capacity to care for him. A month later he was found to have a fractured arm, and a full skeletal survey subsequently revealed old fractures that had gone undetected. Repeated physical abuse had probably been occurring since he was born. Both his parents were arrested and charged with abusing Dabir, who was placed with his maternal grandfather and his partner.

(Dabir: severe risk of harm at identification; safeguarded through separation at age three)

Sexual abuse

Three infants in the full follow-up group (and one in the intermediate group) were considered to be at significant risk of being sexually abused. These children had fathers or grandfathers who were convicted child sex offenders, and had extensive contact with them. In two cases the father was living in the child's home at the time the concerns were first raised. There is evidence that one of these very young children was being sexually abused, but no evidence of this happening for any of the others during the timescale of the study. The sexual abuse cases raise questions about perceptions of the risk of harm, about the limits of confidentiality, and about the ongoing position of adults who have previously abused children. As with the physical abuse cases, they also raise questions concerning the role of professionals in cases where one parent fails to protect a child from their partner's maltreatment. May provides an example of one of the infants for whom the risk of sexual abuse was the predominant concern:

May was identified by children's social care before she was born, following an anonymous referral by the relative of a victim of a serious child sexual assault committed by May's father. The assault had occurred 20 years previously, and May's father had served a prison sentence for it. However, concerns were raised because he had now remarried, and had two young children and another (May) due. It was thought that he might pose a risk of sexual abuse to May and her siblings.

(May: medium risk of harm at identification; low risk, living with birth parent and safeguarded at age three)

Neglect and emotional abuse

Nineteen (44%) infants in the full follow-up group experienced significant neglect during the period of the study; a further two experienced neglect in combination with physical and emotional abuse, and a further ten infants were considered to be at high risk of being neglected. Neglect was by far the most widespread type of maltreatment experienced by the sample children – a phenomenon which mirrors the national picture (see Department for Education 2011a). The evidence from the sample also indicates that neglect is the form of maltreatment most likely to be sustained for a lengthy period after identification: while none of the children apparently experienced physical abuse after their second birthdays, two thirds (12/18: 67%) of those who were neglected before their first birthday continued to be so when they were three years old. The neglect cases demonstrate the importance of developing an understanding of the child and family's previous history; the difficulties of identifying a threshold at which an issue that may initially appear to be of relatively minor concern becomes severe maltreatment with long-term consequences for the child; the challenges involved in taking proactive action where there is no obvious crisis; the difficulties of assessing parents' capacity to change within the child's timeframe; and the problems practitioners have in focusing on the child when the whole family is very vulnerable. All these issues have been identified in other, complementary studies (see, for instance, Daniel *et al.* 2011; Farmer and Lutman forthcoming). Janis was a typical neglect case:

Janis was born with severe visual impairment; his mother also had sight difficulties. Concerns were raised by Janis' older siblings' school because of their poor attendance, poor personal hygiene and behavioural difficulties. Janis' mother used drugs in the home and there were concerns that the baby was accidentally inhaling crack cocaine. The mother was also suspected of using the house for prostitution and having an 'inappropriate relationship' with her father, a known drugs dealer. Janis was often observed by professionals to be unkempt and he was not taken to health care checks, including appointments related to his visual impairment. His poor attendance at nursery meant that he could not make use of the special needs programme that had been devised for him. On several occasions his mother failed to order him the much needed glasses that would significantly help his sight. Janis' experiences of neglect and emotional abuse continued with no evidence of improvement throughout his first three years.

(Janis: severe risk of harm at identification; severe risk, living with birth parent but not safeguarded at age three)

Complex cases

Finally, while many of the children experienced one form of maltreatment, combinations were also common. Two infants who were physically abused were also neglected. There was an element of emotional abuse in all forms of maltreatment, but for some children this was also focused on their witnessing intimate partner violence, often coupled with neglect. The complex maltreatment cases raised all the issues present in those cases where a single type of abuse was evident, but the likelihood of them suffering harm appeared to be greater, and more difficult to address. Nathan was one such child:

Nathan's parents had a volatile relationship, with numerous incidents of intimate partner violence both before and after his birth. The intimate partner violence was exacerbated by his parents' misuse of alcohol, and rendered him likely to suffer both physical and emotional harm. His home was neglected and dirty and he and his mother frequently moved from one relative to another: by the age of three he had had 12 domiciles. His mother threatened to punish his father by leaving Nathan in his pushchair in the road and was eventually arrested when the police found that she had left him alone overnight in the home while she went to visit her boyfriend.

(Nathan: high risk of harm at identification; high risk, living with birth parent but not safeguarded at age three)

Conclusion

Table 2.4 shows the incidence of different types of abuse over which there were concerns. Almost all of the infants were assessed as suffering or likely to suffer significant harm, but not all of them actually experienced abuse or neglect, at least within the study timeframe. Table 2.5 shows the incidence of different types of maltreatment that were actually experienced by the full follow-up group before they reached the age of three.

Table 2.4 Types of maltreatment over which there
were concerns (full follow-up group: n=43)

Type of maltreatment	Frequency	Percentage
Sexual abuse	3	8
Physical abuse/neglect, emotional abuse and physical abuse	8	20
Neglect and emotional abuse	29	73
Total	**40**	**100***
Unclear/missing	3	

* Percentages are rounded figures.

Table 2.5 Types of maltreatment experienced
(full follow-up group: n=43)

Type of maltreatment	Frequency	Percentage
Sexual abuse	1	2
Physical abuse	2.	5
Neglect and emotional abuse	19	44
Neglect, emotional abuse and physical abuse	2	5
No experiences of abuse or neglect	19	44
Total	**43**	**100***

* Percentages are rounded figures.

Given their experience, it is not surprising that a number of children were displaying emotional or behavioural difficulties or delayed development by the end of the study. There was evidence of this in the case papers or from interviews for 13 of the 24 children (54%) who had experienced abuse or neglect. These included nine of the 19 (47%) children who had experienced neglect, one child who had experienced physical abuse, one child who had experienced sexual abuse and both those who had experienced complex patterns of maltreatment.

However, it is perhaps of equal interest that there was no evidence that 19 (44%) of these infants who were at very high risk of harm had ever experienced maltreatment by the time they were three. This is an important finding and is indicative of both the appropriateness of some of the decisions that were made, and of the strengths of some of the parents in overcoming extensive adversity.

The next chapter presents the parents and their circumstances. It explores the risk factors that made abuse more likely and the protective factors that enabled some to overcome the substantial difficulties with which they were struggling. Subsequent chapters then explore the extent to which professionals were able to analyse the risk and protective factors evident in parents and their environment and distinguish those parents who might be able to change from those who might not; the decisions they made and the reasons behind them; parents' views of what happened; and how far the children were safeguarded from further harm.

Summary points for Chapter 2

- It was possible to follow 43 of the original 57 infants until they reached the age of three. Thirty six (63%) children from the full sample were boys, 20 (35%) were girls, and one was unknown. Thirty five (69%) were White British and 16 (32%) were from Black and Minority Ethnic (BME) groups. The diversity of some of the children's heritage added to the complexity of the social worker's task.

- Thirty (64%) of the infants in the full sample had older siblings, all of whom were known to children's social care. In 20 (67%) cases these older children had been permanently removed from their mother's care by the time of the birth/identification of the index child.

- During the course of the study 12 mothers gave birth to another baby. Three of these new siblings were also deemed to be suffering, or likely to suffer, significant harm and have been included in the full sample.

- Thirty two (65%) of the infants in the follow-up groups were identified before birth as being likely to suffer significant harm, and a further 17 (35%) before their first birthdays.

- Information concerning children's developmental needs was only infrequently recorded on core assessments; given that 31 per cent of the babies were exposed to alcohol and/or substance misuse *in utero*, the paucity of information is an issue that needs to be addressed.

- Sixteen (37%) children continued to experience maltreatment while their cases were open to children's social care; concerns about the likelihood of significant harm were still present at the end of the study for 12 (28%) children, and had been ongoing for at least the first three years of their lives.

- Four infants in the full follow-up group experienced physical abuse, and a further six children were living in households where high levels of violence were evident.

- Neglect was by far the most widespread type of maltreatment. Nineteen (44%) infants in the full follow-up group experienced significant neglect during the period of the study; a further two experienced neglect in combination with physical and emotional abuse, and a further ten children were considered to be at high risk of being neglected.

- Three infants in the full follow-up group (and one in the intermediate group) were considered to be at significant risk of being sexually abused.

- While many of the children experienced just one form of maltreatment, combinations were also common.

- All but one of the 43 infants in the full follow-up group were assessed as suffering or likely to suffer significant harm; 24 (56%) of them were maltreated at some stage before their third birthdays. However, there is no evidence of maltreatment of the other 19 (44%) children. This is an important finding for this sample of children who were at exceptionally high risk of harm and is indicative of both the appropriateness of some of the decisions made, and the strengths of some of the parents in overcoming extensive adversity.

3

The Parents and Their Circumstances

Introduction

The infants were completely dependent on the capacity of parents or other adults to meet their needs – if this capacity was reduced, there was clearly a danger that their health or development might be significantly impaired. We know from the previous chapters that almost all these very young children were considered to be suffering, or likely to suffer, significant harm before their first birthday, and that about half of them had experienced abuse or maltreatment by the time they were three. In making decisions that would impact on their future welfare, the professionals involved had to identify the various risk factors posed by parents and the wider environment and assess how far these were mitigated by the presence of protective factors. This chapter focuses on the parents and their circumstances; it discusses their vulnerability and explores the evidence of risk and protective factors at the point at which initial decisions were made. Later chapters will show how the pattern of risk changed over the following years as, for instance, parents overcame (or failed to overcome) damaging behaviours, as relationships between adults and between adults and children changed, and as new information came to light; they will trace in some detail how such evidence of change impacted (or failed to impact) on key decisions concerning the children's future welfare.

The full sample of 57 infants included four sibling pairs. This chapter focuses on their 53 families. This includes 53 mothers and 34 fathers who were involved in the care of their child and/or were living in the same household.

The parents

As must be evident from the previous chapter, many parents were facing substantial adversities. They started out as vulnerable adults, who tended to have been maltreated themselves as children, to have little constructive support from their wider families, and to have few of the skills or qualifications necessary for employment. Before the birth of the index child, many of them had also experienced unstable and chaotic lives, with frequent changes of partner and household.

Unsurprisingly, the interviews with birth parents indicated that almost all the infants were unplanned. A number of birth mothers had considered abortion or had been encouraged to do so by partners or other family members:

> When I found out I was pregnant I was like, oh no…I didn't want him and I went to have an abortion, but I couldn't go through with it. (Birth mother of Martin-Louis: medium risk of harm at identification; low risk, living with birth parent and safeguarded at age three)

Some fathers questioned their paternity, or left when they became aware of the pregnancy:

> Soon as he found I were pregnant, [he] walked out, haven't seen him since. (Birth mother of Janis: severe risk of harm at identification; severe risk, living with birth parent but not safeguarded at age three)

> He's never seen [child's name]… He's never wanted to. (Birth mother of Matthew: severe risk of harm at identification; low risk, living with birth parent and safeguarded at age three)

Nevertheless, almost all birth parents interviewed talked about 'doing the best' for their child. At the point of the core assessment, over half of the parents were living together (34/57: 60%), 21 (37%) infants were living with their mother only, and two (4%) infants were living with their father only. It is noteworthy that at this stage almost two thirds of fathers were involved in supporting both the child and the birth mother. The interviews with birth mothers make it clear that a number of fathers were present at the baby's birth; Martin-Louis' father, for instance, had 'been to all the ante-natal appointments and scans and things' and, with the midwife's help, had delivered the baby.

One of the key findings from this study is the extent to which fathers become excluded as part of the safeguarding process. In many cases, as we shall see, this was an inevitable consequence of their own behaviour, but there was also a widespread expectation that fathers might play only a marginal role in their children's lives. This was initially evident in the paucity of available data about fathers on case files. Even when fathers were extensively involved with the care of the baby, there was a tendency for both case records and practitioners in interviews to focus on the mother as the main caregiver and the father as a secondary figure (see Brown and Ward forthcoming (b)). There was further evidence of this tendency to marginalize fathers in some of the subsequent decisions. The invisibility of fathers in safeguarding practice has been identified in numerous other studies (see for instance Fauth *et al.* 2010; Featherstone *et al.* 2010; Ryan 2000).

Issues affecting parenting capacity

Whatever their initial intentions, it was also evident that many parents were facing substantial problems that were likely to impact on their caregiving. As Chapter 1 has shown, the adverse impact of factors such as physical and mental ill-health, substance misuse, learning disability and intimate partner violence on parents' capacity to meet their children's needs is now well established (see among others Cleaver *et al.* 2007, 2011; Jones *et al.* 2006). The evidence also shows that those who grow up in families affected by these issues are more likely to suffer significant harm (see among others Barnard 2007; Cleaver *et al.* 2007, 2011; Kroll and Taylor 2003; Tunnard 2002). There is also research evidence linking certain parental factors with an increased risk of *recurrent* maltreatment, a pertinent issue in cases where abuse or neglect has already occurred and decisions have to be made about whether a child should remain with or be removed from their birth parents.

Hindley and colleagues (2006) undertook 'an evidence based, systematic review of studies of outcome following identification of child abuse and neglect, in order to provide the most up to date assessment of factors which pertain to the likelihood of re-abuse and other poor outcomes' (Jones *et al.* 2006, p.275). They reported that the most consistently identified factors for recurring abuse were parental conflict and parental mental health difficulties. They also found other factors to be associated with recurrent abuse, although less consistently. These included substance and alcohol misuse, lack of informal support and a history of abuse during the parent's own childhood (Hindley *et al.* 2006, p.751). The following discussion explores the prevalence of such risk factors amongst the parents of infants in the sample.

Parents' previous history

There is considerable evidence to show that many parents who maltreat their children have experienced abusive childhoods themselves (see, for example, Jones 2008; Noll *et al.* 2009; Putallaz *et al.* 1998). Twenty two (22/53: 42%) of the mothers in the sample are known to have been abused as children, either in the UK or in their country of origin. The paucity of information recorded on case files about fathers meant there was only evidence that one had experienced an abusive childhood, undoubtedly an under-estimate. At least 16 (16/53: 30%) mothers and two (2/34: 6%) fathers had been looked after by the local authority for some or all of their childhood. Many of the parents found that their own experiences of abuse were difficult to overcome and impacted, both in terms of poor parenting skills and lack of confidence, on their own parenting capacity.

Mental health issues, alcohol and substance misuse, intimate partner violence and learning disability

We know that adults who have not been able to come to terms with their own experiences of abuse in childhood are more likely to become addicted to alcohol or drugs, to develop mental health problems or to become involved in violent or abusive relationships (Cleaver *et al.* 2011; Noll *et al.* 2009). It is therefore not surprising to find that at the time the first social work decision was made one or more of these factors were considered to be an issue in over three quarters of the families in the sample (42/53: 79%). Our earlier study of very young looked after children (Ward *et al.* 2006) has already highlighted the impact of such factors on decisions concerning the future wellbeing of the child; in that study, none of the babies of parents with mental ill-health, intimate partner violence, or drug or alcohol misuse problems were successfully rehabilitated to their birth families after they had been looked after for a year.

Table 3.1 shows the prevalence of these risk factors at the time of the first core assessment for the study children. The apparently lower incidence of problems experienced by fathers is likely to be an artefact, reflecting the lack of attention given to them (see above) and the fact that at least 21 (21/57: 37%) were no longer involved in the family at this stage, rather than a genuine disparity.

Table 3.1 Issues affecting parenting capacity (full sample of mothers: n=53; full sample of fathers: n=34)

Issues affecting parenting capacity	Issue at first decision (number)	Issue at first decision (percentage*)
Mental ill-health (mother)	24/53	45
Mental ill-health (father)	5/34	15
Substance misuse (mother)	20/53	38
Substance misuse (father)	14/34	41
Intimate partner violence	21/53	40

* Percentages are rounded figures.

MENTAL ILL-HEALTH

A frequently identified issue relating to maternal parenting capacity was mental ill-health. As Table 3.1 shows, for 24 (24/53: 45%) mothers, mental health problems were a concern at the point of the first decision. There were variations in the nature and severity of difficulties experienced: post-natal depression was relatively common, but diagnoses also included schizophrenia, chronic depression and personality disorders. The severity of symptoms ranged from low mood to suicide attempts and/or attempts to harm the baby. Although, as Table 3.1 shows, only five fathers were recorded as suffering from mental health problems, this is likely to be an under-estimate, for the reasons noted above. The conditions recorded were 'post-traumatic stress disorder', 'psychiatric problems and depression', 'agoraphobia and personality pathology' and 'obsessive compulsive disorder'.

In certain circumstances mental health conditions can have a major impact on the parent's capacity to care for a child. Parents with mental health problems can be emotionally withdrawn and have difficulty in forming attachments or meeting the child's other emotional needs; they can find themselves unable to meet the child's physical needs for basic care and safety; in extreme cases they can become delusional and pose a physical threat to their children (Cleaver et al. 2011). Such difficulties are also exacerbated if mental health problems are combined with alcohol or drug problems (Cleaver et al. 2011; Hogan 1998), as was the case for 12 (23%) birth mothers and three (9%) birth fathers.

At the time of the first decision, four of the 24 mothers who had mental health problems were considered likely to physically abuse their children; two were regarded as unlikely to be able to protect their children from partners or family members who posed a threat of sexual abuse; 13 mothers with mental health problems were considered likely to neglect their children; and the data are unclear for the other five.

If parents' mental health problems respond to treatment, their children are less likely to suffer significant harm; the presence of a supportive adult can also be a protective factor (Hindley *et al.* 2006). In some families such factors existed, and these were seen to mitigate the extent to which infants were affected by their parents' ongoing mental health problems.

Scrutiny of case records revealed poor recording in relation to the impact that mental health difficulties had or might have upon a parent's capacity to provide adequate care and protection, and the potential neutralizing power of protective influences.

ALCOHOL AND SUBSTANCE MISUSE

As Table 3.1 shows, substance misuse was identified as a problem that was a current concern for 20 (20/53: 38%) mothers and 14 (14/34: 41%) fathers. These figures may not reflect the prevalence of substance misuse amongst parents whose infants are identified as suffering, or likely to suffer, significant harm, as addiction and a consequently chaotic lifestyle will mean that these parents are less likely to return consent forms and engage in research. Moreover, such a suspicion is supported by the qualitative evidence gained from professionals, who are able to draw on their wider experiences of such cases. Substance misuse among parents was most commonly cited by professional interviewees as one of the issues affecting local communities. Furthermore, discussions with local authority senior managers suggest that it has precipitated increases in the number of very young children entering care or accommodation. Most maternity units have reported an increase in the number of pregnant women with drug problems over the last five years (Advisory Council on the Misuse of Drugs 2003).

Overall, evidence of current drug or alcohol misuse in the parents of sample children was identified in 23 (23/53: 43%) households at the point of the first decision. In 11 of these only the mother was misusing drugs or alcohol, in nine it was an issue for both parents, and in three cases it was a concern regarding only the father. Sixteen (16/53: 30%) mothers continued to misuse drugs and/or alcohol while they were pregnant with the index child.

The nature and type of drug and/or alcohol use was not always clear from case file data but in all cases where it was raised as a key risk factor the parent was using class A substances or alcohol in a problematic or chronic manner. As is common among problematic drug users, most substance-misusing parents were using more than one type of drug (Newcomb and Felix-Ortiz 1992).

The ramifications of drug and alcohol problems are far reaching. In addition to the danger to their mother's health, children living in such families are at high risk of being maltreated throughout their childhood. Parents who tend primarily to their own needs (to satisfy their addictions) are likely to neglect their children's needs (Kroll and Taylor 2003). Alongside neglect, children of addicts are often exposed to the associated problems of criminality, intimate partner violence, and physical and emotional abuse.

Kroll and Taylor (2003) highlight a further issue that is particularly important for babies and very young children: the impact drug and alcohol problems can have on attachment. They question the ability of parents, for whom the 'principal attachment is to a substance', to make attachments to their children (Kroll and Taylor 2003, p.16). The case example of Nathan is revisited below, and demonstrates parental alcohol misuse in context, and the associated neglect and attachment issues:

> Nathan's parents' violent relationship was underpinned by their alcohol use. While his father's alcoholism was seen as more serious, the social worker recounted incidents where Nathan's mother had left him with his father while she went out and got drunk. As Nathan grew older, concerns over his mother's attachment to him were raised by the social worker, who commented: 'The attachment with Nathan appeared to be very weak. So we did a lot of work at the family centre…on issues around attachment so an assessment was done and support was given to [mother] to encourage that bond…and that did make a difference…although I've, in the last probably three or four months, I've had a bit of a question mark about that bond in my own head' (social worker).
>
> *(Nathan: high risk of harm at identification; high risk living with birth parent but not safeguarded at age three)*

INTIMATE PARTNER VIOLENCE

There is a recognized association between problem drinking and intimate partner violence (Coleman and Cassell 1995); indeed around 80 per cent of cases of intimate partner violence are alcohol-related (Velleman 1993). Intimate partner violence was identified as a concern in 21 families (21/53: 40%), as shown in Table 3.1.

Violence during pregnancy can expose unborn babies to direct harm (Humphreys and Stanley 2006). Cleaver and colleagues' (2011) overview of parents' problems and their consequences found that intimate partner violence can have a negative impact on the unborn child through inherited traits (e.g.

parental personality disorder), physical damage to the foetus and the effects of maternal stress. Women in violent relationships may experience an increase in both the severity and frequency of abuse when they become pregnant; moreover 40–60 per cent of pregnant women exposed to intimate partner violence during pregnancy experience punches or kicks to the abdomen, with a consequent risk of physical harm to the mother and/or foetus (see Cleaver *et al.* 2011, p.105). Following birth, children continue to be placed at risk and parent–child attachments may also be affected by exposure to intimate partner violence (Humphreys and Stanley 2006).

Four babies in the sample were exposed to intimate partner violence *in utero*, as their mothers suffered at the hands of violent partners while pregnant. The abuse continued for all of these infants following their birth. Because these children were so young, all of those whose parents were engaged in a violent relationship were at risk of being physically, as well as emotionally, abused, as they were in danger of getting injured during the course of a violent argument. A number had siblings who had been placed away from home because they had either been injured or were considered likely to be physically harmed in these situations. Ava provides an example of an infant for whom the likelihood of witnessing or becoming caught up in intimate partner violence was the primary cause of concern:

Ava's mother had a long-standing history of violent and abusive relationships with various partners; as a result of this and the consequent instability of her lifestyle, Ava's three older siblings had been removed from home. When Ava was born her mother was free of violent relationships; mother and baby had support from Ava's (non-abusive) father and the paternal grandmother. The parents were separated and Ava remained with her mother but had regular contact with her father. However, when Ava was two she and her mother were evicted from their home due to rent arrears. The mother then began a period of entering violent relationships and moving herself and Ava between her partners' homes, and in and out of refuges. The pattern that had led to the older children's adoption was repeating; by the time Ava was three she had witnessed several reported incidents of violent altercations between her mother and her various partners. Ava remained in her mother's care throughout the study period.

(Ava: medium risk of harm at identification; high risk, living with birth parent but not safeguarded at age three)

There were 21 (21/53: 40%) families for whom intimate partner violence was a current concern at the time of referral. These included five couples who were violent to each other, 15 fathers who were violent to their partners and one mother who was violent to the father.

Ava's mother was one of several who had well-established histories of moving from one violent relationship to another, a recognized phenomenon amongst women who have experienced abusive childhoods and have low self-esteem and limited life chances. As time progressed over the three years of the study, this tendency was observed in many of the intimate partner violence cases.

Intimate partner violence was also associated with other types of criminally aggressive behaviour. It is important to note the extent to which some of the infants were at risk of being caught up in violent interchanges between the adults in their lives: Martin-Louis' father, for instance, arrived at the mother's house with a gang of his friends to try to force her to hand the baby over to him; Harry's mother thought herself to be in danger of suffering reprisals from a Yardie gang when she tried to stop misusing drugs; both of Blossom's parents had served prison sentences for assault; both Nathan and May's fathers were alleged to have raped teenage girls; Shay's father had bitten off someone's finger in a fight; and Gary's father had a conviction for armed robbery. In England and Wales, on average two women per week are killed by partners or former partners (Home Office 2002); it seems likely that some of the mothers in the sample were living in similarly dangerous situations.

Cleaver and colleagues (2007) show how fear of violence has an impact on professional decision-making, for 'to confront families on issues which are likely to result in a violent response is frightening, and when practitioners feel unsupported or must visit alone, there is a danger that concerns are not thoroughly investigated' (p.23), a point also raised by a recent review of effective practice to protect children living in highly resistant families (Fauth et al. 2010). Such issues were very real in some of the cases in this study; Blossom's father, for instance, had kidnapped two social workers and held them at knifepoint for several hours. It would be surprising if the fear of violence had not influenced some areas of practice.

In addition to those whose violence posed a threat to the children, there were also three fathers (and one mother) who had Schedule One[1] status at the point of the first social work decision. The presence of both physically and/or

---

1 A Schedule One offender was, until recently, the term commonly used for anyone convicted of an offence against a child listed in Schedule One of the Children and Young Person's Act 1933. It occurred frequently on children's case files and in interviews with professionals, and has therefore been used in this book, although it has now officially been replaced by the term 'presenting a risk to children' (see HM Government 2010, p.323).

sexually abusive men in a household prompted concerns around the ability of some mothers to protect their children from the threat of abuse.

PARENTAL LEARNING DISABILITIES

In a small number of cases other issues were identified as affecting parenting capacity. Adults with learning disabilities can successfully parent children, but they will need extensive encouragement, training and long-term support to acquire the necessary skills to do so. Such support may not be available, particularly on a long-term basis. Cleaver and colleagues (2007) found that 58 per cent of learning disabled parents experienced difficulties in ensuring the safety of their children (see also Cleaver *et al.* 2011). International research indicates that between 40 and 60 per cent of learning disabled parents have their children taken into care following court proceedings (McConnell and Llewellyn 2002). Five mothers (including one with Asperger's syndrome and two in supported accommodation) and three fathers in the current study were identified as having a learning disability. Parental learning disabilities were an issue in a total of six cases.

Interviews with professionals in these cases provide an insight into how learning disability can impact on parenting capacity:

> My biggest concern was that, I think it had got to do with his learning problems, he doesn't show any interest in the child... in an hour's contact he would probably total with the baby for about two or three minutes, and that's it...he wasn't showing any interest in the contact. Mum as well, she doesn't have any interest. (Social worker)

The mother of this infant also had learning disabilities, and the same social worker considered that this made her 'extremely anxious' and suggested this was an obstruction to successful parenting.

Parental learning disability was the sole concern in only two of these cases; in the others the assortment of issues included intimate partner violence, substance misuse, chaotic lifestyle and mental health difficulties, among others (see also Cleaver *et al.* 2007). In two sample cases both parents had learning disabilities, and in both these intimate partner violence was also an identified issue.

Combinations of risk factors, such as those identified above, frequently coexist, and are known to render children increasingly vulnerable to abuse and neglect (see Cleaver *et al.* 2011; Hogan 1998; Klee, Jackson and Lewis 2002). Only two families in the current study were faced with only one risk factor at the point of first decision. In most cases the focus of social work concerns was around a collection of risks. These were often interlinked and reflected some of the issues and challenges present in the wider communities in which these families resided. Combinations of factors render the issues increasingly complex and make the task of addressing them more problematic for practitioners.

Older children removed

At least 20 mothers and an unknown number of fathers had already experienced the permanent removal of older children prior to the birth of the sample child. Such experiences are indicative of the entrenched nature of the risk factors facing the families. However, losing a child to adoption or special guardianship also had a major, ongoing impact on parents' subsequent functioning, for it had left them with an enduring sense of shame and loss.

Research on birth families' views on adoption highlights the ongoing difficulties they face when coming to terms with losing their children. Ironically, the issues in the parents' lives that precipitated the removal of the child may also hamper their ability to deal with the resultant loss (Neil 2007; Neil *et al.* 2010). Indeed, it was not uncommon for birth parents in the current study to respond to the removal of a child by increasing their substance misuse or experiencing more extensive mental health problems.

Neil and colleagues (2010) found that, following adoption, many birth relatives experienced emotional difficulties that remained unresolved; three quarters of those interviewed well over a year after the adoption were still experiencing psychological distress at clinically significant levels. Interviews with parents in the current study confirmed what one might therefore expect: that the adoption of older children presented a substantial emotional challenge. During interviews, one parent explained how 'emotions were everywhere' following the permanent removal of a child, while another told the researcher: 'I can't explain the feeling, I was just devastated, absolutely devastated.'

The responses of positive acceptance, resignation, and anger and resistance identified by Neil (2007) could all be seen in the current sample to some degree, but the latter was most prominent. Several parents spoke of being 'frustrated and angry' about child removal. One father expressed his confusion and fury in the following terms:

> Where was them coming to fucking tell me and explain to me why you took the only thing in my life that matters…you've took something that you're not allowed…you try and get a lion cub off its mother, and it fucking rips your arm off…that's nature, you protect your young. It's instinct in all of us, we're animals…and that's what I say is mine, my young. Now if I was an animal I could kill them and get away with it, but…I'm classed as a human being,

I shouldn't feel that kind of pain…if you show anger, they use it, if you show any emotion to them, they use it, you're not allowed to get angry, you're not allowed to scream, you're not allowed to shout, you're not allowed to swear. (Birth father of Blossom: severe risk of harm at identification; safeguarded through separation at age three)

Blossom's father went on to make the following case against having her adopted:

…couples are screaming for babies, well they're not having my fucking baby, you know, just because they're infertile, tough shit, do you know what I mean? But I'm no fucking excuse for someone to be happy. (Birth father of Blossom: severe risk of harm at identification; safeguarded through separation at age three)

Parents who had experienced the permanent removal of an older child were understandably fearful that the same action would immediately be taken for the index baby, particularly if they had not succeeded in overcoming their difficulties. Three mothers (3/53: 6%) responded to such fears by concealing their pregnancies. The case of Olivia exhibits these fears:

Olivia's mother had experienced the removal of two older children following serious concerns about her parenting capacity and the neglect they experienced. During care proceedings for these older children, Olivia's mother became pregnant. Because she was frightened that Olivia would also be removed, she concealed the pregnancy from Olivia's father, with whom she lived, children's social care and the courts. She succeeded in keeping the pregnancy secret until she started labour.

(Olivia: medium risk of harm at identification; low risk, living with birth parent and safeguarded at age three)

Mothers who took such action tended to enter a vicious circle in that by concealing the pregnancy they were seen to endanger both their own and their baby's health, thereby rendering them more vulnerable and increasing the chances of removal. All these three birth mothers lost the care of their babies.

Risk factors in the wider environment

Financial issues

Other stressors such as financial difficulties were an ancillary concern in some cases. Among the current sample, financial difficulties were substantial enough to be recorded on case files as a risk factor for five families, although it must be remembered that poverty was endemic in the lives of many of the others, and in the communities in which they lived. Financial strain can exacerbate already difficult situations and mean that the impact of other risk factors is more pronounced (Cleaver *et al.* 2011).

Housing issues

Leslie (2005) has drawn attention to the high incidence of housing problems amongst families who receive social work support, and the lack of attention given to this issue. While it was rare for housing issues to be cited as a reason for considering whether a child was suffering, or likely to suffer, significant harm, concerns with regard to housing circumstances were identified for a third of the families (19/53: 36%). Eight of these families were faced with homelessness: this included street homelessness (one case), 'sofa surfing' (three cases), residing in a hostel for the homeless (one case), and in three cases there was a threat of eviction or a parent was about to be released from prison with nowhere to live. The remaining 11 families were living in precarious circumstances in homes that were over-crowded or in a poor state of repair, or in a neighbourhood where the attentions of drug dealers and abusers made it extremely difficult to address their own substance misuse. The following quote from a social worker exemplifies such concerns:

> The people living in and around the flat were all using drugs, which was not really acceptable, but steps had been taken to try and, you know, re-house, but I think with the, with the amount – the demand – in the local area far outstrips the amount of accommodation available, so that was an ongoing issue. (Social worker)

Team leaders were also acutely aware of the problems posed by poor housing, citing it as one of the issues affecting the local community at large:

> Housing is a major feature here now, there's so little council housing, and relations with the housing department are absolutely zilch from what I can gather, from the department as a whole, not just me. (Team leader, children's social care)

The mitigating value of protective factors

There is substantial evidence that certain protective factors can interact positively with the established risk factors and reduce the likelihood of future significant harm. Hindley and colleagues (2006) identified the following parent factors as being among those that are particularly pertinent: the presence of a non-abusive partner; the presence of a supportive extended family; parents' adaptation to childhood abuse; parents' recognition that there is a problem, and their willingness to take responsibility for it; and parents' willingness to engage with services.

Many of these protective factors were evident in the families of the sample children, and served to mitigate the impact of the numerous risk factors.

Presence of a supportive, non-abusive partner

Twenty one of the mothers were no longer involved with the birth father by the time the first social work decision was made, and many of these were either single parents or in fragile relationships. However, seven abusive mothers had partners who could provide a supportive and protective influence, and this appears to have had a positive impact in most cases. For example, Natasha and Olivia's fathers left their partners and looked after their infants themselves, with the support of Residence Orders. However, in Ava's case the general tendency to overlook the father's capacity to act as a supportive parent meant that when the parents separated a Residence Order in favour of the birth father and the paternal grandmother was not applied for, and the child remained with a mother who proved, ultimately, unable to meet her needs. In other cases fathers appear to have helped instigate changes in the mother's lifestyle, thus enabling children to remain with them.

Wider family and informal support

In addition to those who had supportive partners, 15 parents had some form of informal support they were able to draw upon. Networks of informal support were diverse and originated from areas of the community such as the local church, as well as from the extended family. In most instances, however, informal support came from grandmothers and aunts who sometimes came forward to support both the birth mother and the child. Brendan is an example of one such case:

Brendan's mother's mental health problems dominated concerns about whether she could provide him with adequate care. She had a history of self-harm, suicidal tendencies and reported feelings of wanting to harm Brendan. She had been sexually abused as a child; she misused substances and had a chaotic lifestyle.

This vulnerable young woman was largely isolated from her wider family, except for her own mother who gave up her job to support the family. This support was seen to be instrumental in the outcome for Brendan who remained with his mother throughout the study.

(Brendan: medium risk of harm at identification; low risk, living with birth parents and safeguarded at age three)

The issue of wider familial support demonstrates the extent to which complex risk factors interact with one another. Parents who had experienced abuse and/or been looked after by the local authority in their own childhood tended to have diminished or non-existent support from their extended families in adulthood. Pippa's mother, for instance, had been sexually abused and placed away from home during childhood. She had had three children removed previously, and eventually lost Pippa to adoption. The concerns of the local authority in this case were multiple, but the mother's vulnerability, attachment to dangerous adults and isolation were considered to be of key importance. The difficulties she faced were largely attributed to the abuse she had experienced during her own childhood and her subsequent relationship with her own family, which was characterized by feelings of anger towards them.

The isolation of some birth mothers was particularly evident where members of the extended family were Schedule One offenders, and parents had agreed to break off contact with them in order to safeguard their own infants. In the case of Jordan, both the grandfathers and the birth mother's partner were Schedule One offenders. The mother was considered to be emotionally dependent on her own father, who had brought her up, but was required to reduce contact with him and restrict his access to her own child because he had sexually abused two teenagers.

Although there were obvious reasons why some violent or abusive adults should not have had contact with the sample children, birth parents in these situations tended not to have other, supportive members of an extended family to whom they might turn. Many of the birth mothers had poor relationships with their own mothers, who had failed to protect them in childhood. Their social networks were further diminished by low self-esteem and a lack of a supportive network of friends. It is understandable that, given the absence of support from family and friends, some mothers found it difficult to extricate themselves from abusive relationships, as in the case of Isla:

Isla was made the subject of a child protection plan when she was around nine months old because of her parents' intimate partner violence. Social workers attempted to engage the mother and encourage her to end the relationship with Isla's father, who was in and out of prison in the first year of her life. The relationship between the parents was one of break-up and reunification, and the mother had attempted to hide their reunification several times. Efforts to engage with the mother failed and ultimately Isla was placed for adoption when she was 14 months old.

(Isla: severe risk of harm at identification; safeguarded through separation at age three)

The isolation of very vulnerable birth parents has been noted in other research that has focused on similar populations, and has obvious implications for the provision of services. Neil and colleagues' (2010) study of post-adoption support found this to be a key factor amongst the birth parents in their sample. Selwyn and colleagues (2010) found that this was a particular issue for white mothers of mixed ethnicity children who were permanently placed away from home. These women sometimes experienced overt racism from their relatives and were nearly three times as likely not to have any extended family support as white mothers in similar situations. However, this finding was not replicated in the current study, where isolation appeared to be more closely related to the mother's own experience of childhood abuse. There is also evidence in this study that some white mothers of mixed ethnicity children received extensive, positive support from the paternal extended family.

Parents' insight, understanding, and capacity to change

The most important protective factors related to parents themselves, their own understanding of the problem, their willingness to engage with services and their ability to come to terms with those factors within their own childhood and adult experiences that had led them to abuse their children.

Insight and understanding are paramount in prompting behavioural and lifestyle change. Jones and colleagues (2006) note that: 'On occasion a parent can agree to relinquish care of one child, while starting an extended process of change which eventually enables him or her to care for a future child adequately' (p.286). While this was not always evident at the point of the first decision, a number of cases in the current study exemplify a situation where, despite often multiple and severe risk factors, parents managed to make sufficient changes to enable them to meet the needs of the index child. This was true of about one in three of those birth mothers in the full follow-up group who had previously had a child placed for adoption (5/14: 36%).

Classification of families where children are suffering or likely to suffer significant harm

The above exploration of the infants' needs and their parents' circumstances demonstrates the complexity of the professionals' task when there are child protection concerns. All but one of the sample babies were assessed as suffering, or likely to suffer, significant harm and a number had already been maltreated before they came to the attention of children's social care; most of their parents were labouring under multiple difficulties and many had shown themselves unable to safeguard older children. Protective factors were present in some families, in the form of supportive partners or relatives, and many parents showed a willingness to change, but professionals had to decide whether these were sufficient to reduce the likelihood of significant harm in the future.

This chapter has made extensive use of Hindley and colleagues' (2006) systematic review of studies of outcome following identification of child abuse and neglect. The researchers advocate the use of such evidence in social work decision-making, though they are careful to stress the limitations of actuarial approaches and the importance of giving due weight to qualitative assessment of individual factors when real world decisions have to be made that can have lasting consequences for children and their families (Jones *et al.* 2006). Table 3.2 sets out a number of factors that have been found to be associated with an increased likelihood of significant harm, contrasted with those protective factors that have been found to be associated with a decreased likelihood of its occurrence. Those items in italics met the inclusion criteria of the systematic review; the other factors have been identified by other studies that may not have been so rigorous (see Jones *et al.* 2006).

Table 3.2 Factors associated with future harm

Factors	Future significant harm more likely	Future significant harm less likely
Abuse	Severe physical abuse including burns/scalds *Neglect* Severe growth failure Mixed abuse *Previous maltreatment* Sexual abuse with penetration or over a long duration Fabricated/induced illness Sadistic abuse	Less severe forms of abuse If severe, yet compliance and lack of denial, success still possible
Child	Developmental delay with special needs Mental health problems Very young – requiring rapid parental change	Healthy child Attributions (in sexual abuse) Later age of onset One good corrective relationship
Parent	*Personality disorder* • Anti-social • Sadistic • Aggressive Lack of compliance Denial of problems Learning disabilities plus *mental illness* Substance misuse *Paranoid psychosis* Abuse in childhood – not recognized as a problem	Non-abusive partner Willingness to engage with services Recognition of problem Responsibility taken Mental disorder, responsive to treatment Adaption to childhood abuse

Table 3.2 Factors associated with future harm *cont.*

Factors	Future significant harm more likely	Future significant harm less likely
Parenting and parent/ child interaction	Disordered attachment Lack of empathy for child Poor parenting competency Own needs before child's	Normal attachment Empathy for child Competence in some areas
Family	*Inter-parental conflict and violence* Family stress Power problems: poor negotiation, autonomy and affect expression	Absence of intimate partner violence Non-abusive partner Capacity for change Supportive extended family
Professional	Lack of resources Ineptitude	Therapeutic relationship with child Outreach to family Partnership with parents
Social setting	Social isolation Lack of social support Violent, unsupportive neighbourhood	Social support More local child care facilities Volunteer networks

Source: adapted from Jones (1991, 1998). (Reproduced from Jones et al. 2006, pp.277–8.)

This framework was used to classify families in the current study, both at the point of identification and again when the children reached their third birthdays. There were a number of difficulties. Not all the items were appropriate to such very young children; for instance, mental health problems had not yet revealed themselves, and at the start of the study none had had an opportunity to develop one good corrective relationship; for many of the infants, it was also too early at identification for developmental delay and special needs to have been diagnosed. Moreover the data were patchy (particularly those concerning professional competence and resources) and we were reliant on what was written down or revealed at interview: inevitably there were gaps in our information. Data were readily available on parental substance misuse, mental ill-health, intimate partner violence and childhood abuse. However, evidence of protective factors concerning the parents, such as 'responsiveness of mental disorder to treatment' or 'adaptation to childhood abuse', was less consistently available.

Notwithstanding these difficulties, it was possible to utilize evidence concerning those risk and protective factors shown in Table 3.2 to distinguish between those families where the likelihood of children suffering harm appeared to be higher or lower than in others. Because one of the aims of the study was to explore whether it might be possible to identify parents who were able to make sufficient changes to meet their babies' needs within an appropriate timescale, particular weight was given to any evidence that demonstrated their capacity to change. Families were allocated to one of four groups, using a very simple classification system, as follows:

- **Severe risk of harm:** families showing risk factors, no protective factors and no evidence of capacity to change.

- **High risk of harm:** families showing risk factors and at least one protective factor but no evidence of capacity to change.

- **Medium risk of harm:** families showing risk factors and at least one protective factor including evidence of capacity to change.

- **Low risk of harm:** families showing no risk factors (or families whose earlier risk factors had now been addressed), and protective factors including evidence of capacity to change.

Classification was undertaken by two members of the research team, initially working independently. This method resulted in inter-rater agreement on categorization of 36 (84%) of the families at this stage. The remaining seven cases were classified following discussion between the researchers. Most anomalies arose through lack of sufficient information; wherever the position was unclear, parents were given the benefit of the doubt and given the more positive rating.

One reason for classifying the families in this way was to explore how far professional decision-making matched the evidence concerning the likelihood of significant harm. By repeating the classification when children were three, we were able to identify those families where the risk factors had decreased or increased in the years following the initial decision, in order to explore whether certain factors might have been identified at the outset that might indicate which families were most likely to overcome their difficulties – and which were not. Because the exercise was repeated when the children were three, the classification refers to the 43 infants in the full follow-up group.

Table 3.3 Risk of harm at identification (full follow-up group: n=43)

Risk of harm	Frequency	Per cent
Severe	12	28
High	7	16
Medium	21	49
Low	1	2
Outliers	2	5
Total	**43**	**100***

* Percentages are rounded figures.

As Table 3.3 shows, at identification almost half (44%) of the infants in the sample were at high or severe risk of suffering harm, with parents who had shown no evidence of a capacity to change. Twenty one (49%) parents had shown some capacity to change, but nevertheless still displayed risk factors that are associated with significant harm or its recurrence. Only one family fell into the low risk group at identification, thereby displaying no risk factors that are associated with abuse or its recurrence and thus not needing to change. Virtually all families displayed more than one risk factor; moreover, many families displayed other factors, such as prostitution or a concealed pregnancy, which do not appear on Jones and colleagues' (2006) list, and were therefore not included in the classification, but nevertheless are obvious indicators of vulnerability.

Families where there was a severe risk of harm

More than one in four (12/43: 28%) of the infants in the full follow-up group were identified as being at severe risk of suffering harm. The absence of protective factors, including evidence of parents' capacity to change, was the distinguishing feature for this group. Parents who were recorded as 'lacking empathy' were most likely to fall into this group, and there was a slightly higher level of intimate partner violence. Otherwise the *types* of risk factors were similar to those in other groups. However, the average *number* of risk factors (six) shown by these families was greater, with half of them displaying six or more. Peter is an example of a child whose family were in this group:

Peter's mother had been sexually abused in childhood, had a history of substance misuse and a diagnosed personality disorder. His father also had a history of substance misuse and suffered from depression. Care proceedings had been instigated for Peter's five older siblings whilst his mother was pregnant with him. The main concerns were around neglect and emotional abuse as the household was used for drug dealing, the older siblings were not attending school and an older sister, who was under 16 at the time, was allowed to have sexual relationships with older men. The children were also socially isolated and the family were not engaging with services. As the care proceedings had not yet concluded by the time of Peter's birth, he was initially allowed home with his mother and was made the subject of a child protection plan under the category of neglect. One month later the courts decided that Peter and his older siblings should be permanently separated from their parents. Peter was moved to foster care and later placed for adoption.

(Peter: severe risk of harm at identification;
safeguarded through separation at age three)

Families where there was a high risk of harm

Seven (16%) infants were identified as being at high risk of suffering harm. *Types* of risk factor were similar to those in the other groups, though the average *number* (five) was slightly lower than in the severe risk group, with under half displaying six or more. The protective factors, whose presence distinguished this group from that in which children were at severe risk of harm, were either a willingness to engage with services (all but one family) or a supportive extended family. Jaz provides an example of a child whose family were in this group:

Jaz was referred by the hospital midwife before he was born as his mother had previously had two children removed from her care following concerns that they were suffering from neglect because of her substance misuse and her lifestyle. She continued to misuse substances during the pregnancy. Jaz's mother had been sexually abused in childhood and, at the time of identification, was engaged in prostitution. His father was also a substance misuser and had learning disabilities and mental health problems. A month before Jaz's birth he was arrested for storing crack cocaine and was also seriously assaulted by an accomplice. However, Jaz's maternal grandmother was able to offer support and both parents were willing to engage with a range of services including those intended to address substance misuse. Jaz was made the subject of a child protection plan but remained with his parents.

(Jaz: high risk of harm at identification; low risk, living with birth parent and safeguarded at age three)

Families where there was a medium risk of harm

Almost half (21/43: 49%) of the infants were identified as being at medium risk of harm at identification. *Types* of risk factor were similar to those in other groups, although a slightly higher proportion of children (12/21: 57%) came from families where an older child had been permanently placed away from home. The average *number* of risk factors (four) was lower than that in the severe and high risk groups, with under a third displaying six or more. All families in this group had shown some evidence of their capacity to change, the factor which distinguished them from other groups. They also showed more additional protective factors than the high risk group: according to the case papers and interview data many of them were not only willing to engage with services, but also had recognized that there was a problem and taken some responsibility for it. Over a third of them (seven) had support from a non-abusive partner and/or from their extended families. Richard's family were in the medium risk group:

Richard's parents had a history of alcoholism, intimate partner violence and substance misuse. His mother had suffered emotional abuse in childhood (witnessing intimate partner violence) and had mental health problems. Two older children had been permanently placed away from home four years before Richard was born and were now adopted. In the past, both parents had shown an unwillingness to comply with arrangements made by children's social care. However, Richard's mother had since stopped her substance misuse and taken steps to come to terms with her own childhood experiences of abuse. By the time Richard was born considerable progress had been made and both parents were willing to engage with a wide range of services and access the support provided by the paternal grandparents. Richard was made the subject of a child protection plan but remained with his birth parents.

(Richard: medium risk of harm at identification; low risk, living with birth parents and safeguarded at age three)

Outliers and families where there was a low risk of harm

Chlöe was the only child where the risk of harm was low: her sister began to display some behavioural disturbance after their mother left the family home; there were some concerns that this older child might have been physically abused by her father's new partner. However, there were no further concerns, the children were safeguarded by the presence of their grandmother who moved in to the family home and the case was quickly closed.

There were also two infants (outliers) who did not comfortably fit into this categorization. These were babies born into families where both parents had learning disabilities, but where there was no evidence of other risk factors. In both our outlying cases the children were born into supportive extended families and were placed from birth in the care of their aunts who became special guardians. Both case file and interview data suggest that the parents willingly agreed to arrangements where they had open access to their children and were able to participate in their care and upbringing, although there were later concerns about one of the kinship placements (see Chapter 6). These infants are included in the low risk of harm group in some data analysis in later chapters.

Conclusion

Social workers are expected to analyse a vast amount of information on children, parents and the wider community to help inform the decision-making process. The complexity of this should not be under-estimated. The level of need in individual cases and the co-occurrence of specific issues are both factors that are likely to influence decision-making and the determination of what action is necessary to safeguard children from harm. Social work practitioners must analyse the interactions between the risk and protective factors that render maltreatment more or less likely and balance the potentially competing priorities of safeguarding children from harm and respecting parents' needs and rights. Classifying children in the manner described above may assist in such decisions by providing an evidence-based methodology for assessing how likely they are to suffer significant harm. Subsequent chapters explore how far decisions were related to such evidence, and why those which appeared to ignore it were sometimes taken.

Summary points for Chapter 3

- In spite of evidence of substantial problems and professionals' concerns about adverse behaviour patterns, most parents wanted to 'do the best' for their children.

- Almost two thirds of fathers were involved in supporting both the baby and the birth mother at the point of the core assessment; however, during the safeguarding process many fathers were excluded.

- The most prominent issues affecting parenting capacity included mental ill-health, substance misuse and intimate partner violence. At the time the first social work decision was made, one or more of these factors were considered to be an issue in over three quarters of the sample.

- Other evident, but less prominent, risk factors included parental learning disability, financial issues and housing problems.

- Protective factors included wider family/informal support and parents' insight, understanding and capacity to change. These were evident in many families and sometimes served to mitigate the impact of the numerous risk factors. However, isolation was a major issue in some of the most vulnerable families.

- Scrutiny of case records revealed poor recording in relation to the impact that risk factors had upon a parent's capacity to provide adequate care and protection, and the power of protective influences in mitigating their impact.

- Many parents had experienced the permanent removal of older children in the past. Such experiences are indicative of the entrenched nature of the risk factors facing the children's families. They also had a major, ongoing impact on parents' subsequent functioning, for they had left them with an enduring sense of shame and loss.

- Infants in the full follow-up group (n=43) were classified according to evidence of risk factors indicating the likelihood of maltreatment or its recurrence. This framework was used to classify sample families both at the point of identification and again when the children reached their third birthdays, as follows:

    ° **Severe risk of harm:** families showing risk factors, no protective factors and no evidence of capacity to change (12 (28%) infants at identification).

    ° **High risk of harm:** families showing risk factors and at least one protective factor but no evidence of capacity to change (seven (16%) infants at identification).

    ° **Medium risk of harm:** families showing risk factors and at least one protective factor including evidence of capacity to change (21 (49%) infants at identification).

    ° **Low risk of harm:** families showing no risk factors (or families whose earlier risk factors had now been addressed), and protective factors including evidence of capacity to change (three (7%) infants at identification).

- Two infants whose learning disabled mothers had voluntarily relinquished them to family members with whom they shared their care were regarded as outlier cases, although they are included in the low risk of harm group in data analysis in later chapters.

4

Referrals and Assessments

Introduction

Earlier chapters in this book have explored the infants, the likelihood of their suffering significant harm, the types of maltreatment experienced, and the risk and protective factors within the parents and their wider family and environment that made it more, or less, likely that abuse or neglect would occur or be repeated. This chapter considers the decisions that were made at the early stages of concern, during the process of referral to children's social care, and throughout the stages of initial and core assessment.

Early decisions, concerning whether or not a referral should be made to children's social care, were made by individual practitioners and their managers from a wide range of agencies; in addition to concerns about the children, they also reflect some of the issues that act as barriers to smooth inter-agency working, such as different priorities and perceptions of risks and thresholds. After a referral had been accepted, early decisions concerning how children might best be safeguarded were largely made in inter-agency forums such as strategy meetings, child protection conferences, core group meetings and child protection reviews. The forums themselves demonstrate the careful processes in place to ensure that sensible and fair decisions were made, and that children were adequately safeguarded. However, some of the decisions that resulted and the disagreements that occurred further reflect the complexities of inter-agency working in this very difficult field.

Referrals

The national statistics show that between 2005 and 2010 there was a steady rise in both the proportion of referrals that led to initial assessments and the proportion of initial assessments that led to core assessments (Department for Children, Schools and Families 2009b; Department for Education 2011a). The sample babies were all born around the same time as Peter Connelly; lying behind, and largely obscured by the recent crisis following his death, are a number of other factors that were already adding to the pressure on children's social care: these include already increasing levels of risk averseness, improved recognition and responses to abuse and neglect linked to early intervention and prevention strategies, and better professional knowledge and understanding of thresholds for statutory intervention (see Holmes, Munro and Soper 2010). Referrals of infants in the sample, and the responses to them, also reflect some of the underlying tensions between agencies with very different perspectives, and particularly between those which deliver children's and adult services.

Table 4.1 Sources of referral to children's social care (full sample: n=57)

Referring agency	Number	Percentage
Hospital	7*	13
GP/medical centre	4	8
Health visitor	4	8
Midwife	7	13
Police	1	2
Probation	5	9
Leaving care service	1	2
Drug and alcohol service	1	2
Homeless and asylum support team	1	2
Birth parent	1	2
Sure Start	1	2
Anonymous/members of public	2	4
Already known to children's social care – no referral details available	18	34
Total	**53**	**100****
Missing data	4	

* One set of twins were both referred by the hospital.
** Percentages are rounded figures.

Information on the source of referral was available for 53 children in the full sample (see Table 4.1). We have seen that a high proportion of families were already known to, or currently working with, children's social care because of concerns about the maltreatment of older siblings before the birth of the index child. As the table shows, 18 (34%) of the babies had no formal referral from an external agency, presumably for this reason.

With this very young sample, many of whom were identified before birth, it is unsurprising that a high proportion (22/35: 63%) of those who were not already known to children's social care were referred by health professionals. The health professionals caring for the mother during the pregnancy and birth (midwives, general practitioners and 'hospital staff') were the most likely to refer an unborn child where there were concerns about substance misuse, intimate partner violence or the mother's mental health. Their focus is on the child as well as the mother, and at this time they are unlikely to face the same conflict of interests that has sometimes been noted amongst those who provide adult services (see Barnard 2007; Falcov 2002; Tompsett *et al.* 2009). Hospital staff working in accident and emergency departments were also most likely to identify cases of non-accidental injury.

Recent policy developments reinforce the importance of a family-focused approach from agencies that work with adults as well as those that work with children (HM Government 2011). This is in response to evidence that some agencies that focus on adults' needs find it difficult to take account of the extent to which parents' problems may impact on the needs of their children. For instance, Falcov found that a substantial proportion (estimated at somewhere between 20 and 50%) of adults known to mental health services had children, but that much less was known (or indeed asked) about the extent and nature of these children's needs, including their needs for safety and protection (Falcov 2002). One social care team leader in the current study noted that:

> We have had conflicts with adult mental health services, in terms of their client group that they're working with and looking at their best interests and our very different view of looking at a child of that service user. And sometimes there is a conflict there in terms of child protection. (Team leader, children's social care)

It is therefore less surprising, though a matter of some concern, that, although a high proportion of parents suffered from mental ill-health, an issue that was thought to be a factor underlying the maltreatment of several children, there were no referrals from mental health workers.

Similarly, only one referral came from drug or alcohol support workers. Neil and colleagues (2010) found that a high proportion of parents whose children are placed for adoption, many of whom misuse substances, are not accessing support from adult services; however, in the current study, seven (7/17: 41%) of the 17 parents[1] (or sets of parents) who had drug and/or alcohol problems in the full follow-up group were accessing and engaging with drug and alcohol support services, but only one infant was referred by them. The lack of referrals may reflect different agency cultures and the prioritization of adults' needs in this type of service provision. Barnard (2007) notes that practitioners in this area have tended to focus upon the needs of the individual with the drug problem and their treatment and failed to acknowledge adequately the impact on children. Several professionals in the current study echoed this view. Substance misuse workers were perceived as acting as 'advocates' on behalf of parents, and were considered unlikely to alert social workers to the impact of parents' lifestyles on their children's wellbeing. They:

> …have a different perspective to social workers for children, in that they will regard themselves as working for the adults and sometimes they will struggle with the role that social workers have, in that they will want to remain positive and supportive to parents. (Team leader, children's social care)

This is an important omission for, as noted in earlier chapters, substance misuse during pregnancy can affect foetal development and have long-standing consequences for the health and wellbeing of the children concerned (Moe and Slinning 2003); the newborns of drug-dependent parents are also known to be especially at risk of being neglected (Connell-Carrick 2003; Harwin and Forrester 2002).

The different perspectives adopted by substance misuse workers and social workers also meant that parents received mixed messages concerning the extent to which their babies were considered likely to suffer significant harm; there were instances where substance misuse workers were praising the progress parents were making at the same time as social workers were preparing to remove the children:

> Generally, certainly…say, in case of drug-using parents, certainly, there's issues of, in my opinion, over-optimism because identification with parents by, for example, the specialist midwife, drug midwife and so forth, and that sometimes leads to over-optimistic assessments, I think. And the drug agencies. But there is a protocol…to work with. But…again, that's a perennial issue, it's understandable that people are acting as advocates really. They're trying to focus but they're acting as advocates. (Children's guardian)

---

1   17 parents (or sets of parents) of 19 children.

One authority had attempted to promote a closer alignment of perspectives by recruiting an in-house drug and alcohol team, whose role was to 'look at how the lifestyle and the effects of the substance misuse is having an impact on the parenting capacity of a particular adult' (Social worker).

On the other hand, probation services may perceive their role as less partisan, and therefore may face fewer conflicts of interest: five of the infants were referred by probation officers who were concerned about their safety, a factor which reflects the extent of criminality and violent behaviour displayed by the parents in the sample.

As well as the difficulties in balancing the conflicting interests of children and parents, previous research has identified other issues around referrals to children's social care. There are concerns about potential loss of control over what happens once the referral is made, deriving from distrust and lack of confidence in children's social care, particularly following experiences of heavy-handed, intrusive interventions. On the other hand, there are also concerns that too little is done to protect children, that they may be left in damaging situations and that referrals are therefore largely ineffective (see Tompsett *et al.* 2009; Ward and Peel 2002). These are all live issues when referral is being considered, particularly by the providers of adult services.

Health visitors provide a universal service and have regular contact with very young children; therefore they are arguably best placed to notice any signs of abuse or neglect. Given the importance of their role, it is perhaps surprising that they referred only four of the infants. Other studies have found that, in cases of neglect, health visitors perceive their role as referring agents rather than as providers of alternative services, but that they perceive social care as being reluctant to respond to their concerns (Appleton 1996; Brandon *et al.* 2006; Daniel *et al.* 2011). Data from the focus groups held with health visitors replicate such findings.

First, health visitors found it difficult to get referrals accepted, some suggesting that this was due to a lack of resources and the impact of recent cuts:

> But now, the social services input is so hard to get any reaction, any involvement, that they cut down drastically on social workers, haven't they, and we've got these child, like, children advice workers who are not qualified, who will dismiss your [referral]… and it's so difficult to engage with them, isn't it? (Health visitor)

Elsewhere, high thresholds for access to social care were thought to be an issue. In one local authority the feeling was that 'the thresholds are so high… that a lot of referrals you put in, they just bounce back at you' (Health visitor).

Some health visitors felt that their concerns were not taken sufficiently seriously. One commented: 'Actually, trying to get social services to sometimes take a referral, sometimes I feel that the health visitor's concerns are dismissed at that point.' Another health visitor spoke of having to make regular referrals in cases where concerns were particularly serious:

> We've got...I can think of three families on our caseload that we have got grave concerns about, and we must make a referral probably every other week. At least once a month but because it's little bits of things, it just goes: 'Oh, we're not going to take it forward, the case is closed.' (Health visitor)

Such perceptions were echoed in another local authority, where health visitors commented that 'it's got to be absolutely dire to get anywhere and you just get case closed after case closed'. These comments were among several that also indicated concerns that once cases had been opened, they could be closed prematurely, an issue that became evident as we tracked the children's experiences further (see Chapter 5).

Health visitors were also concerned about the lack of proactive engagement that sometimes followed a referral:

> We've also got a group of families who social care are involved with, the families that we're getting most concerned about and you feel absolutely sure from your observations that the children are suffering significant harm, not in a physical way [...we would] be able to measure that, but in lots of other ways, they're in social care, so whenever anybody has any concerns, whether it's A and E, whoever, they phone social care and, and they're sort of keeping a cap on it and they don't seem, even when their concerns rise pretty high, to be able to push it across into child protection, and there's this feeling, I think, don't know where it's from, that, you know, once social care are involved, that that's enough and OK and it isn't...the parents aren't engaging, this isn't being achieved, that's not being achieved...and they still can't push it up into child protection. (Health visitor)

One authority had introduced a 'buddy' scheme intended to help social workers and health visitors work more closely together and understand more about the types of concerns that should trigger further action:

> Each social worker is buddied with a health visitor and that means if they have any general, oh, I wonder what this means, I'll ring my buddy and find out and *vice versa,* so if they have any child protection concerns, they've got someone to ring, [and] if they have any health concerns we've got someone to ring. And I think

there's a bit of a protocol where you spend half a day twice a year
together, you know, doing joint working. (Social worker)

Even when the referral process worked smoothly and infants were identified
early, procedures were not always in place to ensure that the growing evidence
of maltreatment would be sufficiently co-ordinated to elicit an appropriate
response. Dabir, whose circumstances have been discussed in Chapter 2, was one
of a small group of children who might well have had a fatal outcome. Details of
his experiences between referral and core assessment are given below:

Dabir was the subject of an anonymous referral to children's social care
at three weeks old, due to concerns about his parents' rough handling
and capacity to care for him. An initial assessment was undertaken and
he was referred to Sure Start. Over the next four months there were four
incidents of bruising to his arms or forehead, all of which were deemed
by health professionals to be accidental. When he was four months old
a social worker made an unexpected home visit and found bruising to his
arms: this precipitated a section 47 enquiry and he was made the subject
of a child protection plan because he was at risk of being neglected and
physically abused. Over the next six weeks there was a further incident of
unexplained injury. Finally, when Dabir was aged five and a half months,
he was found to have a fractured arm and the consultant paediatrician
recommended a full skeletal survey. This revealed old fractures that had
gone undetected; the parents were arrested and Dabir was placed in the
care of his grandparents.

(Dabir: severe risk of harm at identification;
safeguarded through separation at age three)

Dabir is a classic case of non-accidental injury. The broken arm which
precipitated the full skeletal survey was the seventh recorded injury to this
baby, following which it became clear that he had been continually abused,
probably since birth. Had the series of minor incidents that had previously been
dismissed as 'accidents' been brought together to form a full chronological
picture, and shared with the relevant professionals, it seems probable that more
decisive action would have been taken earlier. It also seems likely that sharing
of research evidence indicating that any bruising on a pre-mobile baby is a
solid basis for child protection concerns (see Brandon *et al.* 2011; Maguire *et
al.* 2005) might also have prompted more precipitate action.

It is evident from many of the case histories of these infants that early identification, followed by decisive action, is of key significance in ensuring satisfactory outcomes, particularly for babies for whom adoption may prove to be the most appropriate option. Failure of adult services to appreciate how parents' problems can impact on their children's wellbeing; concerns over conflicts of interests when the purpose of a service is primarily to support the adults in a family; concerns about the high thresholds for access to children's social care and the futility of referring cases that may still not be adequately safeguarded; and the failure to bring together the different pieces of information into a coherent whole and to relate it to wider research evidence are all factors that need to be addressed in improving the processes of referral and initial response. The issue is not to increase referral rates at a time when children's social care is already over-burdened, but to find ways of ensuring that cases where there is a high risk of harm, such as those followed in this study, are identified early and offered timely interventions before maltreatment escalates.

Core assessments and section 47 enquiries

The national returns for the year in which the majority of the babies were born (2006–7) show that only 17 per cent of all referrals led to a core assessment or a section 47 enquiry (see Department for Children, Schools and Families 2009b). However, this was the case for all the babies in the full sample, and indeed was one of the criteria for selection. Within the very small group of infants who receive core assessments before their first birthdays, we also know that the sample children were significantly more likely than others to be referred before birth; to be offered family support services for children in need; and to be looked after before they were 12 months old. These indicators suggest that, at referral, these infants were assessed as being particularly likely to suffer significant harm; evidence concerning parents' problems and the availability of protective factors that might mitigate their impact has already confirmed that almost all cases displayed risk factors that increased the probability that future maltreatment and other poor outcomes would occur (see Jones *et al.* 2006).

Table 4.2 shows the immediate reasons for the core assessment/section 47 enquiries for 48 of the babies in the full sample. Twenty (42%) were undertaken as a result of parents' previous or current involvement with children's social care, either because an older sibling had been considered to be suffering, or likely to suffer, significant harm, or because the mother was still in the care of the local authority and was thought to be particularly vulnerable. Seventeen (35%) core assessments were undertaken following concerns about issues affecting parenting capacity; these include seven cases where substance misuse was the primary factor, though often combined with other problems, and six where intimate partner violence was the major issue. The remaining 11 (23%) assessments were undertaken because there was some evidence that an infant had already been maltreated or was likely to be in the immediate future.

Table 4.2 Reason for core assessment and/or section 47 enquiry (full sample: n=57)

Reason for assessment	Number	Percentage
Parents' previous history		
Previous children's social care involvement with the family	18	38
Children's social care involvement with mother	2	4
Parents' current circumstances		
Multiple risk factors including substance misuse	5	10
Alcohol/substance misuse	2	4
Intimate partner violence	6	13
Post-natal depression	1	2
Mother's learning disability	2	4
Chaotic lifestyle of parents	1	2
Significant harm/likelihood of significant harm to child		
Contact/potential contact with a Schedule One Offender	4	8
Injury to child	2	4
Injury to sibling	3	6
Child left alone	1	2
Child not thriving	1	2
Total	**48**	**100***
Data unavailable	9	

* Percentages are rounded figures.

Information collected during initial and core assessments/section 47 enquiries

A key function of initial and core assessments and section 47 enquiries is to gather information that makes it possible to identify the strengths and weaknesses within the child, the family and the wider environment that promote or hinder development and make it more, or less, likely that the child will suffer significant harm. Information is therefore collected across the three domains of child development, parenting capacity, and family and environment. This information forms the basis of initial decisions, so its quality and completeness are important. The analysis of the social work case file data suggested that the information was often inadequate, although only two case files did not include a core assessment.

Notwithstanding the above, prior to the first major decision, in most cases some information had been collected concerning the children's developmental needs, the parents' capacity to meet those needs and those factors within the wider family or environment that promoted or impeded their ability to provide a sufficiently nurturing home. Much of this was recorded on the case file notes rather than on the core assessment exemplar, but nevertheless it was available to those who had to make decisions concerning the infants' future. As we have seen, using data concerning known risk and protective factors, it has been possible to classify the families into those where the risk of children being harmed was severe, high, medium or low. This classification is utilized in the following analysis to explore how far the initial actions following the core assessments were based on evidence concerning types of abuse (or their likelihood); risk and protective factors within the children, the parents and their circumstances; and evidence of parents' capacity to change.

Outcome of the section 47 enquiry or core assessment

While core assessments might end with a recommendation from the social workers who completed them, and decisions concerning placement away from home were led by children's social care, other decisions, concerning how children might be safeguarded while living with their birth parents, were made in inter-agency forums such as child protection conferences, core group meetings and strategy meetings. According to one team leader:

> We do formulate views and probably 99 per cent are ones that everybody's agreeable to which way we should go in terms of whether we continue as family support or child in need cases, or whether we need to be looking forward to a legal route. (Team leader, children's social care)

While disagreements may have been rare, social workers sometimes found it frustrating that other professionals did not always put forward their views, preferring to leave the key decisions to children's social care:

> But then people very seldom disagree with social workers at child protection conferences. They should do but they don't…because child protection is still seen as the social worker's job, basically… There are exceptions but as a general rule, and it really pisses me off, nobody will argue with the social worker, people abdicate responsibility really, I think. Still…child protection is ultimately the social worker's responsibility. Doesn't matter how well you work with people, when you get right down to it, it's a social worker's job. There are very seldom, in my experience, arguments about whether a child should be on the register or not at child protection conferences and there should be, sometimes. (Social worker)

By not putting forward their own views, staff from partner agencies were sometimes seen as unwilling to take responsibility for the decisions that were made:

> You can clash, you know, you can clash sometimes, different opinions which sometimes it's healthy, sometimes it's difficult, it's frustrating when they won't, they don't recognize that they've got as much responsibility as what you have…they've got as much of a duty to protect and support and nurture as what we have, so you know again that's frustrating. And there are times when…they'll phone you up and make all these complaints and then you'll get them into a meeting and they'll backtrack and they won't say what they've said to you, as if, you know, they're scared to say it in front of a parent. (Social worker)

Nevertheless, there were some instances where the child protection conference could not agree and subsequent action was decided by the chair or by a vote. In the case of Martin-Louis (Chapter 6), the health authority was strongly in favour of a child protection plan, opposed by children's social care, but in Matthew's case (discussed below) the position was reversed, with children's social care wishing to extend the child protection plan for an infant whom the other agencies thought was already adequately safeguarded.

Those responsible for making these decisions had to analyse evidence concerning the extent to which the child's welfare could be safeguarded in the future. The key factor influencing immediate decisions pending further enquiries and long-term plans was the extent to which the infant could be adequately safeguarded if s/he remained with birth parents. Table 4.3 shows the numbers of infants who remained with their parents, the number who were removed from them and the legislative background to those arrangements made immediately following the core assessment, or the baby's birth if the mother had been pregnant at the time the decision was made.

As Table 4.3 shows, some form of further professional action was deemed necessary in all cases. However, as the data from this study will increasingly demonstrate, all the professionals concerned made extensive efforts to keep children with birth parents, or failing that, within their birth families, sometimes in the face of substantial contra-indications. Notwithstanding the evidence that almost half of the mothers had already had at least one child placed for adoption, it was first thought that the majority (35/48: 73%) of the babies could be adequately safeguarded while remaining with their birth parents, and that only 13 (13/48: 27%) of this sample showing a very high risk of harm would need, at least initially, to be placed away from home.

PLACEMENTS AWAY FROM HOME

Of the 13 infants who were initially placed away from their birth parents, six never returned and, at the age of three, were settled with adoptive carers or in secure kinship placements. This group included five children who were placed at birth, and one who was first placed at six months old, immediately after identification.

The six babies for whom immediate and permanent separation was thought to be the most appropriate course of action included the two outliers, whose learning disabled mothers had voluntarily placed them with relatives with whom they were sharing care, and four infants from the severe risk of harm group. These four all had parents who displayed multiple risk factors, with no evidence of protective factors or of a capacity to change. Three of the mothers had had older children placed away from home within the previous year, and all of them had been unable to demonstrate enough changes in their lifestyle to provide a sufficiently nurturing home for the new baby. The profiles of such families were similar to that of Gary:

This infant was born showing symptoms of substance withdrawal; both his parents were abusing drugs and had a violent relationship; they were described as leading a chaotic lifestyle and were homeless at the time of Gary's birth; in addition, his mother had schizophrenia for which she was not accessing mental health support. The mother had had two older children placed for adoption within the previous year, and since then there had been no evidence of change or of a willingness to engage with services.

(Gary: severe risk of harm at identification; safeguarded through separation at age three)

Table 4.3 Infant's domicile and legal status following first decision or birth (intermediate and full follow-up groups: n=51)

Infant's domicile	Interim Care Order	Police Protection Order	Emergency Protection Order	s.17a	s.17b	S20 single placement regular	Interim Residence Order	Total
With parent/s at home	1	0	0	7	21	1	1	31
With parent/s at assessment	0	1	1	0	1	0	0	3
With parents case closed	0	0	0	0	1	0	0	1
Kinship care	0	0	0	0	0	2	0	2
Foster care	4	1	1	0	0	5	0	11
Total	**5**	**2**	**2**	**7**	**23**	**8**	**1**	**48**
Data unavailable								3

Seven infants were removed from their birth parents immediately following the core assessment and then returned home, although two later returned to the care of the local authority. One of these babies was in the severe risk of harm category; another was a high risk case; and the other five were from medium risk families. They were mostly infants living in exceptionally dangerous situations, with parents who had convictions for cruelty or who had been perpetrators of non-accidental injury, but who had demonstrated a willingness to engage with services and to overcome their earlier problems. They were looked after in order to ensure that they were adequately safeguarded pending assessments of parents and decisions as to whether or not they should be placed for adoption. The one exception was a child at medium risk of harm whose mother had fled from a violent partner; he and his disabled sibling were briefly accommodated to give their mother time to recover from her injuries.

REMAINING WITH BIRTH PARENT(S)

However, placing children away from their birth parents while decisions were being made about their long-term future was relatively rare. Wherever possible, separation was avoided. Eight of the infants in the severe risk of harm group initially remained with a birth parent, all but one of them the subjects of child protection plans. Most of these babies had violent parents and were allowed to remain at home on condition that the perpetrator was excluded from the household. However, two of them were born into families where ongoing, long-term neglect was a major issue and older siblings had not been placed away from home. In one family, after many years of corrosive neglect, care proceedings had finally been instigated by the time the baby was born, and after a month he and all five siblings were placed away from home. In the other family, the extent and the impact of the neglect had not been appreciated; the older siblings were still at home, and so there appeared to be no pressing reason to remove the baby. The difficulties professionals face in identifying and addressing neglect is an issue to which we return in later chapters.

A high proportion of infants in the high and medium risk of harm groups who initially remained at home were also in similar situations, the difference being that their parents had begun to address their difficulties and/ or protective factors were apparent such as a supportive partner or relative. Olivia is an example:

> Olivia's parents lived together, although they were not in an intimate relationship; Olivia's father worked away for most of the time, and had been unaware that her mother was severely neglecting her older half siblings. These children were removed from their mother's care, and care proceedings were in process during her pregnancy with Olivia. However, the mother successfully concealed her pregnancy both from Olivia's father and from children's social care until she started labour. Shortly following the birth, children's social care were alerted and planned to remove Olivia immediately. However, Olivia's father put himself forward as her main carer with the help of the paternal grandmother. He cut all ties with Olivia's mother and gave up work to successfully parent Olivia and one of her older half siblings.
>
> *(Olivia: medium risk of harm at identification; low risk, living with birth parent and safeguarded at age three)*

While, as one might expect, the majority of the babies who remained at this stage with their birth parents were made the subject of child protection plans, seven (7/35: 20%) were thought to be sufficiently safeguarded by being offered family support services under section 17a of the Children Act 1989. The one low risk baby was offered services under this section of the Act, and the case was swiftly closed after a written agreement had been made with the parents. However, another of these seven infants was in the severe risk group, and others who appeared to be at high or medium risk of harm were still not routinely made the subject of a child protection plan if there was evidence that parents had shown some capacity to change and/or that there were sufficient protective factors in place to ensure their safety. Harry's mother, for instance, had had four children permanently placed away from home two years previously, when she had been living in a violent relationship, and this had precipitated her subsequent substance misuse. However, she had since formed a relationship with a new, supportive partner and had succeeded in coming off the drugs before the baby's birth. The child protection conference decided that she had made sufficient progress for it not to be necessary to make Harry the subject of a child protection plan.

Conclusion

Many of the decisions following the core assessment appear to relate relatively closely to the evidence concerning risk and protective factors and parents' capacity to change. Infants who were immediately placed away from home were either in the severe risk of harm group, or were living in violent families where there was, as yet, insufficient evidence that protective factors could be sufficiently robust and the risk factors sufficiently reduced for them to be safeguarded in the future. One could argue that the threshold for deciding that the majority (35/48: 73%) of these very young children could be adequately safeguarded at home while further information was collected was low, but there were relatively few decisions at this stage which are difficult to understand. These few decisions, however, are of particular interest: not only do they give some cause for concern – justified at a later stage in all cases – but they also are early indicators of themes that became more pronounced as time progressed.

The decision to leave two infants at severe risk of harm in families with long-standing and extensive neglect issues will be discussed in a later chapter, alongside other similar cases which later emerged. Neglect is notoriously difficult to recognize (see Daniel *et al.* 2011; Farmer and Lutman forthcoming) and these decisions are not so much difficult to understand as problematic in terms of the long-term consequences for the children concerned.

However, the decision made in Shay's case (introduced in Chapter 3) is one that is less understandable. This baby's mother was socially isolated and had a history of relationships with violent partners. Shay's father was another extremely violent man, who was characterized as a 'serial' domestic abuser. He also had convictions for violent crimes, and had assaulted the mother in the past. Following a pre-birth assessment it was agreed that Shay could remain with his mother, and that he would not need to be made the subject of a child protection plan. Instead, the mother signed a written agreement, formally stating that she would have no further contact with Shay's father. The purpose of this arrangement was 'to allow mother to show she can parent'; however, an older half sibling had been made the subject of a Care Order the year that Shay was born, on the grounds that the mother had been unable to attach to him or protect him from another violent relationship. The mother had a history of false compliance (see Fauth *et al.* 2010), and there was no evidence that she was committed to extricating herself from the relationship with Shay's father, whose criminal activities she was reported as finding amusing. This is the only severe risk of harm case that was not, at the core assessment stage, thought to require either placement away from home or a child protection plan. It is perhaps unsurprising that, within three weeks, the written arrangement was breached, the arrangement broke down and Shay was placed with foster carers. A key point, however, is the view that this mother should be given (another) opportunity 'to show she can parent'. Over the course of the study this argument was put forward in many cases, and for some became a barrier to successful safeguarding.

Finally, the decision made in Matthew's case was controversial at the time and had to be quickly reversed. This infant's mother had been looked after by the local authority for the previous four years; however, she had a history of absconding, misusing drugs and alcohol, and sexual exploitation, and had refused to acknowledge that she was pregnant. When Matthew was born he was found to have syphilis. He came into the severe risk of harm category, his mother showing no protective factors or evidence of her capacity to change, and a pre-birth child protection conference agreed to make him the subject of a child protection plan, on the grounds of neglect. However, Matthew's mother then began to attend ante-natal appointments, parenting classes and a teenage mother's group. Because of her engagement with services the child protection plan was discontinued and the case closed before he was born.

The social worker had opposed this decision on the grounds that:

> It was a short period of time to measure [mother's name] as to how willing or how committed she was to her child…it goes on a majority vote, and the majority voted that his name should be removed from the register, [but] I felt that his name should have remained on the register… I felt that given that [mother's name] was involved with ourselves since the age of 12, a three or four month timescale to measure how committed she was to this child was too short a period of time. (Social worker)

Three months later, when Matthew was two months old, the GP re-referred the case on the grounds that his mother was not caring for him adequately.

These three themes – the withdrawal of support after very brief interventions as evidenced in the above case; the care given to ensuring that, even in cases where there was a severe risk of harm, parents should have every opportunity to develop or demonstrate capacity to care for a child; and the reluctance to take intrusive action in response to neglect – all emerged at a very early stage in the case management of these infants; they became much more evident as cases progressed and children grew older, and will be explored further in subsequent chapters.

Summary points for Chapter 4

- The babies were all born around the same time as Peter Connelly: the referrals and the responses to them reflect some of the growing pressures on children's social care, but they also reflect some of the underlying tensions between agencies with very different perspectives, and particularly between those who deliver children's and adult services.

- A high proportion of infants who were not already known to children's social care were referred by health professionals.

- There were no referrals by mental health professionals and only one from drug and alcohol support workers. This is of concern, given that a high proportion of babies were living in households where parents had mental health problems or were misusing drugs or alcohol.

- Health visitors were concerned that they found it difficult to get referrals accepted by children's social care; that once cases had been opened, they could be closed prematurely; and that referrals were sometimes followed by a lack of proactive engagement.

- Extensive efforts were made by professionals to keep babies with birth parents, or failing that, within their birth families, sometimes in the face of substantial contra-indications.

- Three themes emerged from the initial stages of case management: first the withdrawal of support after very brief social work involvement; second the care given to ensuring that parents should have every opportunity to develop or demonstrate capacity to look after their children, even where the likelihood of their suffering harm was severe; and third the reluctance to take intrusive action in neglect cases.

5

Pathways to Permanence

Introduction

As we have seen, the evidence of significant harm or its likelihood was sufficient for professionals to decide that, following the core assessment, further investigation and/or the provision of services was necessary to safeguard the welfare of all the babies in the study. It was initially thought that nearly three quarters of them (35/48: 73%) could be adequately safeguarded while remaining in the care of their birth families. However, these first decisions were intended as definitive for only seven (15%) infants, in one case leading to the closure of the case with the child remaining with birth parents, and in six cases leading to permanent placement away from home. The vast majority of formal decisions in this early stage were temporary, pending further information concerning the likelihood of a child suffering significant harm, or provisional, pending evidence that parenting capacity had improved or an established risk of significant harm was no longer present. We were able to follow 43 of the infants for a further two to three years, until their third birthdays.[1] This chapter traces the complex decision-making processes that shaped their experiences over these intervening years, as professionals sought to ensure that they were adequately safeguarded.

Support

Following the core assessment, almost all the parents of infants who remained at home were offered extensive packages of practical, social and therapeutic support from social workers, health visitors and adult mental health or substance misuse services, as part of a multi-disciplinary child in need or child protection plan. However, although there is some evidence concerning how far parents valued these services (see Chapter 8), there is little recorded information about the extent to which support packages were accessed or how far they served to ensure that children were safeguarded.

---

1   Please note that, from this point, this and subsequent chapters focus on the 43 children who we were able to follow until their third birthdays. The figures quoted are therefore slightly different from those reported in earlier chapters.

Position of the sample at age three

Following the core assessment, 31 (72%) infants in the full follow-up group remained with their parents, while 12 (28%) were considered to require placements away from home. As Table 5.1 shows, by their third birthdays 28 (65%) were living with their parents and 15 (35%) had been placed apart from them.

Table 5.1 Child's domicile following core assessment by child's domicile at age three (full follow-up group: n=43)

		Child's domicile following core assesssment					
		With parents case open	With parents at assessment	With parents case closed	Kinship care	Foster care	Total*
Child's domicile at age three	With parents case open	2	3	–	–	4	9 (21%)
	With parents case closed	17	–	–	–	–	17 (40%)
	With father on Residence Order	1	–	–	–	1	2 (5%)
	Kinship care with special guardianship	1	–	–	2	1	4 (9%)
	Kinship care Residence Order/Care Order	1	–	–	–	1	2 (5%)
	Foster care	1	–	–	–	1	2 (5%)
	Adoptive care	4	–	1	–	2	7 (16%)
	Total	27 (63%)	3 (7%)	1 (2%)	2 (5%)	10 (23%)	43 (100%)

* Percentages are rounded figures.

The 15 children placed away from home at three years old included seven in adoptive homes and four with special guardians, two children settled with kinship carers on Care Orders or Residence Orders, one child who had recently been placed in temporary foster care, pending a permanent placement, and one child who had been placed in a mother and baby foster home and was now awaiting an adoptive placement. Two of the children placed with kinship carers/special guardians and six of those placed with adoptive carers had initially been supported while remaining with their birth parents (including Matthew, whose case, it will be remembered, had been closed before he was born, but had, however, subsequently been reopened).

Although by their third birthdays about a third (15/43: 35%) of the sample were now permanently placed away from home, two thirds (28/43: 65%) were not. Six children had originally been placed in foster care and were now living with a birth parent; three others had been reunited but then separated again; and one was now living in a mother and baby foster home, with the foster carer and the birth mother jointly participating in his care. Two children were now living with birth fathers under Residence Orders; both of them had only limited contact with their mothers, by whom they or their siblings had been maltreated. However, it is perhaps more important to note that, of the 28 children who were living with their birth parents at age three, 21 (75%) had never left home.

Although the constellations of risk and protective factors changed over the course of the study, not all these very young children were adequately safeguarded, and there was still ongoing social care involvement in a number of cases. By the children's third birthdays, 30 (70%) cases were closed and 13 (30%) were still open, six of them reopened following closure and a subsequent re-referral. Nine of the 13 cases that were still open were children living with birth parents, one other was living with a birth mother with regular periods in respite care, two had recently been removed from the care of a birth mother and were now in foster care with a view to adoption, and the final open case was a child living in a fragile kinship placement where there were concerns about the quality of care.

By the time they reached three the children had fallen into three groups of relatively similar size: those who were adequately safeguarded and were living with birth parents, now apparently at low risk of suffering harm (16/43: 37%); those who were not adequately safeguarded and were living with parents at medium, high or severe risk of harm (12/43: 28%); and those apparently safeguarded and permanently separated from parents (15/43: 35%). This chapter considers the pathways the infants and their parents followed to reach this position. Later chapters will explore the factors that influenced the decision-making process; the services families received to help them overcome their difficulties; how far children had moved from one risk of harm category to another; and the extent to which safeguarding had been achieved.

Decisions

The decisions that form the basis of the discussion in this chapter were all formally made as part of the case management process, and recorded on case files. Although these showed all the shortcomings of poor recording, inadequate analysis and gaps in information that have been noted by numerous other studies (Cleaver and Walker with Meadows 2004; Sinclair *et al.* 2007; Ward *et al.* 2008), at least three quarters of them demonstrated a meticulous, not to say tortuous, decision-making process. Moreover, by the end of the study the children's position also closely matched our classification at identification: the 15 children who were permanently placed away from home at age three included 11 of the 12 infants who had initially been classified as at severe risk of harm; one infant first classified as at high risk and one at medium risk of harm (both now in temporary foster care pending adoptive placements); and the two outliers, whose learning disabled parents had placed them voluntarily with relatives with whom they were sharing their upbringing. Furthermore, all but one of the 21 infants who had been classified as at medium risk of harm at the start of the study were still living with a birth parent at the end. Thus for the majority of the children in this study decisions concerning permanence bore a relatively close relationship to objective evidence of the likelihood of significant harm. However, as we shall see, it sometimes took several months before these definitive decisions were reached, and in the interim many infants were exposed to abuse and neglect for extensive periods, with long-term consequences for their future life chances. Moreover decisions did not follow evidence of risk of significant harm in just over a quarter (28%) of sample cases.

As Chapter 2 has shown, the children were very young at referral. Twenty three (53%) of those in the full follow-up group were referred before birth; 36 (84%) before they were three months old. Only two babies were older than six months at referral. Initial decisions following the core assessment were also made at a relatively early age, with only seven (16%) made after infants were six months old. However, there then followed an extensive decision-making process, as professionals tried to ascertain which children could be permanently safeguarded from harm while remaining with their birth parents, and which could not. On average it took 14 months for a definitive decision (i.e. one resulting in a viable permanence plan) to be made, and a further six months before this was completed (i.e. for a child to remain with parents without further social care involvement or for a Special Guardianship or Residence Order to be made). Adoption Orders often took longer, and many of them had not been completed by the children's third birthdays, although by then most infants for whom this was the permanence plan had been placed with adoptive carers.

At least in the early stages of case management, decisions made by all professionals (psychologists, psychiatrists, children's guardians and the judiciary, as well as by social workers) were almost always made in the expectation that the infants would eventually be adequately safeguarded while living with birth parents. Early decisions were therefore almost always temporary, pending the results of assessments of parenting capacity, or provisional, pending evidence of parental progress in overcoming the risk factors that jeopardized their children's long-term wellbeing. Almost all early decisions were made with the proviso that parents might be able to overcome their difficulties – for instance, all but one of the four babies born into families where the risk of harm was severe, and placed for adoption at birth, were twin tracked, with the alternative option being to return to birth parents if their situation improved. However, while a protracted decision-making period ensured that parents' rights were properly protected, such decisions rarely took account of infants' timeframes. Specifically, while professionals waited for parents to overcome their difficulties, questions were rarely raised concerning the impact of long-term exposure to chronic neglect or emotional abuse on the neurobiological and emotional development of these very young children, or the need to make swift decisions concerning permanent separation in view of the evidence concerning the development of attachment in early childhood.

Types of decisions

For the purposes of analysis, decisions were classified according to whether they were taken pending further information or the outcome of an assessment, pending progress made by parents or carers, or whether they were definitive, that is, moving towards permanency. Many decisions could be made for either of the first two reasons (and sometimes for both of them) but it was important, and relatively simple, to ascertain their purpose. For instance, decisions to place infants temporarily in foster care could be made either in order to protect the child while professionals waited for the results of an assessment of parenting capacity or the potential quality of kinship care (decision pending assessment) or pending evidence that the parents had sufficiently overcome their difficulties to provide a safe home for their baby (decision pending progress). Definitive decisions marked a clear step towards permanency and case closure; they included decisions to end or not to make a child protection plan; decisions to end family support services; decisions that a child should be placed for adoption or that a Residence or Special Guardianship Order should by sought; and decisions to close a case.

Timing of decisions

All decisions made before infants were born were temporary, awaiting the outcomes of assessments designed to ascertain whether parents had sufficiently overcome problems such as substance misuse and intimate partner violence to provide a nurturing home, and whether they had the necessary capacity to meet the baby's needs. Such assessments continued after birth; although the majority had been undertaken before infants were six months old, assessments of parenting capacity continued beyond this timescale in 14 (33%) cases and were ongoing in eight (19%) cases after the children were one year old and in two (5%) cases after they were two.

Definitive decisions were postponed, pending evidence of parents' progress, in seven cases until after the infants were six months old, in four until after they were one year old and in one case until after the child's second birthday.

Definitive decision-making was therefore frequently postponed pending further assessments of parenting capacity and parental progress. As a result, although eight (8/39: 21%) children had decisions leading to permanence made before they were six months old, and 11 (11/39: 28%) between six months and one year, 20 (20/39: 51%) were over a year old before a viable definitive decision was made, including six (6/39: 15%) who were over two.

As we shall see, some parents were able to overcome their difficulties at a very early stage, and cases were kept open in order to provide ongoing support while ensuring that early improvements were adequately sustained. However, in those cases where substantial progress had not been made within the first six months, concerns about maltreatment persisted and were still evident at the third birthday. After infants were six months old there was increasingly less likelihood that the outcomes of parenting assessments would be positive or that parents would succeed in overcoming their difficulties. Such children were likely to remain in damaging situations, usually characterized by chronic neglect, while the difficult decision to place them outside the parental home was continually, and sometimes permanently, delayed.

Safeguarded through parental change (16 children: 37%)

The majority (13) of the 16 children whose parents appeared to overcome their difficulties sufficiently to meet their needs were classified as at medium risk of harm at the start of the study; however, this group also included two children from families where the risk of harm was high and the one low risk case. Although there was a high preponderance of infants at medium risk of harm, many of the parents in this group had previously put other children at severe risk, but had begun to address their difficulties before the birth of the index baby (see Chapter 6 for further details). Seven of the infants in this group were referred before birth, and all were aged under six months at identification. Only three children in this group ever left the care of their birth parents; by their third birthdays all were living at home and all cases were closed except for that of one child who was the subject of a full Care Order and placed with her mother.

Although they were living with birth parents at age three, two children in this group had come close to adoption. One had a social worker who appeared to be determined to follow his own agenda, without regard to the absence of evidence of significant harm or the interests of the child. This was the only case that appeared to be driven by a determinedly negative view of the parents, and led to a formal complaint. Overall, plans to separate children unnecessarily were extremely rare and did not reach fruition, although as we discuss in Chapter 7, over-optimistic assessments of parents' capacity to change were common. The other child, Natasha, was placed in foster care at birth. There were concerns about her mother's neglect and physical abuse of two older children, who had both been removed; her father had also lied about his previous involvement with children's social care. However, when Natasha was 12 months old, and after the best interests panel had recommended that she be placed for adoption, she was returned to the care of her father on a Residence Order. The social worker decided that because her father had separated from her mother and had established a good bond with Natasha during contact sessions, he should be given one last chance; at three she was living with her father, with support from the extended family, and there were no ongoing concerns. These are the only two cases where children were on the verge of being unnecessarily separated from their birth parents. In both of them there were genuine and justifiable concerns about the children's safety; the late emergence of protective factors led to a change in direction.

Decision-making in the majority of cases in this group was relatively straightforward and there were examples of very careful case management, with support offered when necessary, and then gradually withdrawn as the situation appeared to improve. One such example is that of Simon:

Simon's mother was a prolific crack cocaine user. This continued throughout her pregnancy and Simon was made the subject of a child protection plan pre-birth. However, after giving birth and holding Simon for the first time his mother took the decision to come off drugs and change her lifestyle; she convinced her social worker of her determination to do so. A court hearing when Simon was one week old directed an Interim Care Order and residential parenting assessment. During this time Simon's maternal grandmother was also assessed as a potential carer should his mother be unable to look after him. However, the parenting assessment was positive and Simon and his mother returned home with the added support of the grandmother who came to live with them. The child protection plan ended when Simon was eight months old; shortly afterwards a psychological assessment concluded that his mother had made progress and was determined to stay off drugs. Around the time of Simon's first birthday a Supervision Order was granted for 12 months in place of the Interim Care Order; shortly after his second birthday this lapsed and the case was closed. Simon's mother had intensive health visitor and drugs service support throughout, and this continued following case closure.

*(Simon: medium risk of harm at identification; low risk,
living with birth parent and safeguarded at age three)*

Simon's case was open for at least two years, and closed following a gradual withdrawal of services. Many of these cases showed a similar reduction in intensity, with, for instance, a child protection plan followed by a few months of family support services before closure. However, most of these cases were open for a relatively short time – ten months on average – and some parents who had been struggling with extensive difficulties appeared to experience the withdrawal of support before they felt ready to cope without it.

Pre-birth	**Pre-birth:** Temporary decision pending assessment: child protection plan Forum: Child protection conference
0–1 year	**One week:** Temporary decision pending assessment: Interim Care Order granted Forum: Court Domicile: Parent
	One month: Temporary decision pending assessment: residential parenting assessment Forum: Court Domicile: Parent (residential unit)
	Four months: Temporary decision pending assessment: assessment of potential kin carer (twin track) Forum: Court Domicile: Parent (residential unit)
	Four months: Temporary decision pending progress: following positive parenting assessment mum and child move to own home; maternal grandmother moves in for added support Forum: Court Domicile: Parent
	Ten months: Temporary decision pending progress: end child protection plan Forum: Unclear Domicile: Parent
	Ten months: Temporary decision pending assessment: psychological assessment of mother – outcome positive Forum: Unclear Domicile: Parent
1–2 years	**One year one month:** Temporary decision pending progress: Supervision Order granted for 12 months Forum: Court Domicile: Parent
2–3 years	**Two years one month:** Definitive decision: lapse of Supervision Order – case closed Forum: Court Domicile: Parent

Figure 5.1 Timeline: decisions made for Simon *(medium risk of harm at identification; low risk, living with birth parent and safeguarded at age three)*

In Chapter 3, Jaz was cited as an example of a case with a high risk of harm at identification. The reader will remember that there were multiple risk factors relating to his parents, including drug and alcohol problems, prostitution, and mental health and learning difficulties. His mother had continued to misuse drugs throughout the pregnancy and the family was also under financial strain; just before the birth his father had been arrested and charged with drug dealing with a strong possibility of a custodial sentence. His parents were, however, willing to engage with services and were supported by the maternal grandmother. The following decisions were made after the pre-birth assessment:

A child protection conference was held a week before Jaz was born, and he was made the subject of a child protection plan on the grounds of neglect. This was a provisional decision, pending evidence of the parents' ability to engage with services and sustain the changes they had begun to make to their lifestyles; a detailed plan was drawn up, offering a comprehensive package of services to both parents. When Jaz was two months old, a child protection review decided that the plan should be extended, pending evidence that the progress made so far could be sustained. Six months later the review decided unanimously that Jaz was no longer suffering, or likely to suffer, significant harm, and the case could be closed. Parental care had been 'first class' throughout. Although there were still some outstanding concerns regarding the father, who was still receiving support to overcome his substance misuse, it was agreed that the mother was able and willing to provide appropriate protection for the baby and prioritize his needs.

(Jaz: high risk of harm at identification; low risk, living with birth parent and safeguarded at age three)

Pre-birth	**Pre-birth:** Temporary decision pending assessment: child protection plan Forum: Child protection conference
0–1 year	**Two months:** Temporary decision pending progress: remain subject to child protection plan Forum: CP review Domicile: Parents
	Eight months: Definitive decision: end child protection plan – case closed Forum: CP review Domicile: Parents

Figure 5.2 Timeline: decisions made for Jaz *(high risk of harm at identification; low risk, living with birth parent and safeguarded at age three)*

Jaz was only eight months old when his case was closed, and his mother was one of a handful of parents who felt that support had been withdrawn too swiftly, before she was certain that she had overcome the many difficulties that had precipitated the removal of her older children. Although it had been made clear to her that she could still access the family centre that had been providing her with support over the previous months, and she was aware that she could ask for further advice and support when necessary, she nevertheless would have preferred the child protection plan to have continued for longer:

> I says keep him on [child protection plan] another three months, I asked to be kept on it. For that bit more support, I didn't want to go back to my old lifestyle. (Birth mother of Jaz)

Not safeguarded (12 children: 28%)

Decision-making was relatively straightforward for most of the 'safeguarded at home' group because their parents succeeded in following child protection plans and in making the changes required of them. The 12 children who were living at home and not considered to be safeguarded at the end of the study were placed in this category because their parents had not succeeded in overcoming their difficulties by the time they were three, and, consequently, they remained likely to suffer significant harm. One child in this group was identified as at severe risk of harm at identification, four at high risk and seven at medium risk. By the end of the study, one parent had overcome some difficulties (although risk factors still persisted) and six had remained unchanged; the situation of five other parents, however, had deteriorated, largely because initial evidence of capacity to change had not been sustained. By their third birthdays, one of these children was (still) at severe risk of suffering harm; eight were deemed to be at high risk; and three at medium risk. Nine of these cases were still open at the end of the study (although six had at some stage been closed and then reopened). There were persistent, ongoing concerns in the three cases that were closed at the child's third birthday; one of these cases had been showing considerable deterioration at the time of closure and was highly likely to be re-referred.

All but one of these very young children experienced neglect and/ or emotional abuse during their first three years, most of them persistently. However, there were different degrees of maltreatment, and there appeared to be at least two patterns of experience. Five (42%) children in this group could be considered as being at *intermittent* risk of suffering harm. Their parents all had mild to moderate mental health problems, and although these were not overcome, they were manageable with support from a range of children's and adult services. This does not mean that the children were always safe: in some instances the risk of harm was severe – for instance Bella's mother did not feed her properly and at 12 months old she was very small and presented as a six-month-old baby; Morgan's mother felt unable to cope with the care of his disabled sister and occasionally threatened to abandon or kill both children. However, the parents were able, at least intermittently, to overcome their difficulties if they were provided with adequate support to do so. Thus Bella's mother's debilitating depression lifted somewhat when her home was condemned as unfit for human habitation and she was moved elsewhere; Morgan's mother was able to look after her children when offered a package of respite care. It seems possible that, although these parents showed little capacity to change, they might have been able to provide adequate care for their children if extensive, ongoing multi-agency support were available and accessible. This had, for instance, been acknowledged in the case of Lily, who was placed with her own parents on a Care Order that was intended to continue at least until she started school. However, support such as the respite care offered for Morgan was time-limited, and the situation liable to deteriorate if it was withdrawn. Under the current economic climate it seems likely that the long-term support required by these parents may well become increasingly difficult to access.

The other seven (58%) children in this group followed a rather different pathway. They were all categorized as at high or severe risk of harm at the end of the study, and included all but one of the group whose parental circumstances had deteriorated over the three years. Their parents were struggling with substance misuse and intimate partner violence; in five cases an older child had already been removed. These seven infants were subject to numerous provisional decisions as practitioners waited in vain for solid evidence of parental progress. A major issue for decision-makers was that there often *were* improvements, but these were either not sustained, or were insufficient to ensure that children were adequately safeguarded. However, the impression that genuine progress had been achieved had led to four infants being returned to birth parents from foster care, or not being placed at the very last moment, two of them at the point of a decision to separate them permanently. Six cases had also been closed on the grounds that the child was adequately safeguarded. Although no child had, as yet, returned to the care of the local authority, five of the closed cases were now open again on the third birthday, and the sixth was showing evidence of an increase in the parent's problems. Madeleine is one of these children. Risk factors at identification included both parents' prolific heroin use, concerns about possible intimate partner violence, housing problems and harassment from neighbours. Madeleine's father had previously had two children placed permanently away from home. Protective factors were her parents' apparent ability to keep their substance misuse under control and reduce it. The following decisions were made after the pre-birth assessment:

One month before Madeleine's birth her parents had made no preparations and were continuing to use heroin and lead a chaotic lifestyle. Professional concerns were such that at birth she was immediately placed in foster care on an Emergency Protection Order. A parenting assessment commenced and Madeleine's parents responded well. This subsequently led to Madeleine being rehabilitated to her parents when she was three months old on an Interim Care Order under placement with parents regulations. Madeleine's parents were at this time working well with services and attending a drugs programme. However, although their heroin use decreased, it did not entirely stop. When Madeleine was 11 months old the Interim Care Order was replaced with a 12-month Supervision Order. During this time her home circumstances deteriorated; her parents' relationship became fraught and their heroin use increased. The Supervision Order expired just before Madeleine's second birthday and the case was closed. Just before her third birthday, a re-referral was made because of intimate partner violence between the parents, but the case did not reopen. Instead a letter was sent to the parents advising that they seek professional help with anger management. Further evidence also suggests that by this time Madeleine's parents' drug use had substantially increased and her mother was prostituting to pay for it.

(Madeleine: medium risk of harm at identification; high risk, living with birth parent but not safeguarded at age three)

Pre-birth	**Pre-birth:** Emergency Protection Order at birth Forum: Child protection conference Domicile: Unborn
0–1 year	**Birth:** Temporary decision pending assessment: parenting assessment Forum: Court Domicile: Foster care (s.20)*
	Three months: Temporary decision pending progress: Interim Care Order – placement with parents regulations Forum: Court Domicile: Parents
	Eleven months: Temporary decision pending progress: Supervision Order for 12 months Forum: Court Domicile: Parents
1–2 years	**One year 11 months:** Definitive decision: lapse of Supervision Order – case closes Forum: Court Domicile: Parent
2–3 years	**Two years 11 months:** Referral regarding intimate partner violence. Letter sent to parents advising father seek anger management help. Case remains closed.

* Children looked after under section 20 of the Children Act 1989 are accommodated by the local authority with the agreement of their parents.

Figure 5.3 Timeline: decisions made for Madeleine *(medium risk of harm at identification; high risk, living with birth parent but not safeguarded at age three)*

Children such as Madeleine appear likely to experience neglect and abuse for much of their childhoods. Their cases raise numerous concerns, and are constantly referred and re-referred to children's social care. There are now some interventions that are known to be effective in addressing the consequences of neglect and emotional abuse (see Barlow and Schrader McMillan 2010), but these tend to be less effective as children grow older. It seems probable that many of these children will hover on the verge of care, and some may become looked after in the future; however, the longer this decision is delayed, the less their chance of achieving long-term, stable placements (see Farmer and Lutman forthcoming; Wade *et al.* 2011; Ward *et al.* 2008). At three years old, their chances of achieving successful adoptions are already beginning to diminish. This group of children resemble those who are later separated (see below), and their wellbeing is likely to be similarly compromised.

Safeguarded through permanent placement away from home (15 children: 35%)

As Chapter 4 indicated, six infants were permanently placed away from parents following identification. These included the two outliers, whose learning disabled mothers had voluntarily placed them with relatives, and four babies in the severe risk of harm group, whose parents displayed multiple risk factors, an absence of protective factors and minimal capacity to change. During the course of the next three years, decisions were made to separate nine other children permanently. Seven of these were also in the severe risk of harm group at identification; the parents of the other two had shown some capacity to change, but this proved insufficient for them to provide long-term care for a child.

There were five decision points that impacted on the life trajectories of infants in the permanently separated group: the age at which they were identified; the age at which they were removed from an abusive situation; the age at which permanent separation was agreed; the age at which they moved to their final home; and the age at which the arrangements were finalized.

Our previous study of very young children in care and accommodation (Ward and Munro 2010; Ward et al. 2006) focused on those who followed this pathway, and identified a substantial difference between permanence as experienced by the children, and the finalization of all procedures to secure their situation (see also Jackson and Thomas 1999). From the children's point of view, the definitive time points would have been the points at which they moved towards psychological, familial and domiciliary permanence, that is, the day they were separated from abusive parents and the day they moved to their final placement. Administrative or legal permanence, achieved through decisions to open the case, to make the separation permanent or to finalize a Special Guardianship or an Adoption Order, are unlikely to have been noticed by them, although they had a direct impact on many of their experiences.

Research on child development indicates that early separations are probably less damaging than those that occur later because, for the first six months of life, having positive interactions *per se* appears to be more important than interacting with specific people (Tannenbaum and Forehand 1994; Van den Dries et al. 2009). More preferential attachment behaviours and stranger anxiety begin to set in at seven months; from this age children start to develop secure attachments, the loss of which, particularly in the early years, are sources of considerable and enduring distress. Moreover, children who are left in abusive situations start to develop maladaptive attachments from about this age (Howe 2005; Schore 2010). There is therefore substantial evidence of a need for urgency, both in removing children from abusive and neglectful parents and in placing them permanently; delays risk disadvantaging children twice over, first by leaving them too long in abusive situations and second by separating them from interim carers to whom they have become attached. Those who develop close attachments to foster carers are likely to find it difficult to transfer attachments to adoptive parents. Van den Dries and colleagues (2009) found that infants who were adopted before 12 months of age were as securely attached as their non-adopted peers, whereas those adopted after their first birthday showed less attachment security than non-adopted children.

All the 15 children in the permanently separated group in the current study were identified before they were eight months old, eight of them before birth. However, it took on average 7.5 months between the decision that the infant was suffering, or likely to suffer, significant harm and the decision to place them away from birth families, and a further seven months between the decision to separate them and the decision to make this arrangement permanent, either through Residence Order, special guardianship or adoption. Where children were placed for adoption, it then took at least a further five months for a suitable home to be found and in some cases much longer. Table 5.2 shows the children's ages at the time points that would have had the greatest impact on their future development – the day they were separated from abusive parents and the day they reached their permanent placement.

Table 5.2 Age at separation by age at permanent placement (permanently separated children: n=15)

	Age at permanent placement				
Age separated	0–6 months	7–11 months	12–23 months	24 months plus	Total*
0–6 months	3	2	3	–	8 (53%)
7–11 months	–	1	1	1	3 (20%)
12–23 months	–	–	1	2	3 (20%)
24 months plus	–	–	–	1	1 (7%)
Total	3 (20%)	3 (20%)	5 (33%)	4 (27%)	15 (100%)

* Percentages are rounded figures.

As the table shows, over half of this group were separated from abusive situations before they were six months old, and about three quarters before their first birthdays. However, four children were more than a year old before they were finally separated, at ages 13, 16, 18 and 28 months. Furthermore, only three infants had been permanently placed by the time they were six months old, and only six by their first birthdays. Of the nine (60%) children who were more than a year old before they were permanently placed, two were aged two, and two were aged three.

Children who were permanently placed at an early age tended to be those who were first placed with kinship carers, with whom they then remained. Dabir, whose case history has been discussed at some length in preceding chapters, was one such infant. Although it took several months for the professionals concerned to recognize that this child was being repeatedly subject to physical abuse, once the decision to separate him from his parents had been made, he was placed immediately with his maternal grandfather and partner who were approved as kinship carers. The birth parents both asked to be considered as permanent carers and were given an extensive parenting assessment, but when it transpired that they were jointly responsible for his injuries, Dabir's placement with his grandparents became permanent. Two of the infants who were placed for adoption followed similarly simple pathways, and were permanently placed before their first birthdays; a major factor that contributed to their achieving permanence so swiftly was, in both cases, the decision to separate them from birth parents before they were four months old.

Later separations: double jeopardy

The nine children who were not permanently placed until after their first birthdays tended to follow rather different pathways, with lengthy delays between identification and the decision to separate and/or between the decision to separate and finding a suitable placement. Those children who had no suitable relatives available to look after them on a long-term basis were particularly likely to experience delays, for they spent on average 15 months in temporary placements pending the move to an adoptive home. This timescale is identical to that identified by our previous study of very young children looked after by local authorities (see Ward et al. 2006, p.87) and is of concern, for the chances of these nine children becoming securely attached to permanent carers are likely to have been diminished by the delays in decision-making. There was plenty of evidence of twin and even triple tracking, with infants being placed with carers with alternative plans for reunification with birth parents, or adoption if insufficient progress was made. However, there was no evidence of concurrent planning, whereby children are placed with foster carers who will later adopt if reunification proves impossible, thus reducing the chances of their developing attachments which are later disrupted. This initiative was being piloted at the time of our earlier study; although the results were promising (Monck, Reynolds and Wigfall 2003), it has not been widely taken up. The service is currently provided by Coram Family but, although recently there has been increased interest, in the 11 years since the project was established, only 59 children have been placed for concurrent planning (Coram Family 2011).

This service is not appropriate for all babies and very young children placed in the care of local authorities, some of whom, as this study shows, have parents who are able to look after them. However, it can speed up the decision-making process and reduce the risk of 'double jeopardy' in circumstances where, as was the case with the permanently separated children in our sample, from an early stage the birth parents show evidence of multiple risk factors, no protective factors and insufficient capacity to make the changes necessary to provide a nurturing home for a child.

One child who exemplifies the experiences of these late separated children is Matthew, who was introduced in Chapter 4 as an infant whose case was closed, possibly prematurely, shortly after the pre-birth assessment. It will be remembered that Matthew's mother was a teenager and looked after by the local authority herself when she became pregnant. She had a long history of substance misuse, and of absconding from residential and foster homes, and was vulnerable to sexual exploitation. She had also refused to acknowledge that she was pregnant. Matthew was made the subject of a child protection plan before birth, but his mother then began to engage with services and, against the social worker's recommendation, this was rescinded and the case closed before he was born.

When Matthew was two months old his GP re-referred him to children's social care as he was not receiving adequate care. Matthew was made the subject of a second child protection plan and was temporarily placed with his maternal grandmother. When he was nine months old, he and his mother began a residential parenting assessment. However, this was terminated prematurely, and Matthew was returned to his grandmother. When Matthew was 14 months old, a court hearing granted an Interim Care Order and directed a second residential parenting assessment of his mother and a kin care assessment of the grandmother with whom he had lived for eight months. The kin care assessment was negative because of concerns about intimate partner violence. However, the parenting assessment was positive and Matthew and his mother returned home. Within one month, when Matthew was 19 months old, the reunification failed due to concerns of neglect and physical abuse and he was placed in foster care with the plan changing to adoption. He was finally placed with his adoptive family 16 months later, just before his third birthday.

(Matthew: severe risk of harm at identification; safeguarded through separation at age three)

Pre-birth	**Pre-birth:** Temporary decision pending assessment: child protection plan Forum: Child protection conference
	Pre-birth: Definitive decision: end child protection plan Forum: CP review
0–1 year	**Four months:** Temporary decision pending assessment: child protection plan Forum: Child protection conference Domicile: Kin care
	Nine months: Temporary decision pending assessment: residential parenting assessment Forum: Unclear Domicile: Parent (residential unit)
	Eleven months: Temporary decision pending assessment: place in kin care parenting assessment unsuccessful Forum: Unclear Domicile: Kin care
1–2 years	**One year:** Temporary decision pending assessment: Interim Care Order granted. Second residential parenting assessment to take place Forum: Court Domicile: Parent (residential unit)
	One year five months: Temporary decision pending assessment: assessment of kin carers – outcome negative Forum: Court Domicile: Parent (residential unit)
	One year six months: Temporary decision pending progress: written agreement signed. Mother and child live independently Forum: Unclear Domicile: Parents
	One year seven months: Temporary decision pending assessment: written agreement not adhered to; child placed in foster care Forum: Unclear Domicile: Foster care
	One year ten months: Definitive decision: plan changes to adoption Forum: Adoption best interests panel Domicile: Foster care
	One year 11 months: Definitive decision: Care and Placement Orders granted Forum: Court Domicile: Foster care
2–3 years	**Three years:** Definitive decision: child moves in with adoptive family Forum: Unclear Domicile: Adoptive family

Figure 5.4 Timeline: decisions made for Matthew *(severe risk of harm at identification; safeguarded through separation at age three)*

Matthew, who was classified as being at severe risk of suffering harm before he was born, spent 19 months living with a mother who physically abused and neglected him, or being passed between his mother and his grandmother, where he was witness to intimate partner violence, before finally being placed in foster care. He then spent a further 16 months, presumably becoming attached to foster carers, before he moved to his adoptive home, by which time professionals had noted signs of behavioural problems and delayed speech. His chances of achieving wellbeing in his adoptive home had been doubly jeopardized by his early experience.

The potentially adverse consequences of such delayed decision-making did not go unnoticed by some of the birth parents:

> He is in foster care waiting to be adopted…but I doubt he will now, he's getting too old for that, he's three years old, he's four next year, so you know, they don't normally take them for adoption at that age, it's normally a bit younger than that. So I'm thinking that he might be the same as what I went through, being passed from pillar to post through foster care basically. (Birth mother of Cassie speaking of an older child: medium risk of harm at identification; high risk, living with birth parent but not safeguarded at age three)

> If they can't get a family [they should] send him back, and they never even did that, they just dragged it on and dragged it on and then a three-year-old gets adopted by someone he doesn't even know. (Birth mother of Stephen: severe risk of harm at identification; safeguarded through separation at age three)

It is difficult to identify how far the experiences of these children reflect those of other infants placed for adoption in England, although findings from other research amply confirm that children's long-term wellbeing can be doubly jeopardized by late separation from an abusive birth family followed by delays in finding a permanent placement (Biehal *et al.* 2010; Farmer *et al.* 2010). The most recent national data show that of the 3050 children adopted in the year 2010-11, 1910 (63%) became looked after before their first birthday, but only 60 (2%) were adopted before they were one. The national longitudinal data suggest that over the last five years an *increasing* proportion of infants who are eventually adopted become looked after before their first birthday. However, the average length of time looked after before adoption is 31 months. Moreover, *fewer* children now reach their adoptive home within 12 months of a decision to adopt, and *fewer* children are adopted before they are one (Department for Education 2011b). The implications are that although there may have been some improvement in early identification, there is still little emphasis on the need for swift decisions when children are very young, and the adverse experiences of so many infants in the sample are likely to reflect those of several hundred others each year.

On the other hand there is greater evidence of stability of placements for these very young children who become looked after than was found in our previous study, although the numbers are too small for the findings to be more than indicative. Our earlier study demonstrated a close relationship between delayed decision-making and placement instability for these children (Ward *et al.* 2006, pp.43–5). There is less evidence of instability for those who became looked after in the current study, with only 20 per cent (three) of these children having three or more placements as compared with 65 per cent (25) in the earlier study, which tracked a similar sample of infants who were identified about ten years earlier.

Conclusion

This chapter has explored the decisions that shaped the experiences of the children from the time of the core assessment until their third birthdays. At that stage they had fallen into three similar sized groups: those who were adequately safeguarded because their parents had overcome their difficulties; those who were living with parents who had not succeeded in overcoming significant problems, and were therefore not adequately safeguarded; and those who were safeguarded through permanent separation. Within these groupings, 16 children (over a third of the sample) were particularly disadvantaged: the seven children who waited in limbo while their parents' situation deteriorated or showed only minimal positive change, and the nine children who faced the double jeopardy of late separation from abusive parents followed by disrupted attachments from interim foster carers. The three themes that emerged in the preceding chapter – the early withdrawal of support from children's social care in some cases; the care given to ensuring that parents should have every opportunity to demonstrate their capacity to change; and the reluctance to take intrusive action in the face of neglect – are all evident in the decisions that shaped the lives of these infants. However, this chapter has simply explored what happened; the subsequent chapters consider further evidence concerning which children were safeguarded at the end of the study, and the factors which shaped the decisions discussed above.

Summary points for Chapter 5

- Following the core assessment, 31 (72%) infants in the full follow-up group remained with their parents and received support from children's social care, while 12 (28%) were considered to require placements away from home.

- By their third birthdays, 28 (65%) children were living with their parents and 15 (35%) had been placed away from home, almost all of them permanently. Twenty one (75%) of those living with their birth parents had never left home.

- Not all the children were adequately safeguarded by their third birthdays, and there was still ongoing social care involvement in a number of cases. Thirty (70%) cases were closed and 13 (30%) were still open, six of them reopened following closure and a subsequent re-referral.

- By the time they were three, the children had fallen into three groups of relatively similar size:
  - ° Sixteen (37%) children who were adequately safeguarded and were living with birth parents, now apparently at low risk of suffering harm.
  - ° Twelve (28%) children who were not adequately safeguarded and were living with parents at medium, high or severe risk of harm.
  - ° Fifteen (35%) children who were apparently safeguarded through permanent separation from abusive or neglectful birth parents.

- Decisions concerning permanence bore a relatively close relationship to objective evidence of risk levels for the majority of children. However, it could take several months before definitive decisions were reached, and in the interim many infants were exposed to abuse and neglect for extensive periods, with long-term consequences for their future life chances.

- Decisions did not follow evidence of risk of harm in over a quarter (28%) of sample cases.

- Decisions were classified according to whether they were taken pending further information, pending progress made by parents or carers, or whether they were definitive, that is, moving towards permanency. For the sample as a whole, it took on average 14 months for a definitive decision to be made, and a further six months before this was realized.

- Early decisions were almost always temporary, and made with the proviso that parents might be able to overcome their difficulties. While a protracted decision-making period ensured that parents' rights were properly protected, such decisions rarely took account of these very young children's timeframes.

- After infants were six months old there was increasingly less likelihood that the outcomes of parenting assessments would be positive or that parents would succeed in overcoming their difficulties.

- Where children were safeguarded through permanent placement away from their birth parents, it took on average 7.5 months between the decision that the child was suffering, or likely to suffer, significant harm and the decision to separate, and a further seven months between the decision to separate them and the decision to make this arrangement permanent, either through Residence Order, special guardianship or adoption.

- The national statistics indicate that although there may have been some improvement in early identification, there is still little emphasis on the need for swift decisions when children are very young; the adverse experiences of so many children in the sample are likely to reflect those of several hundred others each year.

- However, there is less evidence of instability for those who entered care in the current study than in our previous research, which tracked a similar sample of infants who had been identified ten years earlier.

6

How Far Were the Children Safeguarded?

Introduction

The previous chapter tracked the infants' experiences from the time of the core assessment until their third birthdays. As we have seen, by then the sample had fallen into three groups of roughly similar sizes: the 16 (37%) children who were living with birth parents who had overcome their difficulties; the 15 (35%) children who were permanently separated from birth parents who had been unable to change sufficiently to safeguard them; and the 12 (28%) children living with birth parents who had made insufficient changes and were still suffering, or likely to suffer, significant harm. Children were considered to be safeguarded through parental change and at low risk of being harmed in the first group, and safeguarded through separation in the second; children in the third group were not considered to be safeguarded and to remain at medium, high or severe risk of suffering harm. The criterion for judging that parental change had been sufficient to ensure safeguarding was that all known parental risk factors[1] had been addressed. For instance, substance misuse or intimate partner violence would need to be completely overcome with no recurrence within the study timeframe.

This chapter focuses on the children at the age of three: it compares the 16 (37%) children whose parents overcame their difficulties with the 27 (63%) whose parents did not, and it explores the evidence of how abuse and neglect had or had not impacted on children's subsequent development and behaviour.

---

1   For one parent if caring for the index child independently, or for both parents if caring for the index child together.

Risks of harm and how they changed over time

It was possible to use the classification described in Chapter 3 to analyse the progress of parents in terms of increased or decreased risk factors. As the reader may recall, there are four categories of risk of harm in our classification:

- **Severe risk of harm:** risk factors, no protective factors and no capacity for change.

- **High risk of harm:** risk factors, protective factors and no capacity for change.

- **Medium risk of harm:** risk factors, protective factors and capacity for change.

- **Low risk of harm:** no risk factors or previous risk factors addressed, protective factors and capacity for change.

Table 6.1 compares the risk of harm at identification with that at the children's third birthdays.

None of the 12 parents (or sets of parents) whose children were categorized as at severe risk of harm at identification had demonstrated protective factors or a capacity to address their problems by the end of the study. By this stage, 11 had seen the removal of the index child; the twelfth was an abusive mother whose child (Janis) had remained with her throughout the study and whose circumstances have been considered in previous chapters. Four of the seven parents whose children were at high risk of harm showed no change (one of them being separated from the index child), one showed evidence of some capacity to change and two appeared to overcome their earlier difficulties, at least for the three years of the study. Thirteen of the 21 parents with children at medium risk of harm showed sustained capacity for change and overcame their earlier problem behaviours; two of them remained much the same throughout the study; and six parents in this group deteriorated, one to the point where her child was placed for adoption. This group of six parents were all classified as at high risk of harming their children by the end of the study, and five of them had children living with them throughout the three years.

Table 6.1 Risk of harm at identification by risk at child's third birthday (full follow-up group: n=43)

	Risk of harm at age three							Total*
	Severe risk	High risk	Medium risk	Low risk	Severe risk child removed	High risk child removed	Outliers	
Risk of harm at ID Severe risk	1	–	–	–	11	–	–	12 (28%)
High risk	–	3	1	2	–	1	–	7 (16%)
Medium risk	–	5	2	13	–	1	–	21 (49%)
Low risk	–	–	–	1	–	–	–	1 (2%)
Outliers	–	–	–	–	–	–	2	2 (5%)
Total	1 (2%)	8 (19%)	3 (7%)	16 (37%)	11 (26%)	2 (5%)	2 (5%)	43 (100%)

* Percentages are rounded figures.

Parents who overcame difficulties (sufficient change group)

Fourteen of the 15 sets of parents whose children were adequately safeguarded at the end of the study had overcome considerable difficulties to do so. Broadly speaking, there were two ways in which they succeeded in addressing their adversities sufficiently to safeguard the index child: one was through overcoming their own internal problems, such as substance misuse or mental ill-health; the other through extricating themselves from a relationship with an abusive partner. The situation was rarely clear cut, for most parents had multiple problems to address; for instance, many parents with substance misuse problems were also in violent relationships. Nevertheless, for the majority it was possible to identify either external or internal factors as the primary cause of their difficulties.

It was extremely rare for parents who had shown no capacity for change at the beginning of the study to have apparently overcome their difficulties by the time the index child was three. This occurred in only two cases, including that of Jaz, whose case was described in some detail in Chapters 3 and 5. The mother of this child had had previous children removed, but appeared to overcome substance misuse, prostitution and a chaotic lifestyle sufficiently to safeguard Jaz. Both parents made strong signs of addressing their problems from an early stage and accessed support both formally and informally. They were considered to have made sufficient progress for the case to be closed when Jaz was around eight months old, an example of the tendency to withdraw services after relatively short interventions when things appeared to be going well. However, there were no subsequent referrals by the time Jaz was three. The social worker attributed the 'sufficient change' outcome to the parents' willingness to engage, and noted that such remarkable change is rare when the risk factors are so considerable:

> I think a big part of the success was that both [parents] kind of actively embraced the child protection plan, very seldom that you get parents with that background displaying such a kind of openness, willingness to co-operate, and there was quite a lot of demands being made on them in terms of appointments, but both of them kept to that. (Social worker)

The majority of parents who succeeded in overcoming internal difficulties had already made some progress in doing so before the birth (and sometimes before the conception) of the index child. Thus Richard's mother had already overcome her alcohol addiction before she and her partner decided to have another baby. Because these parents had previously had children removed from them, they took the (unusual) step of consulting with their GP concerning the chances of social care allowing them to bring up a subsequent child before Richard was conceived.

Parents with continuing problems

Children living at home and not safeguarded

Three of the 12 sets of parents whose children were living with them but not adequately safeguarded by the age of three had shown some protective factors and some capacity to change, but had not succeeded in overcoming all the risk factors they had shown at identification. The remaining nine sets of parents had shown less evidence of progress: four of them had shown no capacity for change, and five had been unable to maintain their initial progress; for instance, substance misuse had initially decreased but had continued, or intimate partner violence had ceased at identification but then recurred by the time the child was three. This group included all those seven (sets of) parents identified in Chapter 5 for whom professionals waited in vain to overcome their difficulties, as well as two who only succeeded in overcoming their problems intermittently, with substantial support from children's social care.

Jack's case is typical of those where the likelihood of significant harm remained relatively high and the parent showed little capacity to change:

Jack's mother had relinquished responsibility for her previous children who were being cared for by their extended family. Jack was the subject of a child protection plan from birth and he and his mother went to live with relatives, although conditions were very cramped and professionals did not deem them safe for a baby. Jack and his mother then moved to supported housing, but were evicted and moved to their own tenancy. When Jack was 11 months old it was noted that his mother was not giving him adequate care, that he was grubby and often left in dirty nappies. Shortly after they were evicted from the supported housing, the case was closed. The mother had not addressed her substance misuse issues and was still thought to be prostituting herself; however, she did have a supportive extended family. The police made a re-referral to children's social care when Jack was almost two years old as they found him alone with 'youths' who were taking drugs. The case remained closed. A further re-referral was made a few months later by a paediatrician who was concerned about Jack's developmental delay; however, the case remained closed. It was not until shortly after Jack's third birthday that a section 47 enquiry was undertaken following concerns that he was being physically abused and having contact with a Schedule One offender. This resulted in a second child protection plan for Jack, who remained in his mother's care.

(Jack: high risk of harm at identification; high risk, living with birth parent but not safeguarded at age three)

In all these cases there were ongoing concerns about the parents' ability to safeguard; the evidence of maltreatment was not thought to be sufficiently severe to warrant their removal, but nonetheless there remained a strong probability that these very young children would suffer significant harm. Parents such as Jack's mother received a substantial range and level of services, particularly in the early years. For instance, during the first child protection plan, she was offered a community resource worker, financial assistance, supported housing and support from the family centre. However, once the case had been closed following little progress, it was difficult to get it reopened, despite high levels of concern. Children such as Jack often followed a pattern of bursts of intensive intervention interspersed by periods of little or no attention as their cases were continually opened and closed. One of the key problems in cases such as these is how to safeguard children who suffer levels of abuse that are always close to, and sporadically pass, the threshold of causing significant harm.

The comments of professionals shed some light on the difficulties of managing risks of harm in such cases. In the words of one team leader:

> With some families it's just continual, the standard of parenting is always just going to be above or below good enough, and it's what do you do with those cases…we know that we wouldn't want to remove these children. If they did go to court, we wouldn't even get agreement for it, and it's how do we get them to a level that they can consistently remain at throughout their children's lives? (Team leader, children's social care)

Undoubtedly one could argue that in several cases the threshold was too high, and some children would have benefited by removal. Nevertheless, there remains the issue of how services can adequately support those children who suffer intermittent abuse, or continuing, low-level neglect that is never sufficiently serious to warrant intrusive interventions but that nevertheless is likely to compromise their life chances to a greater or lesser degree.

Children safeguarded through separation

The children were safeguarded either because parents changed or because they were separated from parents who did not change. By the end of the study the 16 children in the sufficient change group were considered to be safeguarded through parental change, and the 15 children permanently placed away from home were considered to be safeguarded through separation. The 12 children living with parents in the insufficient change group were not considered to be safeguarded. The parents of the children in the safeguarded through separation group had made few if any changes to their lifestyles; their characteristics are discussed later in this chapter, in the analysis of the insufficient change group.

By their third birthdays, two of the 15 permanently separated children were living in foster care pending permanent placements, seven were placed with adoptive carers and six were permanently placed with relatives on Special Guardianship or Residence Orders. Two of these children were placed with grandparents, three with aunts and uncles and one with a family friend. We only had access to one child after they were placed for adoption, but the six placed with relatives and the two in temporary foster care continue to be tracked.

Because most adoptive parents have not consented to further involvement, we do not know whether there have been any re-referrals for these children nor whether their placements have been successful. However, closer analysis of the kinship placements reveals a number of concerns.

As our earlier study of infants looked after by local authorities also found (Ward *et al.* 2006), there was a lower standard of approval for kinship carers and children were sometimes placed with relatives who had extensive criminal records or whose own children had been abused or maltreated. This issue is discussed further in Chapter 7. By the end of the study, three of the six kinship placements were raising concerns because of the carer's own adverse behaviour patterns. Craig's case is one of these:

Craig was placed with a maternal aunt at birth and his care was shared with his learning disabled mother. From the start the placement caused some friction with other members of the extended family who felt the baby should have been placed with them. Less than a year after the maternal aunt was approved as a kinship carer, Craig was admitted to hospital with a fractured femur. An older cousin had been left to care for him and sat him on the sofa with his leg twisted under him. A written agreement was put in place to ensure the cousin did not have sole care again, but other concerns about the family continued beyond Craig's third birthday. As he approached four, the aunt reported that she was pregnant and there were concerns around her former partner, the unborn baby's father, who was a Schedule One offender. This child was now the subject of a child protection investigation and the social worker was considering removing Craig both because of the aunt's association with her former partner and because there were concerns about the quality of care and the unsatisfactory home circumstances. Perhaps unsurprisingly, there were also concerns about Craig's development; according to his aunt he needed constant reassurance, still wore nappies at night-time and lacked the kind of 'understanding' that you would expect of a child of his age.

(Craig: outlier case; separated at age three)

In the other two problematic kinship placements there were concerns about the carers' past criminal activity and their current risk-taking behaviours including recreational drug-taking and driving illegally. Overall, of the six children who were permanently placed in kinship care at age three, two were receiving good quality care and their needs met within their placement. However, the placements of the other four children were not meeting their needs, and three were on the verge of breakdown.

Factors indicative of parental change

Fourteen (14/37: 38%) parents (or sets of parents) succeeded in making and sustaining sufficient changes and were able to safeguard their children adequately, at least until they were three. These were the parents of all 16 children who were at low risk of harm at age three, except the one family who had been classified as low risk at the outset and thus did not need to change. There was also one set of twins in this group. The remaining 23 (62%) parents (or sets of parents) did not succeed (and in some cases did not attempt to succeed) in making and sustaining changes. This includes all parents (or sets of parents) of the 12 children who were at medium, high or severe risk of harm at age three and were not adequately safeguarded living at home, and the parents (or sets of parents) of 13 children who were permanently removed. The two outlier cases where birth mothers had moderate to severe learning disabilities, and voluntarily placed their children with relatives with whom they could share care, have not been included in the following discussion. There were also two sets of siblings in this group.

It is possible to compare the two groups of parents who showed *sufficient change* with those who showed negative or *insufficient change* in order to gain more understanding of those factors that distinguished between them. As we discuss below, the key factors that appeared most to influence these different trajectories include: types of risk factors; types of protective factors; the nature of abuse; and the timing of parental change.

The reader should bear in mind first that the sample is very small; comparisons have not been subject to formal statistical analyses of probability as the numbers in each cell are so small. The findings should be tested out with a much larger group of families before they can be regarded as definitive. Second, we have only followed the parents for three years: we do not know how far sufficient changes will be sustainable in the future, particularly in times of stress or adversity. Nor do we know whether those parents who were unable to make sufficient changes to safeguard the index child were able to do so later on for a subsequent child; there are, for instance, some indications that the three parents in the insufficient change group who had begun to address their problems may have continued their progress and in the future been able to provide a nurturing home, even though their current problems impacted on the infant upon whom we focused. Finally it is important to note that it was a significant achievement for any parent in this sample to overcome the complex combinations of risk factors that inhibited their parenting capacity; to do so they had to make extensive changes to their lifestyles and behaviour and to sustain these changes throughout the study period.

Internal and external risk factors

As the reader will remember, the children in this sample were more likely to suffer significant harm than comparable populations. Therefore, the parental risk factors within this population were also likely to be particularly severe. Those risk factors that were most prevalent in both the sufficient change and the insufficient change groups include substance misuse, mental ill-health, intimate partner violence, experience of abuse in parents' own childhoods and previous maltreatment of older children. However, there were differences in type and prevalence of these risk factors between the two groups of parents; these can best be explained by comparing the prevalence of internal risk factors, such as substance misuse and mental ill-health, with external risk factors such as intimate partner violence, or child abuse from an associated adult.

The insufficient change group had a higher incidence of mental health problems (9/23: 39%) than the sufficient change group (4/14: 29%), and their problems appeared to be more entrenched, as parents in this group were less likely to recover or respond to treatment. However, the two groups of parents showed a similar incidence of other internal risk factors. For instance, almost half the parents in each group had problems with drug and/or alcohol use: 6/14 (43%) in the sufficient change group and 10/23 (43%) in the insufficient change group. Almost all (5/6) of the parents who were able to address their addictions were accessing help from a drugs/alcohol counsellor, and we do not have data on the one exception. These parents were engaging in regular counselling sessions, usually every one or two weeks, and over the course of several months. These services were provided by the voluntary sector and parents greatly valued the therapeutic and adult-focused support that they offered (see Chapter 8 for further details).

In contrast, there is evidence that only three of the ten parents (or sets of parents) who failed to overcome alcohol or substance misuse were accessing and engaging with drug or alcohol services. Some of the parents in this group accessed psychotherapeutic interventions such as counselling or a therapeutic domestic violence programme. However, five parents in the insufficient change group, whose substance use was cited as a problem, were not in receipt of any specialist services. This may, however, be more indicative of their unwillingness to engage than a shortage of resources; there is evidence that at least two of these parents were offered services but declined them.

Parents with substance misuse problems in the insufficient change group whose children had been removed were more likely to have shown little or no evidence of addressing their addiction. Those in this group whose children remained with them had often taken slight steps to overcome their addictions but had not been entirely successful and experienced repeated relapses during the course of the study. For example, Madeleine's parents were prolific heroin users who continued to use throughout the pregnancy; whilst they did reduce drug consumption and made improvements to their lifestyle with the result that Madeleine remained with them, their substance misuse did not entirely stop and both parents had several relapses throughout the three years. During this time, they also engaged with a drugs worker and undertook a methadone programme. In contrast, those parents in the sufficient change group who successfully addressed substance misuse maintained abstinence throughout the three-year study period with no known relapses. For instance, Harry's mother also had an addiction to heroin. However, before she became pregnant with Harry she had already taken steps to address this by joining a drugs detox programme and she began to engage with drugs counselling. Harry's mother was determined to be completely drugs free in time for the birth – which she achieved. She appears to have remained abstinent throughout the study.

The prevalence of external risk factors such as intimate partner violence, or the presence of an associated adult who abused children, differed between the two groups. Intimate partner violence had been a feature in half the families (7/14: 50%) where parents made sufficient changes compared with 39 per cent (9/23) of those where few or no changes were seen. There were no instances of fathers being the victims of intimate partner violence in the full follow-up group.

Three sets of parents were able to end the violence within their relationship, and ultimately stayed together. In one of these cases the violence ceased when their drug and alcohol addiction was addressed. It is unclear what factors facilitated the end of violence between the other two couples who remained together except that the problem appeared to be related to stress caused by housing and financial problems and to cease once these had been dealt with. We cannot, of course, be certain that there was no further violence in any of these households; however, there was no further evidence of any police or other reported incidents on the case files by the children's third birthdays.

An additional three mothers ended their relationship with an abusive partner during the study. One other mother had experienced intimate partner violence in the past, but had later started and maintained a relationship with the index child's father who was supportive and not abusive. Those parents who took their own initiative to end their violent relationship were more likely to succeed in sustaining change; this may be because in order to do so they needed to have overcome some of the psychosocial problems such as low self-esteem that were both associated with intimate partner violence and with their own poor parenting (Cleaver *et al.* 2011; Office of the Tánaiste 1997).

Adult services targeted at overcoming intimate partner violence were less widely accessed than services for drug or alcohol problems. There is evidence that four (4/16: 25%) parents who were the victims of intimate partner violence in the full follow-up group were accessing these types of services, but no evidence that any services were offered for perpetrators. There is no evidence that any of those parents who overcame violence within their relationship were in receipt of targeted domestic violence services.

The following two examples show how approaches to intimate partner violence differed between those parents who were successful in extricating themselves from such relationships and those who were not. Nathan's parents misused alcohol and had a violent relationship; the potential impact on his welfare has been discussed in earlier chapters:

> The police were called several times during incidents in which Nathan was held up and used as a shield between his parents. The father's violent behaviour, combined with other criminal activity, resulted in a prison sentence. During this time, Nathan was thought to be adequately safeguarded. Despite intensive input from intimate partner violence support workers and sanctuary schemes, Nathan's mother did not succeed in extricating herself from this destructive relationship; as soon as the father was released from prison it was resumed and the violence repeated. At the age of three, Nathan remained in his mother's care at high risk of suffering harm. His mother was no longer in a relationship with his father, but had begun an abusive relationship with a different partner.
>
> *(Nathan: high risk of harm at identification; high risk, living*
> *with birth parent but not safeguarded at age three)*

Nathan's safety was based on external factors (a prison sentence) over which his parents had no control, rather than on any decision made by his mother to end the relationship to protect herself and her son. In contrast, Martin-Louis' mother managed to extricate herself from a similar relationship. His father had been violent towards her for a long period and had beaten her during the pregnancy and following Martin-Louis' birth. He had also been arrested for an alleged rape of a 15-year-old girl. The mother realized she was not happy in the relationship and wanted it to end; she responded to the threat of more intrusive action from children's social care by making the decision to extricate herself:

> I co-operated because they [children's social care] said that obviously if I didn't co-operate and you know resolve this problem or come to some agreement with [ex-partner] that my kids would be put on the at-risk register, and I wasn't having that. And things did need sorting out, you know because we weren't all happy living together. (Mother of Martin-Louis: medium risk of harm at identification; low risk, living with birth parent and safeguarded at age three)

With the help of her family, domestic violence workers within the police and a community psychiatric nurse specializing in post-natal depression, she succeeded. The father made several unsuccessful attempts to gain access to her house; however, the police domestic violence worker helped her to keep him away. Martin-Louis was still living with his mother at age three and was considered to be at low risk of suffering harm. No new risk factors had emerged and there had been no further incidents of violence in his home.

For five (36%) families in the sufficient change group and one in the insufficient change group, concerns were centred on an associated adult's past or current maltreatment of children. This was another parent in five cases and a grandparent in one. In these families one parent needed to address the risks posed by the associated adult by ending their involvement with them and not allowing the index child unsupervised (or in some cases any) contact. Jordan was the only child whose parent (in this example the mother) was unable to extricate herself entirely from such risks. Jordan's grandfather was a convicted paedophile; although his mother ended her association with him, she later formed a violent relationship with a man who also placed Jordan and his brother at risk of sexual abuse.

The five parents who succeeded in disassociating from partners who were known perpetrators of child maltreatment included two fathers and two mothers; one other mother ended her relationship with an abusive partner who was violent towards both her and their children. The case of Blair (on the following page) is a typical example of one parent overcoming the risks of harm posed by their partner.

Overall, external factors from either intimate partner violence or children being abused by associated adults were apparent in 11/14 (79%) cases where parents made sufficient changes compared with 9/23 (39%) cases in the insufficient change group. Where parents overcame these types of risk factors, one parent either ended their connection with the abuser, or both parents addressed the violence in their relationship.

> Shortly after Blair's parents met, his mother became pregnant. About four weeks after the birth, a health visitor who saw the family for a routine check recognized Blair's father. He had served a prison sentence for very serious acts of cruelty to a baby daughter from a previous relationship. The health visitor informed children's social care, who notified Blair's mother. She had known nothing of her partner's cruelty towards his other child, or of his prison sentence, and the news came as a great shock to her. She immediately cut all ties with Blair's father to safeguard her son.
>
> *(Blair: medium risk of harm at identification; low risk, living*
> *with birth parent and safeguarded at age three)*

Removal of older children

Prior to the birth of the index child, a large proportion of parents had had long-standing involvement with children's social care, either through having been abused themselves as children and/or through having already experienced the removal of older children, two factors which were inter-related.

About the same proportion of parents in both the sufficient and insufficient change groups had experienced the removal of an older child: five out of 14 (36%) in the former compared with nine out of 23 (39%) in the latter.[2] There is, however, a more marked difference if the parents in the insufficient change group who continued to look after their children are compared with those who were separated from them. Six (6/12: 50%) of the former group had experienced the removal of an older child, in contrast with three (3/11: 27%) of the latter. This finding should be tested out with a larger database, for if it proves to be valid it would have important implications. It is counter-intuitive, and may represent a tendency to give parents who have already been separated from one child every opportunity to prevent the loss of a second. It may also be indicative of professionals' variable perceptions of the quality of parenting. In families where older children have been removed, the required distance travelled between parents' starting points to them adequately meeting a child's needs is greater. However, professionals may perceive any small steps achieved

---

2   This is a lower figure than the number of children whose older siblings had been permanently placed away from home given in Chapters 3 and 4. The discrepancy occurs because the former chapters explored data from the full sample, rather than the smaller, full follow-up group, and also because the presence of sibling pairs in the sample means that there are more children than parents.

as greater progress than might be considered to be the case with other families. Without further monitoring and support, and in some cases more intrusive action by children's social care, this can place children at greater risk of being abused or neglected.

Parents who had experienced the removal of an older child had displayed adverse behaviour patterns that were extremely difficult to overcome. There were also indications that, in some circumstances, these were reinforced by the experience of losing a child, so that, for instance, those whose alcoholism had precipitated the separation then drank more to dull the pain (see also Neil *et al.* 2010).

> Because I'd lost the boys and everything I went through a bit of a bad stage, and I started drinking a little bit…it was just me that screwed up obviously because of what had been going on with the boys. (Mother of Ava: medium risk of harm at identification; high risk, living with birth parent but not safeguarded at age three)

In order to break free of the adverse behaviour patterns that had led to the removal of an older child, parents first had both to become reconciled to the loss and to acknowledge the part that their own behaviour had played in the decision. Only a very few were able to achieve this; where they did so, their ability to confront the presenting problems was indicative of them developing the insight and maturity needed to provide a nurturing home for the index child. There was very little evidence that parents who had experienced the removal of an older child were in receipt of any services to help them come to terms with the ensuing sense of shame and loss (see Neil *et al.* 2010). Only one of the five parents (or couples) who successfully made this transition was accessing post-adoption support.

Richard's parents were amongst those who became reconciled to the removal of an older child. They both had a history of alcohol misuse and related conflict and intimate partner violence. Before Richard's birth they had had two older children removed because of neglect and physical abuse. Yet they had been able to come to terms with this decision and understand why it had been made. Richard's mother explained:

> I fell pregnant four weeks after my first son was born, so obviously there was only ten months between the two of them, and me more than anyone went off the rails a bit, neglecting them, and then social workers got involved…I started lying to social workers…at the time I thought they were just stabbing me in the back, telling me one thing and going back telling and doing the complete opposite and that resulted in us losing the children. I was lying to them,

telling them that I'd given up drinking when in actual fact I hadn't. They obviously knew that, they're not stupid, and in the end they were taken off us. (Mother of Richard: medium risk of harm at identification; low risk, living with birth parents and safeguarded at age three)

It is important to note that Richard's parents, whose older children would have been categorized as at severe risk of harm when they were removed, had made significant progress by the time he was conceived, and thus were able to provide a nurturing home for him *within an appropriate timeframe.*

In contrast were parents who had not developed sufficient insight into their own behaviour to understand the reasons why older children had been removed. Cassie's mother had been both a victim and a perpetrator of sexual abuse. She had difficulty comprehending the need to protect her older son from Schedule One offenders in her own family. She had been unable to provide basic care for him and, even with extensive support, had failed to feed him. He had been removed before she had started her relationship with Cassie's father. She could not comprehend why her son had been separated from her, and blamed other factors, such as his refusal to eat. She explained:

So I was left just with this child, didn't know what to do with him, it was like really stressing…he wouldn't drink, he wouldn't eat basically, tried it but he just didn't want the food. That's it really, that's really why he went. (Birth mother of Cassie: medium risk of harm at identification; high risk, living with birth parents but not safeguarded at age three)

At age three, Cassie was the subject of a child protection plan, and her parents were denying any professional access to her and her younger brother. Both children also had unexplained injuries. Blaming external factors for removal of previous children was a common theme; very few parents, and only those in the sufficient change group, had insight into their own harmful behaviour and understood why children's social care had removed older children.

Coming to terms with the loss of children was a near-impossible task for parents who frequently had to contend with their own childhood experiences of abuse and other adversities. It is important to note that many of the homes of these parents displayed large pictures of the children they had lost, and they eagerly (and unrealistically) anticipated 'the day' their child would return looking for them when they reached the age of 18. Parents also waited impatiently for birthdays and Christmas to send a card to the children they had lost and longed for this letterbox contact to be reciprocated.

Parents' experience of childhood abuse

Experiences of abuse in childhood can have severe and long-lasting consequences for wellbeing in adulthood (see Jones 2008). Data concerning childhood abuse was extremely limited for the fathers of sample children. However, it is perhaps unsurprising that experiences of childhood abuse were less common for mothers in the sufficient than in the insufficient change group (3/14: 21% versus 10/23: 43%). Importantly, mothers who had experienced childhood sexual abuse tended to have multiple risk factors, and to be less likely to sustain change. Only one of the three mothers in the sufficient change group who had experienced childhood abuse had been sexually abused, whereas this was true of eight of the ten mothers who had been abused as children in the insufficient change group.

Parents who had been abused as children often had limited informal support networks, both because their low self-esteem made it difficult for them to form or retain friendships, but also because members of their extended family, to whom they might otherwise have turned, had often either been perpetrators or compliant in their abuse. Isla and Dylan's parents, for instance, claimed that they had both been physically abused as children, and the mother had also been sexually abused. Their relationship with their own parents was volatile, and had apparently ceased by the time of the younger child's birth:

> *Birth father:* Yeah. My mum lives almost, well, round the corner, doesn't she? She's remarried. We don't, but we don't have anything to do with her, or I don't have anything to do with her. Or she has nothing to do with me. We have [nothing] to do with each other. And my dad, he's on his third marriage and I don't see him.
>
> *Interviewer (to birth mother):* And what about you? Have you got family in the area?
>
> *Birth mother:* Yes. But I have nothing to do with them.
>
> (Birth parents of Isla and Dylan: severe risk of harm at identification; safeguarded through separation at age three)

Informal support networks can be a key facilitator in sustaining change. In their absence some parents may have found it impossible to overcome their adversities and to maintain any progress they had achieved.

In summary, while the prevalence of substance misuse, mental ill-health and the removal of older children was similar in both groups of parents, there were clear differences. Parents who successfully changed were:

- less likely to have experienced abuse in childhood and substantially less likely to have experienced childhood sexual abuse
- more likely to have been subject to intimate partner violence
- more likely to have been associating with an adult who was likely to harm children.

However, these parents were also able to:

- initiate the end of a violent relationship
- initiate the end of a relationship with an adult who was likely to harm children
- come to terms with the removal of older children and acknowledge the part that their actions had played in this decision.

These were the key factors that distinguished them from the parents who were unable to make or sustain sufficient changes to their lifestyles. They indicate that parents may have found it easier to dissociate themselves from external risks posed by other adults than to overcome internal risks engendered by their own problems. However, they also indicated the growth of confidence and insight that were precursors to parents overcoming their adverse behaviours in order to provide a nurturing home for the index child.

Protective factors

Chapter 3 has already discussed how the presence of protective factors such as the support of a non-abusive partner and/or an extended family and parents' willingness to engage with services can both help them to overcome destructive behaviour patterns and mitigate their impact (see also Cleaver *et al.* 2011; Jones *et al.* 2006). Protective factors for the parents in this sample were key facilitators in promoting and sustaining change; differences in their type and prevalence were evident between the two groups. Overall, those protective factors that appear to have had the most impact include informal support and parents' ability to acknowledge risks, with limited or no protective factors acting as the greatest barrier to parental change.

INFORMAL SUPPORT NETWORKS

The presence or absence of informal support networks was an important distinguishing factor between the two groups. Nine of the 14 (64%) parents in the sufficient change group compared with five of the 23 (22%) who were unable to make sufficient changes had informal support networks they could rely on. Informal support was provided by extended families, such as aunts, uncles and grandparents, non-abusive partners and, in some cases, foster carers.

Much of this informal support was intense and round the clock. Grandparents moved into the home to support the parents, or aunts and uncles were always on hand to offer sanctuary from violence. Many members of extended families were also included in formal meetings, and were relied on to notify children's social care if they believed the children were being abused or neglected. For instance, the mother of Simon, whose experiences were explored in the previous chapter, was able to move away from her substance-misusing lifestyle, and remained free from drugs from his birth onwards. Simon's grandmother, aunts and uncles were key facilitators of this change. The grandmother moved into the home he shared with his mother to offer help with his care and also support for his mother in her new life. She was still living with them at the most recent research visit, around the time of his fourth birthday, and was regarded as a vital element in their lives.

DEVELOPMENT OF INSIGHT

We have already seen that the parents' ability to acknowledge the risks that their behaviour and lifestyles had posed to their children was a key factor in distinguishing those who were able to make sufficient changes after the removal of an older child. Similarly this development of insight served as a protective factor when children remained with them. Eleven out of 14 (79%) parents in the sufficient change group showed some insight into the impact of their destructive behaviours, compared with only one in the insufficient change group. Such understanding was conspicuously absent amongst those parents whose safeguarding was inadequate. For example, the mother of Wayne was a heroin user; although she had previously been separated from an older child, Wayne remained with her. She could acknowledge that in general parental heroin use might have a damaging impact on children, but did not accept that her own drug-taking could potentially harm Wayne:

> Well, I could understand [about children's social care involvement] because I was on drugs, do you know what I mean, but I know I would never have infected him [Wayne]. But I suppose you have to look at it from their [children's social care] point of view. There are people [drug users] that I know that do neglect [their children]. (Birth mother of Wayne: medium risk of harm at identification; high risk, living with birth parent but not safeguarded at age three)

This mother's drug-taking fluctuated over the three-year study period; Wayne remained with her throughout and was exposed to extensive substance misuse within his household: when Wayne was three years old he could demonstrate how to prepare heroin for consumption.

Parents' willingness to engage with services is another known factor that mitigates some of the risk factors and reduces the likelihood of sustained or recurrent maltreatment (Jones *et al.* 2006). Half of the parents in the insufficient change group (11/23: 48%), and all of those in the sufficient change group, engaged with services. However, when the insufficient change group is split between those whose children remained at home and those whose children were removed, stark differences in engagement with services are evident. Eight out of 12 (67%) parents whose children remained with them but were not safeguarded engaged with services compared with two out of 11 (18%) parents whose children were removed. Moreover, the two children who were separated even though their parents engaged with services were only removed after their second birthdays; at the age of three, they were both still in temporary foster care pending a permanent placement. It appears that mere engagement with services, in the sense of attending appointments and giving access to social workers, was a misleading indicator in that it gave no real evidence of a parent's desire or ability to change.

As we know, many parents had long-standing involvement with children's social care, and as a result were well rehearsed in the right things to say and do to achieve a desired outcome. Blossom's father, for example, described a psychological assessment that he had undertaken:

> So these tests have come from America, and apparently they tell your personality on just one sheet of paper, 40 questions, yes or no answers. They reckon these tests are infallible. I've got a book that shows how to beat them. (Birth father of Blossom: severe risk of harm at identification; safeguarded through separation at age three)

This particular assessment concluded that the father's parenting capacity was satisfactory and recommended rehabilitation. However, during the rehabilitation period he was arrested for being drunk and disorderly and for stealing nappies whilst Blossom was in his care and she was removed and later adopted. Other parents indicated that they knew the processes of children's social care from their past experience, and were therefore better able to persuade practitioners that they could safeguard their children, regardless of their desire or ability to change their lifestyles. Such 'false compliance' was a feature of the Peter Connelly case (Haringey Local Safeguarding Children Board 2010), and findings from other studies confirm that practitioners often lack confidence in their ability to distinguish between those families who are genuinely engaged in treatment and those who are simply going through the motions (Fauth *et al.* 2010).

To summarize, those protective factors that were most indicative of parents' capacity to change were:

- the presence of strong informal support networks
- sufficient insight to acknowledge the risks posed by their destructive behaviour patterns
- the ability not simply to engage with services but also to make positive use of the support they offered.

The timing of parental change

Timing was a key component in parents' overall ability to make sufficient changes to safeguard their children's welfare. This was particularly evident where they needed to address internal risk factors such as substance misuse. We have already indicated that five of the 14 parents in the sufficient change group succeeded in overcoming problematic drug and/or alcohol use, three more responded successfully to treatment or recovered from mental health problems and one overcame both substance misuse and mental ill-health to successfully parent her child. The time at which this process occurred was an important indicator of a parent's capacity to overcome the risk factors that jeopardized their ability to safeguard the index child. Of those parents who successfully overcame substance misuse, two did so before pregnancy, three during the pregnancy and one immediately after giving birth. No parent overcame substance misuse if they continued to use drugs after the child had been born. In addition, all but one of those parents who succeeded had an informal support network that helped them to maintain their abstinence. Parents who recovered from mental ill-health (or accepted and responded to treatment) also did so within similar timeframes. Two parents recovered/responded to treatment before conception, one during pregnancy and two parents recovered from or were responding to treatment for post-natal depression before the child was six months old. Apart from these two parents, those who overcame these types of internal risk factors all did so as a result of either planning to become pregnant, the pregnancy itself or, at the latest, the birth.

Apart from the parents with post-natal depression, those who made sufficient changes at a later stage all extricated themselves from either intimate partner violence or the threat of child abuse from an associated adult; and all but one of these parents did so within the first six months of the infant's birth. By extricating themselves from these abusive relationships, parents could address the external risk factors which were closely linked to, but not necessarily engendered by, their own destructive behaviours. The one exception was the case of May, where the severe risk of harm posed by her father did not become apparent to her mother until after she was six months old.

Overall, of the 14 parents who made and sustained sufficient changes, 13 addressed all known risk factors before their child was six months old.

Wake-up calls

A number of parents, including four of those who overcame substance misuse, spoke of a 'wake-up call' that acted as a catalyst for change. This was a defining moment when they realized they would need to make substantial changes to their lifestyles if they were to parent successfully, and it took various forms. Harry's mother, for instance, was devastated when her older child was removed from her care, and realized that she would not be able to care for any future children unless she changed her lifestyle; Blair's mother was shocked to discover that her partner had a long history of physically abusing children and immediately took steps to dissociate herself from him in order to protect her baby; and Richard's mother had two older children placed for adoption and then saw her own mother die from alcohol misuse in her early 40s: she realized that she would need to take drastic action to stop herself following the same pathway. It is noteworthy that no parents in the insufficient change group spoke of such an epiphany.

Several parents developed a growing attachment to their baby; this, combined with the knowledge that they might be separated, acted as the necessary wake-up call. Simon's mother was one such case. Before becoming pregnant she had been a prolific crack cocaine user for five years, and drugs were embedded within every aspect of her life. In her own words: 'I'd been doing drugs really hard, I didn't have a life…I just gave up really,' and she had continued to use drugs throughout the pregnancy. However, her 'wake-up call' came when she gave birth and met her son for the first time. She became terrified of losing him, and from then on did not take drugs again. With the help of a supportive grandmother, a straight-talking social worker and intense health visitor input, she managed to sustain her abstinence and was still drugs free at Simon's fourth birthday. Her reasons for such drastic changes to her lifestyle are best described in her own words:

> [About her change] My son being born, my son being born, definitely. And I think the scare what social services gave me was a kick up the arse and the scare that I needed… They were going to put [Simon] into foster care… And I thought to myself, I just cannot, you know, you know what, I felt like a movie, I felt like, oh my god, my baby, not my baby. And he was so tiny, I felt like, oh no my baby, I felt like, and I thought you're having a laugh, I couldn't believe, you know… A big shock, a big shock, it was a big wake-up call and it was just a terrible feeling, I couldn't believe it. (Mother of Simon: medium risk of harm at identification; low risk, living with birth parent and safeguarded at age three)

It seems clear that the pregnancy and birth of the index child were significant factors in helping some parents overcome destructive behaviour patterns as they realized that they would need to respond to the baby's needs. Those parents who had not responded in this way by the time the baby was six months old were not safeguarding them at their third birthday. This is an important finding that needs to be tested out with a larger sample, for if it proves to be valid it has major implications for the development of policy and practice.

Experience of maltreatment

Although about two thirds of the children were adequately safeguarded by their third birthdays, many had experienced maltreatment. The types of maltreatment varied, and included forms of physical abuse, sexual abuse, emotional abuse and neglect. Neglect was by far the most common type of maltreatment and included inadequate basic care and supervision because of parents' intake of drugs or alcohol; poor hygiene and lack of food, warmth and clothing; being left alone or with inappropriate adults and runaway youths; and missed health appointments and health needs remaining unmet. It was often accompanied by emotional abuse including threats of abandonment and witnessing intimate partner violence, or physical abuse, including assaults on the mother while she was pregnant with the baby. Table 6.2 shows the types of maltreatment experienced, cross-tabulated with data concerning the extent to which the children were eventually safeguarded.

Although 19 (44%) children did not appear to have experienced abuse or neglect, the rest of the sample had. Some infants ceased to be maltreated when they were permanently separated from their parents, although as we have seen, concerns still persisted for a small number of this group; maltreatment ended for others when their parents changed their behaviour; a third group continued to experience abuse or neglect up to and past their third birthdays. As we have already seen in this and previous chapters, infants who were safeguarded through parental change stopped being abused by the time they were six months old; those who were safeguarded through separation were on average six months old when they were removed from abusive parents (although four were more than twice that age); and 11 of the 12 children who were not safeguarded continued to experience maltreatment throughout the study period. It is therefore perhaps unsurprising that, by the time they were three, many of these children were showing signs of emotional and behavioural difficulties as well as delayed development.

Table 6.2 Experiences of abuse and neglect by position at age three (full follow-up group: n=43)

	Safeguarded, sufficient parental change, living at home	Safeguarded, permanent separation	Not safeguarded, insufficient parental change, living at home	Total*
Sexual abuse	0	0	1	**1 (2%)**
Physical abuse	1	1	0	**2 (5%)**
Neglect and emotional abuse	5	4	10	**19 (44%)**
Neglect, emotional abuse and physical abuse	0	2	0	**2 (5%)**
No abuse	10	8	1	**19 (44%)**
Total	**16 (37%)**	**15 (35%)**	**12 (28%)**	**43 (100%)**

* Percentages are rounded figures.

Emotional and behavioural difficulties and delayed development: the children at age three and over

> Child maltreatment…is associated with behaviour and emotional negative outcomes. This is hardly surprising, but the links between maltreatment and particular outcomes…are so strong and specific as to be considered causal, and, furthermore, are known to extend to physical health…and to persist into adult life. (Jones 2009, p.291)

It is well known that abuse and neglect in the early years of life can stunt children's physical, cognitive and emotional development and can be associated with significant problems in the longer term (Barlow *et al.* 2005; Daniel 2006; Daniel *et al.* 2011; Farmer and Lutman forthcoming; Jones 2009). Over half of the children for whom sufficient data were available and who did not have special health care needs or disabilities[3] (16/28: 57%) were showing signs of emotional and behavioural difficulties and/or delayed development at age three. Eleven of these children were receiving professional interventions for their behaviour and/or development; five other children were not receiving interventions but their behaviour patterns and/or development were a cause of strain and anxiety to their families.

Many (10/16: 63%) of these children displayed behaviours indicative of anger and frustration. This manifested itself in actions such as deliberately hurting other children or animals, 'lashing out', biting, kicking and 'trashing' the nursery. Six children (6/16: 38%) were showing signs of speech and language delay, and this coincided with aggression and frustration for four of them. In addition, one child was described as having 'attachment' difficulties by professionals, and for another there were concerns about obesity and a potential eating disorder. The aggressive behaviour shown by many of the children is of particular concern because by their age it could no longer be considered as the typical behaviour of a toddler and should have begun to decline. If it persists beyond the age of four it will be highly predictive of later problems with aggression (Rutter and Rutter 1993, cited by Daniel 2006; see also Selwyn *et al.* 2006). Liam was one example:

Liam was physically abused and neglected by his birth parents, but was not separated until he was almost two, when he was placed with kin carers. Early into the placement the carers had noticed evidence of his previous maltreatment; he became very upset if he were to spill anything; he had never learnt to chew solids and he was found searching in the waste bin for food. As Liam became older the carers' concerns grew: by the age of four he had deliberately hurt the family pet, was aggressive to other children at nursery and had tried to harm the carer's baby grandchild. The carers could not get the professional support they thought they needed and struggled to cope with Liam's behaviour. They had been told by the social worker that, because Liam was young at the time of placement (two years), there would be no problems, and they felt that they had been naïve in agreeing to look after him.

(Liam: severe risk of harm at identification; safeguarded through separation at age three)

---

3   Children with special health needs or disabilities have not been included in the following analysis as different milestones indicate that it would not be appropriate to compare their development with that of the normative population (see Aldgate 2006).

As a consequence of their behaviours some of these children were segregated from their peers, either by being given one-to-one care at nursery, or by their parents/carers not taking them to places where they might meet other children, such as the park. They therefore missed out on the social, fun and play opportunities that mixing with their peers would give, to the detriment of their social development. Ranjit was one such child:

> Ranjit was two when his mother left the foster placement they had shared, and his care plan then changed from rehabilitation to adoption. He remained in the same foster placement but, by the time he was three, his behaviour had become extremely difficult to manage. Ranjit was given one-to-one care from nursery because of the danger he posed to other children; he had also on occasion 'trashed' the playgroup. His foster carer found him difficult to cope with, and needed extra support to look after him. The nursery refused to accept him immediately after contact with his mother, due to the increase in the aggression and anger this triggered.
>
> *(Ranjit: medium risk of harm at identification; safeguarded through separation at age three)*

The children's emotional and behavioural problems were already a source of considerable strain to birth parents and carers. Liam's carer, for instance, described how these difficulties were 'testing out the family as a whole'. Both birth parents and kinship carers tended to give negative attributes to these children; words such as 'monster', 'challenging' or 'difficult' were common. Connotations that the children were to blame for their own behaviour, or that they had inherited a condition that could be to blame, were more likely than an acceptance that their environment, experiences or parenting could be detrimental to their wellbeing.

The children's experiences of maltreatment offer insight into their emotional and behavioural difficulties and delayed development. Out of the 16 with difficulties, 13 had experienced some form of maltreatment, including nine children who had experienced neglect, one child who had been physically abused, one child who had been sexually abused and two children who had experienced complex patterns of abuse and neglect.

Of the 16 children who were displaying signs of emotional and behavioural difficulties and/or delayed development, four had parents (or sets of parents) who had made sufficient changes and were deemed to be safeguarded living at home. Twelve had parents who had not made sufficient changes: these children were either deemed not safeguarded while living at home (seven) or were permanently separated (five). The proportion of children with difficulties in each of these groups differed and suggests that children with difficulties were more likely to be in the insufficient parental change group and either living at home, or separated, than in the sufficient parental change group. Four out of 11 (36%) children in the sufficient parental change group had difficulties compared with seven out of nine (78%) in the insufficient change group and living with parents and five out of eight (63%) in the insufficient change group and separated.[4]

Development of children with parents in the insufficient change group
CHILDREN LIVING WITH PARENTS WHO MADE INSUFFICIENT CHANGES

Those children who remained living with parents who had made little or no progress in addressing risk factors showed greater evidence of poor social, behavioural and developmental outcomes. Of the nine children in this group, two were aggressive towards other children, one had an eating disorder, three had speech and language delay (including one who also had observed attachment difficulties) and one child had behaviour issues that were not described in more detail by the professionals.

Some of these children will be remembered as they have been mentioned several times in previous chapters. They include Jordan, who was witness to intimate partner violence and had close contact with a Schedule One offender who admitted to masturbating with him on his lap; Wayne, whose mother continued to use heroin throughout his life; Nathan, who was witness to intimate partner violence and whose mother neglected him by leaving him alone; Madeleine, whose parents' use of heroin fluctuated throughout her first three years; Jack, whose mother prostituted herself to pay for drugs and left him alone with runaway 'youths'; Bella, whose mother forgot to feed her as a baby and took her to nursery inadequately dressed and 'grubby'; and lastly Cassie, who at age three had unexplained injuries and whose parents were denying any professional access to her.

There were, however, two children who remained living with birth parents in the insufficient change group and who appeared to be making satisfactory progress at the age of three. Both were receiving extensive respite care. Morgan was spending every weekend with foster carers to help his mother who was struggling to cope with caring for him and his older, severely disabled sister and had sometimes threatened to kill them. Ava lived with her mother and a series of violent boyfriends and frequently witnessed intimate partner violence. However, she received regular respite care at least once a week from her non-abusive father. Respite care is known to be an effective means of supporting

---

4   Where data were available and not including children with special health care needs and/or disabilities.

very vulnerable families (Aldgate and Bradley 1999); that provided for Morgan and Ava may have been instrumental in developing their resilience to the neglect and emotional abuse to which they were subject.

CHILDREN SEPARATED FROM PARENTS WHO MADE INSUFFICIENT CHANGES

A high proportion (5/8: 63%) of children who were permanently separated from parents in the insufficient change group also showed emotional and behavioural difficulties and/or delayed development. Five of the eight children in this group for whom we have data were showing signs of aggression, and two were also showing delayed speech and language development. Their experiences during their first three years perhaps offer explanations of why, following separation, they still appeared to be showing such problems. Of these five children, one was placed with his permanent kin carer from birth; however, the placement was unstable and there was a child protection investigation open at his third birthday. The other four children were only separated from birth parents after several months of maltreatment: at five months, 13 months, 18 months and two years old. Three of these four infants experienced the 'double jeopardy' of late separation followed by late permanent placement.

A lack of permanence or unstable placements may well have had a detrimental impact on these children's wellbeing. Ranjit, for example, who was described earlier in this chapter, had remained in a mother and baby foster home until age two, when his mother left and his plan changed to adoption. Although he remained in the same foster placement, his foster carer noted significant deterioration in his behaviour at times of contact with his mother, and described him as confused.

It will be remembered from earlier chapters that Dabir had experienced severe physical abuse during his first few months of life before, at five months old, he was placed with his grandparents. By the time he had reached his third birthday these carers were in despair over Dabir's aggressive and disruptive behaviour; by the time he was four, the situation had so far deteriorated that the placement was approaching disruption. His grandparents described Dabir as having a very high pain threshold. He would purposefully administer pain to himself, and was also deemed a danger to other children. These carers were receiving very little support to deal with Dabir's increasingly worrying behaviour; they felt that they had been let down by children's social care, and left alone to cope.

Craig had been in the same placement with his aunt from birth; however, it will be remembered that this was always unstable. His aunt was concerned about Craig's disruptive behaviour and what she perceived as developmental delay. She attributed this to an inherited condition from his mother (who had learning disabilities); however, this may not account for all (or any) of his difficulties.

> Although a child may have inherited disabilities, the environment can still make a difference; children brought up in a warm and stimulating environment will have better outcomes than those who are not. (Cleaver *et al.* 2011, p.101)

The three permanently separated children who were not displaying emotional or behavioural difficulties or delayed development at age three had all been removed at birth, and had not experienced lengthy periods of maltreatment. They had also experienced less delay than the other separated children, and had all reached their permanent placement by their first birthday (one with an adoptive family, and two with kin carers).

Development of children with parents in the sufficient change group

It was a remarkable achievement for parents to overcome destructive behaviour patterns and lifestyles and provide a safe, loving and nurturing home for their children. The children of parents who made sufficient changes to safeguard them adequately appeared to be less likely to be experiencing emotional and behavioural difficulties and/or delayed development by their third birthdays, though once again the numbers are too small for formal comparison. However, four (4/11: 36%) of these children were displaying difficulties, including aggression and speech and language delay. These children include Simon, whose mother, it will be remembered, was a drug user throughout her pregnancy; Brendan, whose mother recovered from post-natal depression; Gareth, whose mother became his sole carer after his father had given him a severe head injury by 'shaking' him when he was five months old; and Martin-Louis, who witnessed his father beat his mother until she took steps to end the relationship. Three of these four children experienced some form of maltreatment before their parents made the necessary changes. It is also important to note that whilst four (36%) children of parents in this sufficient change group were displaying signs of difficulties, seven (64%) were not.

It is also noteworthy that all four parents of the children mentioned above had sought advice and help for their children's developmental problems. In all cases they did this through approaching their health visitor; none of them approached children's social care for help. Perhaps further routine monitoring and support by health visitors for these parents, as well as for others who are able to make such changes to their lifestyles, would ensure that they continue to meet their children's needs.

Conclusion

Professionals who are responsible for safeguarding the wellbeing of children suffering, or likely to suffer, significant harm are faced with the problem of distinguishing between those families which may be able to make sufficient changes to provide a nurturing home within a child's timescale, and those which may not. This chapter identifies a number of indicators which may well prove valuable in making such decisions. It appears that those parents who can make sufficient changes have, for instance, overcome substance misuse by the time the child is born; overcome other adversities at least within the first six months of the child's life; are likely to have experienced some defining moment when they accepted that they needed to make changes to their lifestyles; have some insight into the harm caused by their destructive behaviour patterns – including the reasons why other children were removed; and are able not only to engage with services but also to make positive use of the support they provide. The pregnancy and birth of the baby should be a catalyst for making such changes – if they have not been made by the time the child is six months old, then they are unlikely to be made within a reasonable timescale. The changes required may well be substantial, and parents are more likely to succeed if they have a partner, a relative or other strong informal support networks to help them through this difficult process. It may also prove easier for parents to overcome external risks, such as initiating the end of a relationship with a violent partner, than internal risk factors such as experience of sexual abuse in childhood, which require engendering change within themselves. These indicators all need to be tested out with a larger sample.

Evidence concerning extensive developmental delay and emotional and behavioural difficulties at age three amongst over half of the sample children for whom data were available is related to their experiences of maltreatment. It provides a vivid demonstration of the reasons why early interventions are necessary when very young children are suffering, or likely to suffer, significant harm, and the importance of improving methods of identifying at an early stage those parents who may not be able to make sufficient changes within the child's timescale.

Summary points for Chapter 6

- None of the 12 parents (or sets of parents) whose children were at severe risk of harm at identification had demonstrated protective factors or a capacity to address their problems by the end of the study; four of the seven parents with children at high risk of harm showed no change, one showed evidence of some capacity to change and two appeared to overcome their earlier difficulties; and 13 of the 21 parents whose children were at medium risk of harm showed sustained capacity to change, but the problems increased for six parents in this group.

- Fourteen (38%) parents (or sets of parents) succeeded in making and sustaining sufficient changes and were able to safeguard their children adequately, at least until they were three. Twenty three (62%) sets of parents did not succeed in making sufficient changes: the insufficient change group included 12 sets of parents whose children remained living with them and 11 whose children had been removed.

- Four of the six kinship placements were providing poor quality care and/or nearing breakdown by the end of the study.

- Although some children in the insufficient change group would undoubtedly have benefited from removal, others suffered intermittent maltreatment or continuing, low-level neglect that was never sufficiently serious to warrant intrusive interventions but that nevertheless was likely to compromise their life chances to a greater or lesser degree. How to provide adequate support for such children remains a continuing problem for services.

- Parents in the insufficient change group who had already been separated from an older child appeared to be less likely to be separated from the index child than those who had never had a child removed. It may be that in extreme cases professionals may perceive any small improvements as greater progress than might be considered to be the case with other families.

- Broadly speaking, there were two ways in which parents succeeded in addressing their problems sufficiently to safeguard the index child: one was through overcoming their own internal problems, such as substance misuse or mental ill-health; the other through extricating themselves from a relationship with an abusive partner.

- Parents who successfully changed were:
  - less likely to have experienced abuse in their own childhood and substantially less likely to have experienced childhood sexual abuse
  - more likely to have been subject to intimate partner violence
  - more likely to have been associating with an adult who posed a danger to children.

These parents were also able to:
  - initiate the end of a violent relationship
  - initiate the end of a relationship with an adult who posed a danger to children

- ° come to terms with the removal of older children and acknowledge the part that their actions had played in this decision.

- Protective factors that were most indicative of parents' capacity to change were:

  - ° the presence of strong informal support networks

  - ° sufficient insight to acknowledge the potential harm caused by their destructive behaviour patterns

  - ° the ability not simply to engage with services but also to make positive use of the support they offered.

- Engagement with services, in the sense of attending appointments and giving access to social workers, was a misleading indicator in that it gave no real evidence of a parent's desire or ability to change.

- Of those parents who successfully overcame substance misuse, two did so before pregnancy, three during pregnancy and one at the point of giving birth. No parent overcame substance misuse if they continued to use drugs after the child had been born.

- Thirteen of the 14 parents who made and sustained sufficient changes had addressed all known risk factors by the time the child was six months old.

- A number of parents, including four of those who overcame substance misuse, spoke of a 'wake-up call' that acted as a catalyst for change. No parents in the insufficient change group spoke of such an epiphany.

- Over half (16/28: 57%) of the children for whom sufficient data were available were showing signs of emotional and/or behavioural difficulties by the time they were three. In some cases these were extreme and included deliberately hurting other children and animals, 'lashing out', biting, kicking and 'trashing' the nursery. Delayed speech and language were also evident.

- Children were more likely to be displaying signs of emotional and behavioural difficulties and/or delayed development by age three if they had been maltreated, if parents made insufficient changes to safeguard them adequately and they remained at home or had been late separated, or if they were living in a placement that was not expected to last.

- Parents in the sufficient change group sought professional advice for their children's emotional or behavioural difficulties. None of them approached social workers, though they did consult with health visitors.

7

Professional Perspectives

Introduction

We know that by the end of the study the majority of the children were adequately safeguarded, either through separation or through living with birth parents who had successfully overcome their difficulties. We also know that about a third of the birth parents (or sets of parents) overcame significant adversities and were able to provide a nurturing home for the index child, at least until they were three. However, by their third birthdays over half of the children had experienced maltreatment (24/43: 56%), and 12 were still living in families where there was a continuing or sporadic likelihood of significant harm. Seven of those children who were separated had experienced several months of maltreatment and neglect before being placed away from home, and nine had been doubly jeopardized, first by being left too long in abusive situations and then by experiencing the disruption of a relationship with temporary foster carers. It is not surprising to find that over half (16/28: 57%) of those children for whom information was available were displaying emotional, social or behavioural problems and/or delayed development by the end of the study. Thus although this study has some very positive findings concerning the extent to which parents are able to overcome destructive behaviour patterns to meet their children's needs, it also raises numerous concerns about the extent to which those children whose parents are unable to change are adequately safeguarded.

While previous chapters have focused on the decisions made by professionals and their consequences, this chapter seeks to understand the various factors which influenced them. It explores questions such as why parents were continually given further chances to demonstrate their capacity to look after a child, why those who did succeed in overcoming adverse behaviour patterns sometimes saw a premature withdrawal of services, why some children were left too long in abusive situations, and why neglect in particular was so difficult to identify. These questions relate to themes which have recurred throughout this book; this chapter seeks to explore the reasoning behind the actions taken, and the manner in which different assumptions shaped the decision-making process.

Finally, this chapter focuses on those factors that made it difficult for professionals to take decisions that were always in the best interests of the child. It necessarily takes a critical approach, with the objective of identifying those issues that need to be addressed if children are to be better safeguarded. However, the reader should also bear in mind that this is only part of the picture: the study also identified areas of good practice and, in particular, dedicated professionals who were able to ensure that children were adequately safeguarded from significant harm.

As Chapter 5 has shown, the majority of decisions concerning permanence bore a relatively close relationship to objective evidence of the likelihood of children suffering significant harm. However, such decisions were often delayed, and in the process of reaching them some children were exposed to continuing abuse and neglect. The factors that influenced decisions, discussed in the following paragraphs, frequently accounted for these damaging experiences.

Why were parents continually given another chance?

> The most important principle is to ensure that the children live within their families; I mean if the local authority can do as much as they can for the children to keep them within their families, I think that is the most important principle. (Social worker)

The above quotation comes from one of the social workers interviewed. It epitomizes a view held by some (not all) professionals from a range of agencies: that their primary role was to preserve the family, sometimes, albeit unintentionally, to the detriment of the child's welfare. This was a major reason behind the evidence that shows how parents were continually given another chance to prove that they could look after a child. The case material amply demonstrates how professional decision-makers made extensive efforts to keep families together. Sometimes such decisions appeared to be contra-indicated by the evidence of parenting problems. Janis, for instance, remained at severe risk of harm throughout the study, in a home where crack cocaine was smoked in front of the children, his mother prostituted herself for drugs and was in an 'inappropriate relationship' with his maternal grandfather who dealt in heroin, and appointments to correct his visual impairment and programmes of support with his special educational needs were not taken up. However, the determination to keep families together was not only evident in decisions made by social workers, but also in those made by judges, magistrates, psychologists and children's guardians.

There were numerous factors which contributed to this position. First, the Children Act 1989 is based on the principle, also enshrined in the United Nations Convention on the Rights of the Child, that 'children are generally best looked after within the family, with both parents playing a full part' (Department of Health 1989, p.1). This principle is reflected in the duties laid on local authorities to provide a range and level of services to safeguard and promote the welfare of children in need in their area and, 'so far as is consistent with that aim, to promote their upbringing by their families' (s.17.1); to ensure contact between looked after children and their parents whenever possible (s.34.1); and to enable these children to live with a person connected to them unless that would not be practicable or consistent with their welfare (s.23.6). These precepts are obviously in the best interests of the vast majority of children in need, but they have sometimes led to the expectation that all children are best looked after within the family, making it difficult to identify and safeguard the few who are not. As Jones (2009) points out:

> We have to acknowledge that some situations cannot be changed for the better, and that some families are simply untreatable... These situations are major challenges for children's social care and other services, but must be faced and responded to by front-line workers and their supervisors. These cases do not represent failure, but in fact successful professional practice, to the extent that a sustained focus on child welfare has been achieved. (p.302)

Parents' rights

The expectation that all children are best looked after within the family is underpinned by concerns about parents' rights, which tended to shape decisions made by the courts, local authority solicitors and some professionals in adult services. The Human Rights Act 1998 specifies a right to respect for private and family life (Article 8) and to a fair trial (Article 6) and lays on public authorities a legal duty not to act in a way that is incompatible with a convention right (Section 6); these articles support arguments against separating birth parents from their children. However, children, too, have rights: not to be subjected to inhuman and degrading treatment (Article 3) and to a family life, including, if necessary, one outside the birth family. However, the courts often appeared to be more focused on ensuring that parents' rights were respected than that children's welfare was promoted. This was particularly true of decisions concerning adoption, which judges and magistrates tended to view as a draconian measure that was deeply destructive of family life, rather than as a means of ensuring that children might be permanently safeguarded from harm:

> One has to remember that if you're removing a child, it's a life sentence very often, if it's going to be adoption. (Judge)

> …a draconian order of very last resort, which means young children will be taken out of their families never to return and be adopted elsewhere. (Judge)

European Court of Human Rights judgements have adopted a similar point of view. Where children have been separated at birth, these have found in favour of parents, on the grounds that:

> The taking of a new-born baby into public care at the moment of its birth was an extremely harsh measure. There needed to have been extraordinarily compelling reasons before a baby could be physically removed from the care of its mother, against her will, immediately after birth. (*K & T* v. *Finland* 2001)

It is therefore not surprising that, although 63 per cent (32/51) of the children in the full sample were identified during pregnancy, only five of those who were permanently removed from their parents' care were separated at birth, and two of these were the children of learning disabled mothers who would be sharing their care within the extended family.

The Children Act 1989 firmly lays down the fundamental principle, that 'the child's welfare is the paramount consideration when a court determines any question with respect to his upbringing' (Department of Health 1989, p.16). In many cases in this sample it was evident that the child's welfare would not be properly served by remaining with birth parents. Nevertheless, it was common for parents to contest social care decisions; their rights, and the extent to which they might have been forfeited, could not be ignored in the decisions that were made.

Empowerment and its limits

For social workers, both the expectation that children will be looked after within their birth family and their understanding of parental rights are further underpinned by a value system which promotes the importance of a non-judgemental, strengths-based approach, informed by theories of empowerment and anti-oppressive practice as the basis for interactions with service users (see for instance Adams, Dominelli and Payne 2009, *passim*). Such an approach may be appropriate for much of the social worker's task, but it can prove problematic when children are suffering, or likely to suffer, significant harm; in such cases judgements are sometimes unavoidable, and some of them cannot but be disempowering. Because child protection decisions can conflict with their underlying value base it may be particularly difficult for practitioners to acknowledge the lack of progress made by some parents, or the extent to which their destructive behaviours are compromising their children's life chances. These issues have also been raised by, among others, the case of Peter Connelly (Haringey Local Safeguarding Children Board 2010), by Brandon and colleagues' (2009) analysis of serious case reviews and by Farmer and Lutman's (forthcoming) study of looked after children reunited with families who had previously neglected them.

A focus on empowerment can also lead to an over-identification with birth parents, as was evident in the absence of information concerning infants' needs in the case papers, and in the numerous, ultimately fruitless, opportunities given to some parents to demonstrate that they had made sufficient progress in overcoming their problems to provide a nurturing home for a child. It was particularly apparent in the repeated chances given to parents who had, themselves, been looked after children. The mothers of Ranjit, Matthew and Liam were all recent care leavers: their children were all eventually removed, but not until they had experienced 28 months, 18 months and 13 months, respectively, living with parents who were ultimately unable to meet their needs.

Fairness

Underlying many of the decisions regarding children made in this study was also a determination to ensure that parents were treated fairly. This was particularly evident in arguments that advocated a clean slate approach that would ignore local authorities' previous involvement with families or parents' previous history in order to eliminate the potential for pre-judging a case. For instance, some children's guardians appear to have taken the view that the courts needed to commission independent assessments of parenting capacity because local authority assessments, undertaken by people who knew the parents, would be intrinsically biased:

> Our reports are based on 12, 13-hour sessions, it's about direct observation of their parenting, it's about questionnaires, it's about seeing progress the parents make or not make, it's much more considered, and yet, you know, I'm sorry, that's the local authority's, so it can't be independent, you know, let's have an independent assessment. It's expensive, it's unnecessary; it's had some perverse outcomes sometimes in terms of the result... (Senior manager, children's social care)

Similarly, some social workers argued that parents should have an opportunity to demonstrate whether they had the capacity to look after *each* of their children, whatever their past history. In one authority, in order to ensure that such decisions were unbiased, there was a policy to allocate a new pregnancy to a different team if care proceedings had been completed for an older child, however recently that may have been:

> We always get a different team to manage it, to look at another pregnancy; in other words…we could be seen as…it's a foregone conclusion, mother can't have this kid, look we've got the one in care, let's get on and whip the other one away as soonest. Whereas to avoid that in a situation like this it always goes to a different team, with a different manager, to try and create a degree of independence, of separation from this decision-making process. So I don't actually know anything about the new situation, and that's deliberate. (Social worker)

The older child in this case was going through care proceedings when the younger child was born. The decision not to take account of the previous history meant that the new baby spent 16 months moving between foster care and the birth parent while temporary decisions were made, pending sufficient evidence of the mother's progress; this infant became one of the doubly jeopardized children, for a definitive decision to separate was not made until she was almost three years old; on her third birthday she was in temporary foster care pending a permanent placement, and likely to remain there for several more months.

Even where the same social worker was responsible for all the children in the family, similar concerns about eliminating bias could lead to situations which were confusing to both practitioners and service users. For instance, Ava's three older siblings had all been removed from her mother's care because they were being physically abused and neglected. Proceedings were still ongoing at the time of Ava's birth, and the same social worker who had removed the older siblings was supporting the mother in her attempts to parent this new baby. This was confusing for Ava's mother who could not understand why her social worker had allowed Ava to remain with her, yet removed her three older children. She believed that as she was able to care for the new baby, her older children (in permanent placements) could now be returned. According to Ava's mother, her youngest son, who was in therapeutic foster care, could not understand why his sister lived at home and he could not return. By the time Ava was three the same pattern of violence and instability that had led to the removal of the older children appeared to be re-establishing itself, and she was considered to be at high risk of being harmed.

The scrupulous attention given to ensuring that birth parents were treated fairly was also evident in the sharing of information. In a number of instances, information that could be considered necessary to the successful safeguarding of the child was not shared between professionals in order to preserve parental confidentiality. Drug and alcohol teams could be reluctant to share information with children's social care because they focused on 'the adult's ability to move and grow and develop and change, but that doesn't always mean there's an appropriate focus on the child' (Social worker). Madeleine was one of the children who, at the age of three, remained with a birth parent even though she appeared increasingly likely to suffer significant harm. The social worker claimed that the substance misuse team were refusing to share information concerning parental heroin consumption that was necessary to the decisions they had to make about her care.

> Well, they don't voluntarily keep us informed of anything. I have asked for information…I've asked in an incredibly detailed way as to what information I require…[but they only] answer my written enquiry in the most general and vague kind of way; it's as if they have an idea that they're doing a service for the parents by obscuring the reality of the drug use that the parents might be indulging in… For example, I asked…clearly, tell me all of the negative tests that the couple have had in the past 12 months and I didn't get a reply to that. I got a reply that said they're making very good progress and we are very pleased with them and nothing to say actually they've had some negative tests and there is evidence they have used heroin in the past 18 months. (Social worker)

Similar scruples prevented Jordan's mother from being given full information concerning the sexual abuse offences committed by her father, despite these being the reason she was asked to sign a written agreement stating that she would not allow him to spend time alone with the baby. According to the team leader in this case, probation were reluctant to give full details of the risk of harm posed by the grandfather in case they were held accountable if Jordan was abused:

> In cases like this where probation notify us of an offender, in particular, because they are perceived as high risk cases, I think, they are perceived like that by the agencies and, and I think they'd be reluctant to, you know, put their views across or be accountable for joint decision-making, in case something happens and the child is abused. (Team leader, children's social care)

Assessments

Concerns over human rights issues, fairness and the importance of a non-judgemental, empowering approach are epitomized in the attention given to assessing parental capacity. Formal assessments were undertaken in all cases, and included initial, core and some specific assessments undertaken by social workers and other non-specialist practitioners as part of their routine case management responsibilities. The latter could be extremely lengthy; they also duplicated areas already covered by other assessment procedures such as core assessments. The Emotional Abuse and Neglect Checklist devised by the local safeguarding children board in one authority, for instance, was designed to help practitioners identify whether a family had reached the threshold for significant harm in these areas. It was an extremely comprehensive document, based on extensive research, but it must have been time consuming to complete, as it attempted to alert a professional with little expertise in this area to the full range of issues of which they might not necessarily be aware. The alternative was to commission specialist assessments.

Specialist assessments were undertaken by psychologists, psychiatrists, independent social workers, assessment foster carers, and staff in family centres and residential units. They were commissioned by children's social care and the courts, as part of the process of decision-making. The parents of the 43 children in the full follow-up group had 35 specialist assessments; these included residential and community-based assessments of parenting capacity (20) and formal psychological or psychiatric assessments (15). Although it was not always clear who had commissioned these assessments, 23 were carried out during court proceedings and were probably required by the courts. It is likely that the remaining 12 were commissioned by children's social care. Some of the latter took place shortly before proceedings began, and were likely to have been requested following advice from local authority legal departments as part of the Public Law Outline arrangements before care proceedings were instigated.

Some assessments of parenting capacity could take up to three months and were designed as interventions to support parents in learning to meet their children's needs as well as straightforward assessments of their capacity to do so. However, these did not provide long-term, intensive support, as they ended once sufficient evidence had been collected to make a recommendation, and suggestions for further work with parents were not usually taken up as they fell outside the work commissioned. In nearly half the cases (19/43: 44%) at least one specialist assessment was carried out, and in around one in five more than one was undertaken. For instance, in the course of care and adoption proceedings, Peter's parents, who had grossly neglected all five of their children, were assessed by four different experts: a child and adolescent psychiatrist, a different psychiatrist, a clinical psychologist and a consultant forensic psychologist.

The case papers reveal several instances where parenting capacity was assessed in spite of obvious contra-indications: Isla's mother, for instance, was advised that she would be unable to resume care of her children unless she could separate from their father, who was serving a prison sentence for assaulting her. Her failure to do so eventually resulted in the children being placed for adoption. Nevertheless, during the decision-making process *both* parents were given a nine-week assessment of parenting capacity. Similarly, Gareth's father, who was undergoing a police investigation following an incident in which one of his twin babies had suffered a head injury after being shaken by him, nevertheless appears to have been given a parenting assessment. In these two cases it seems likely that parenting capacity was assessed in order to prove that parents' rights had been properly acknowledged rather than to ascertain whether they might realistically provide adequate care for their children.

Twenty three of the specialist assessments appear to have been undertaken at the request of the courts, often following recommendations from children's guardians, in the process of care or adoption proceedings. One of the judges interviewed criticized the practice of having 'too many witnesses who are expert witnesses doing too many assessments in a high proportion of the cases'. However, others tended to regard the enormity of the decision to place a child for adoption as sufficient justification:

> So every avenue ought properly to be explored... So sometimes, it's very difficult to say I'm not prepared to agree as a judge to this case being adjourned for a psychological assessment when you know that the parent is going to be losing the child or may be losing the child. (Judge)

> And it's only fair...that the family and the social workers, if they've got some apparent doubts about it, have the freedom to go to as many independent experts as possible...so as to accumulate more and more evidence to get to the right conclusion. (Judge)

A number of respondents claimed that the part played by parents' solicitors increased the proliferation of expert assessments. The Law Society states that good practice for solicitors representing parents is to instruct experts and admit their evidence only:

> ...where necessary: that is, in cases where other available evidence does not deal with the relevant issue and where the welfare of the

child dictates that such further evidence should be obtained. (Law Society 2010, p.19)

Solicitors are also advised to ask themselves 'whether the instruction of an expert is justified in the light of the Children Act 1989, s.1 (2) (the no delay principle)' (Law Society 2010, p.19).

Nevertheless, parents' solicitors tended to cite 'human rights' as their argument for a specialist assessment, and this could make such requests very difficult for a judge or magistrate to decline. The role of parents' solicitors was to advocate the parents' point of view, and in the struggle to ensure that their rights were adequately considered the welfare of the child could be overlooked:

> I think it's easy to lose sight, particularly when mum and dad have got solicitors and they're in there and they're fighting tooth and nail for their client... But why are we here? We're here because this child has been abused, or this child has been neglected, and I think parents' advocates can try and focus more on what [the local authority] hasn't done than actually why we're really here, what the child really needs, and sometimes the wrong decision is taken, kids are returned and there's drastic consequences because they've got their rights...but it can have a consequence on the child and what is right for the child. (Social worker)

Cassie's circumstances were described in Chapter 6. Her parents were in the insufficient change group, and an older half brother had been placed for adoption the year before Cassie was born. At identification there had been concerns about the father's substance misuse, the failure of both parents to understand the risks of harm posed by Schedule One offenders in the mother's family, the mother's inability to meet the older child's needs, and their refusal to engage with services. Her subsequent experiences exemplify the issues raised above:

When her mother became pregnant with Cassie, the local authority decided there was no point in undertaking any further assessments, as both parents had been assessed less than a year previously, at which time they had been considered unable to provide adequate care for a child. The application for a Care Order was contested by the parents, who did not accept any of the concerns raised by children's social care; their solicitor succeeded in persuading the court to agree to a further parenting assessment. Both parents spent three months with Cassie in a residential family assessment centre, where they successfully learned, in a supervised environment, how to meet her needs. Following this, the Interim Care Order was reduced to a 12-month Supervision Order. However, a year later, both Cassie and a new baby brother were made the subjects of a child protection plan on the grounds of neglect and physical abuse; this was still in place at Cassie's third birthday, by which time the parents were refusing to co-operate with child protection reviews or to allow social workers to see the children at home.

(Cassie: medium risk of harm at identification; high risk, living with birth parent but not safeguarded at age three)

Many assessments were intended to explore whether parenting capacity had improved since an earlier occasion. However, in some cases, such as that of Cassie, they had been undertaken with an older child in the course of care or adoption proceedings within months of their being requested for the index baby and there was little chance that any significant change would have occurred. Masson and colleagues (2008) found that recent care proceedings relating to a sibling were a factor facilitating the quick determination of cases in court, but in some cases in the current study assessments continued regardless of the parents' previous history. For instance, Pippa's mother, who had had three children previously placed for adoption, had already had parenting assessments by the same psychologist in each of the two preceding years, but nevertheless had two further parenting assessments concerning her capacity to care for her new daughter; these were within four months of one another. The last one was severely criticized by the children's guardian as being unnecessary:

> I could see there'd just been no change, the dynamics were just the same, but they had, there had been a decision for some reason that there would be a mother and baby placement for her, residential, which I couldn't believe...I looked at it, I thought, why? What has changed? So I said to the court...I really don't think this is the right interim care plan...this isn't, this is not going to work and really, and I felt a bit bad saying it, but I said to the judge, you

know, this isn't going to work. And because it was all in place and as a consequence of the PLO [Public Law Outline], it didn't work, they went ahead with the assessment, and it absolutely didn't work and the police were involved. (Children's guardian)

One magistrate stipulated that she would not accept a request for an additional assessment if a previous one had been conducted within the past 12 months. Twenty children in the full sample had siblings or half siblings who had already been removed from their parents' care; nine were born either during or within months of court proceedings for their older siblings. In all these cases it seems likely that recent assessments would have been undertaken for the older child, although we did not have access to their case papers. Yet in six (67%) of these cases further psychological or parenting assessments were undertaken in respect of the new baby. Many of these very young children were classified as at severe risk of harm at identification, and again it seems likely that assessments were undertaken in order to provide evidence that due consideration had been given to parental rights rather than to explore whether the infant would, or would not, be adequately safeguarded.

RELIABILITY OF RECOMMENDATIONS

Considerable weight was given to specialist assessments in decision-making; indeed the recommendation or overall opinion of the assessor was followed in all 34 of the specialist assessments for which data were available. In view of the weight that is given to assessors' opinions, it is important to explore the extent to which their recommendations ensured that children were adequately safeguarded.

At least one specialist assessment was carried out for 19 children in the full follow-up group, and data on the recommendations of assessments were available for all but one of these. The recommendations or overall opinion of the assessor was negative for five of the 18 children for whom data were available, indicating that the parents could not adequately meet their needs; these children were permanently placed away from home. No recommendation was made for one child. However, the recommendations or opinions in two thirds of cases (12/18: 67%) were positive, indicating that parents were now able to meet their children's needs. Where multiple assessments were carried out, in all but one case the separate assessors made the same recommendations.

In the 12 cases where positive recommendations were followed, the babies remained with their birth parents or returned to them. Four of these children had been at severe or high risk of harm at identification and eight at medium risk.

In five of these cases parents made good progress, addressed risk factors and showed substantial capacity to change; protective factors such as abstaining from drug misuse and the presence of a protective partner were still apparent when the children were three. On the other hand, in the remaining seven cases, children do not appear to have been adequately safeguarded. Three of them were later permanently removed from their parents following an unsuccessful rehabilitation attempt. During this period, all were at high risk of being harmed, all were left in unsafe situations by their parents and one also sustained an injury. The other four children remained with their birth parents at age three; however, by then three of them were classified as at high risk of harm, for parental risk factors had not been addressed, and there was little evidence of their capacity to change; there were ongoing concerns that these children were continuing to experience chronic neglect. One of these children was expected by the team leader to spend the rest of his childhood receiving sporadic and increasingly ineffective interventions from children's social care.

Where the overall opinions of the assessors were positive, on average one less assessment was undertaken than where the overall opinions were negative. It therefore appeared that where there was a greater likelihood that children would be permanently separated from their parents, professionals carried out further assessments to ensure that parents' rights were upheld. However, this could also lead to postponing the inevitability of permanent separation, and ignoring children's timeframes.

It is important to ask why less than half (5/12: 42%) of the specialist assessments were successful in identifying those parents who would be able to meet their children's needs. There are questions about whether some psychologists saw themselves as supporting adults rather than making judgements concerning the future welfare of children: in some instances there were also conflicts of interest as assessors were both working therapeutically with parents and evaluating the success of their own interventions. There are also questions concerning the extent to which assessors saw themselves as offering recommendations that would determine children's immediate care rather than their long-term future. With such a very small sample we can only ask questions whose value should first be verified with a larger database. Given the importance of taking decisive action to make permanent plans to secure the long-term welfare of these very vulnerable children, this is clearly an area that would merit further research.

ASSESSMENT AND DELAY

Data from interviews revealed unanimous agreement from all professionals that too many specialist assessments were being undertaken, and that these contributed substantially to delays in decision-making. Not only could such assessments take several weeks to complete, but there were also long waiting lists for them. Specialist parenting assessments were completed for the parents of ten infants after they were six months old, eight infants after their first birthdays and two after their second birthdays. All but one of those parents who overcame their difficulties did so within the first six months of the baby's life, so that as children grew older, the chances of a positive assessment diminished. Yet these continued to be undertaken and to act as a major cause of delay. Their focus on the parent also meant that there was very little acknowledgement of the impact of delayed decisions on children's welfare. Moreover their often over-optimistic assessment of capacity detracted attention from the impact of parental problems on the child. It is significant that apart from notes on files as to whether milestones were being achieved or immunizations given, there was no evidence of specialist paediatric assessments being undertaken to ascertain whether maltreatment, and specifically neglect, was having an adverse impact on these infants' health and development.

Supporting families where parents were unable to change

Where birth parents were unable to look after children, extensive efforts were made to place them within the extended family, in line with current legislation and policy. However, as Chapter 1 has shown, research evidence concerning the benefits of kinship care is inconclusive, a point that is reflected in the experiences of the babies in this study.

Ours was a sample in which the risk of harm was particularly high, and many of the infants' relatives had considerable difficulties themselves. As with birth parents, professionals made extensive efforts to find out whether relatives had adequate parenting capacity, sometimes in the face of strong contra-indications. For instance, Matthew's mother had been looked after by the local authority for much of her own childhood; nevertheless, a lengthy period was spent assessing the maternal grandmother and her partner before the recommendation was made that their application to become long-term carers should not be progressed 'due to historical concerns around their ability to parent and their ongoing involvement with the local authority in respect of their own children'. Placements with relatives are often made on an emergency basis and then followed, rather than preceded, by an assessment. As we have seen (Chapter 5), where relatives can provide high-quality, long-term care, such placements have the added advantage of reducing the time that children spend in limbo, pending permanent arrangements; however, where, as in the case of Matthew's grandmother, the quality of care is unsatisfactory, such placements can increase the time that children are exposed to maltreatment. Matthew spent seven months in the care of his grandmother before she was assessed as being unsuitable. When, at 19 months, he was finally placed with approved foster carers, his delayed speech and behavioural problems were indicative of the neglect he had encountered.

Assessments of numerous relatives could delay the development of permanence plans, an issue raised by other studies (see Harwin *et al.* 2011). For instance, Liam was left in the care of his father who severely neglected him until, at the age of 13 months, he was finally placed in foster care. His aunt, his maternal great-grandmother, his paternal grandmother and his mother were all then negatively assessed as potential long-term carers before, five months later, he was eventually placed in the care of friends of the father's family who applied for special guardianship. Relatives sometimes came forward as the result of a family group conference, but if these were organized late in the progress of the case, as happened with Liam, the subsequent assessments could add to the delays in children reaching a permanent placement. Ranjit's experiences show how assessments both of parents and of potential kinship carers could add to the time that children spent in temporary care, contributing to the double jeopardy effect noted in Chapter 6.

Ranjit's mother was in the care of the local authority when she became pregnant with him at the age of 15. A few weeks after his birth, a mother and baby foster placement became available, and they both moved there while the carer made a formal assessment of her parenting capacity. This assessment was extended until he was a year old, and repeatedly concluded that it was not yet safe for Ranjit to live independently with his mother, though this might be a viable future option. At the request of the court the following assessments were then undertaken: a parenting assessment of the father and his partner; an assessment of the maternal grandfather as a potential family network carer; a psychological assessment of the mother; and a further assessment of the mother's ability to meet the child's long-term needs. Assessments of the extended family proved negative; indeed they resulted in the father being advised to seek mental health support and his partner to access domestic violence services. The mother's assessment concluded that it would be inadvisable for her to manage the demands of lone parenting currently, but that she could one day manage this within the child's timescale; however, much psychological, practical and behavioural work would need to be undertaken before this could happen.

Ranjit was 28 months old when it was finally decided that he could not safely remain with either his mother or her extended family. An adoptive home was sought for him, but had not been found by the end of the study; by his third birthday he had developed serious behavioural problems that threatened to jeopardize his future wellbeing.

(Ranjit: medium risk of harm at identification; safeguarded through separation at age three)

The mothers of Ranjit, Liam and Matthew had all spent much of their childhood and adolescence looked after by local authorities themselves; presumably their relatives had been comprehensively assessed on previous occasions. Other children had relatives who had had opportunities to come forward or be assessed during recent care proceedings for older siblings. It should be possible to speed up the process by, for instance, identifying indicators that would automatically disqualify inappropriate applications without the need for further assessment.

Some studies have shown that there may be lower standards of approval for kinship carers (see Ward *et al.* 2006); we also know that social workers are more likely to rate the quality of these placements less favourably than those provided by other carers (Sinclair *et al.* 2007, p.232). Some of the kinship carers who were approved to look after these very young children had attributes that might well have disqualified them as potential adopters or local authority carers. Edward, for instance, was placed permanently with a grandfather who had a number of convictions including assaults against the police, had served time in prison in the past, was currently misusing substances and was now caring for eight other children; Wayne's substance-misusing mother was asked by a neighbouring authority to apply for a Residence Order for her nephew, although her own child was deemed to be 'in need'.

There are obvious advantages in placing children in the care of close relatives who are already well known to them and who can preserve their links within an extended family. At least five of the sample children (and/or their parents) were already well known to kinship carers at the time of placement, as is usually the case (see Farmer and Moyers 2008); however, others were not. For example, Erin was placed with a distant cousin whom she had never met and who had not seen her mother since childhood. A chance meeting at a wedding had led to the placement. Liam was placed permanently with friends of his putative father; after the placement had been made a negative paternity test showed that their connection was tenuous in the extreme. Such cases raise issues concerning the purpose and the limits of kinship placements. We need to ask at what point a tenuous link with birth parents ceases to justify less rigorous approval procedures or lower standards of care. Extensive efforts to keep children within the extended family, regardless of the strength of the link or the likely quality of care, mirror the focus on keeping children with birth parents. Some of the experiences of the infants show that where the focus on family preservation ignores or pays too little attention to the evidence of maltreatment and long-term neglect or the consequences of lengthy delays in the planning process, it can be detrimental to children's welfare.

VIOLENT AND/OR SEXUALLY ABUSIVE MEN

The only cases where efforts were not made to keep families together were those where intimate partner violence or sexual abuse were a significant feature. These were treated very differently from neglect cases, the primary objective being to remove the abuser from the family. Whereas neglectful mothers were given extensive, non-judgemental support, those who found it difficult to extricate themselves from relationships with violent or sexually abusive men were often criticized as being unable to put their children's needs before their own. The most obvious example was that of May's mother, whose four children were very nearly placed for adoption because she initially refused to leave her husband; her children were all under the age of five when he was recognized as having committed serious sexual offences against two girls 20 years previously. It took her some months to absorb the new information and to acknowledge the risk of harm he posed, leading to concerns that she was unable to prioritize her children's needs over those of their father (he was disabled, and she was his carer) and that her attachment to him prevented her from viewing the situation objectively. May's mother told the researcher that she had been faced with an impossible choice. The issue was resolved when a new allegation was made against the father and she filed for divorce.

There was also sometimes little understanding of the dangers and difficulties of separating from a very violent man: Blair's mother, for instance, was criticized for giving her violent partner her mobile phone number, although not to do so until she was able to move from the address where he could find her would have placed her in greater danger of a further assault. Support for mothers in the cases of intimate partner violence appeared to be directed at providing practical and emotional help that would enable them to extricate themselves from these relationships. Although some services were available for perpetrators of child sexual abuse, there was very little evidence of services offered to violent men. One father was advised that he could not access an anger management programme unless he had been convicted of an assault. The solution advocated by professionals was almost invariably for the man to leave the home, and indeed many of them were an obvious danger both to their partners and their children. However, those who were successfully excluded from one home then often went on to form another family and the abuse continued.

Information about fathers is noticeably absent in the case papers and also in many of the interviews with professionals. The exclusion of violent men, although obviously justified in terms of safeguarding children, is perhaps another example of the way in which men are marginalized in the child protection process. There is an obvious need to develop programmes to deflect young men from becoming perpetrators of intimate partner violence, and to help those who do abuse their partners to restrain their behaviour.

Why was there sometimes a premature withdrawal of services?

The emphasis on preserving families, on empowering parents and acknowledging their rights and on placing children within the wider family wherever possible was closely linked to a focus on providing less intrusive services and promoting parental responsibility. Again this is reflected in the Children Act 1989, which 'seeks to protect children from the harm which can arise from failures or abuse within the family and from the harm which can be caused by unwarranted intervention in their family life' (Department of Health 1989, p.5).

The actions taken to safeguard the children followed this principle in that less intrusive interventions were almost always favoured above those that introduced greater levels of coercion. Thus, as we have seen, wherever possible children remained with their families rather than being placed away, and they were offered services under the Children Act 1989, section 17(a), rather than as part of a child protection plan. Possibly for similar reasons, parents who were perceived as needing additional support were referred to universal or targeted services such as mother and toddler or young parents' groups rather than to more intensive interventions, tailored specifically to the needs of themselves and their babies; there is, for instance, no evidence of any parents receiving support from programmes such as Family Nurse Partnerships or Parents Under Pressure, although admittedly these are still relatively difficult to access.

Children's social care involvement was also often of very short duration. Thirty (30/43: 70%) cases were closed during the course of the study, 11 of them within a year. Twenty five children were made the subjects of child protection plans; about half of these led to more intensive interventions such as interim and full Care Orders, but where they did not, half of the child protection plans were for 32 weeks or less and all but three were for less than a year. Similarly, unless there was a plan for adoption, children on Interim Care Orders tended to remain or return quickly to their parents, with the final disposal being a time-limited supervision order. Only two of the children remaining with birth parents at the end of the study were subject to Care Orders, although many others continued to be likely to suffer harm. Care Orders appeared to be used as relatively short-term measures, to protect children pending adoption or to ensure that those placed tentatively with parents could be swiftly removed if the situation deteriorated; they rarely appear to have been intended as a long-term means of ensuring that a child could be adequately safeguarded during the lengthy period that they might remain vulnerable. Lily's case exemplifies this issue:

Lily's mother had mental health problems; four older children had been removed on grounds of emotional abuse before Lily was born. Following her birth, Lily spent five months in foster care before being reunited with her parents for a 12-week residential assessment. This proved positive and she returned to live with them on a Care Order under placement with parents regulations. There was an explicit statement that 'these arrangements should remain in place at least until she attends a state-funded education provision/nursery'. However, when Lily was three and a half, the review discussed whether the Care Order should be reduced to a Supervision Order. The health authority opposed this on the grounds that Lily was epileptic and a continuing Care Order would make it easier to access services; however, the social worker thought that the order should be rescinded as 'unnecessary orders are detrimental to progress'. At three years old, Lily was considered to be inadequately safeguarded and at continuing risk of future harm.

(Lily: medium risk of harm at identification; medium risk, living with birth parents but not safeguarded at age three)

The evidence suggests that children who are the subjects of Care Orders receive higher levels of support than those who are not (Wade *et al.* 2011); however, this shift in the use of Care Orders to support relatively short-term interventions where children remain at home has also been noted by Farmer and Lutman (forthcoming).

Social workers were occasionally under pressure to close cases prematurely because of a shortage of resources: 'We don't prevent, we do "blitzkrieg" intervention, and we don't always have the necessary time to follow up and they relapse' (Social worker). However, there were also indications that cases were closed in order to ensure that parents took responsibility for themselves and their children, and did not become too dependent on children's social care:

> Sometimes I think we do close cases too soon, but then it's a very
> fine line, isn't it, because you don't want to encourage that culture
> of being dependent or, you know, you want to be, you want to
> enable families to move on and sort out issues for themselves.
> (Social worker)

The issue, yet again, was that these were largely cases where parents had entrenched and deep-seated problems and their children were extremely likely to suffer significant harm. As we have seen, while a few managed to overcome their difficulties sufficiently to provide adequate care for the index child, many others did not. In these instances, attempts to ensure that they shouldered their responsibilities and did not become dependent could be damaging to the baby's welfare. As one of the team leaders said:

> …it's a big gap in the way, in services, in the way they respond and expect that, you know, people will be, people who have, you know, huge historic issues will, you know, [overcome] them in… two months… (Team leader, children's social care)

There is some evidence that parents whose infants were removed after lengthy delays received the most intensive packages of services. There were also some indications to suggest that interventions in families where at age three children were living with parents who had apparently overcome their difficulties were generally shorter than those in the group who were living with parents but apparently not safeguarded. In the former group, cases were open for a mean length of 39 weeks, and child protection plans for 32 weeks, as compared with means of 78 and 68 weeks in the latter. However, concerns were expressed by both groups that support could be withdrawn or reduced before they were ready or able to cope without it.

We have already seen that some parents who succeeded in turning their lives around were surprised not to be monitored further. Cases were often closed with the proviso that the parent 'knows who to contact should they need help in the future'. However, it was unrealistic to expect those who ran into further difficulties to re-refer themselves, for they were understandably fearful that evidence of further problems would lead to the removal of their children (see also Daniel *et al.* 2011). It is significant that none of those parents whose children were displaying emotional or behavioural difficulties asked for help from social workers. Moreover, there were sometimes concerns as to whether the managers of universal services, where parents might present themselves, would feel able to refer appropriate cases on to children's social care.

Farmer and Lutman (forthcoming) vividly demonstrate how, in an attempt to promote responsibility and prevent parents becoming dependent on services, neglected children who have been looked after are sometimes returned to damaging home circumstances that are undoubtedly detrimental to their long-term wellbeing. The current study found that services that might well have benefited the children were sometimes withdrawn if parents did not meet their responsibilities: Ava, for instance, came near to losing the place at the nursery that might have compensated for her neglectful home circumstances because her mother 'could not even take responsibility for paying a third of the costs'.

Some of those parents who were unable to safeguard their children sufficiently accepted that they were dependent on services:

> Whatever happens I will always need someone there that I can talk
> to more than anything, and know she'd listen to me…take my
> points into account… If it wasn't for the fact that I had, I know I
> can go to them, I'd probably feel lost… (Mother of Jordan: high
> risk of harm at identification; high risk, living with birth parent
> but not safeguarded at age three)

Jordan's mother had mental health and housing problems and was subject to
intimate partner violence; she was considered to have difficulty in putting her
child's needs first. She had strong support from community psychiatric services,
and the case was sporadically open to children's social care. Jordan himself had
been referred for professional help with aggressive behaviour by the age of
three. In cases such as these, expecting parents to meet their responsibilities is
likely to increase the likelihood that their children will suffer significant harm.
There needs to be more clarity as to the type and level of services required –
and perhaps some acknowledgement that long-term dependency on services
may be a necessary concomitant of ensuring that children are safe.

Written agreements

Issues concerning the extent to which very vulnerable parents should be
expected to fulfil their responsibilities without support in situations where
children are suffering, or likely to suffer, significant harm were crystallized
in the use made of written agreements. These were used to formalize
arrangements made between parents or carers and the local authority and its
partner agencies to ensure that children would be adequately safeguarded and
that efforts would be made to overcome the factors that had placed them at
risk of suffering harm. Although they have no legal force, they are presented
as a formal contract between the parties involved.

Written agreements were used for 18 babies, and covered a variety of
issues. The central purpose of seven agreements was to prevent contact with
someone thought to pose a danger to the child, often a Schedule One offender
or a perpetrator of intimate partner violence who was a parent's partner or
family member. In other cases the purpose was to set out requisite standards
of care (e.g. 'no rough handling'; 'child to get three healthy meals a day') or
to formalize an agreement that a member of the wider family would supervise
care of the child.

Written agreements might be seen as a concrete expression of the
relationship between the authority and the parent, whereby parents are, at least
theoretically, working in partnership with practitioners, and the responsibilities
of both sides are articulated. Thus a number of them also specified what the

parents should expect of practitioners (e.g. openness, reliability, honesty) as well as what the authority might expect from parents.

However, it is clear that written agreements were often ineffective; their terms were frequently broken and children whose parents had entered into them continued to suffer harm. Out of a total of 19[1] written agreements, eight (42%) were breached. Although breaches could, and did, lead to a change of plan, with three children moving towards adoption as a result, in the majority of cases there were no adverse consequences – a point also noted by Farmer and Lutman (forthcoming). Nathan's mother, for instance, breached two written agreements with impunity:

> The key risk factors in this case were neglect, intimate partner violence and the mother's inability to break away from Nathan's violent and alcoholic father. The terms of both written agreements precluded contact with the father and stated that the mother had to cease the relationship. Both were broken with no direct consequences; monitoring was increased but Nathan remained in the care of his mother. By the time Nathan was three, professionals were concerned about his delayed speech and his 'attachment' difficulties.
>
> *(Nathan: high risk of harm at identification; high risk, living with birth parent but not safeguarded at age three)*

The fact that so often there were no consequences for breaching such agreements indicates, at the very least, conflicting views over the extent to which parents with multiple problems should be held responsible for ensuring that children are safeguarded. Although written agreements have the potential to clarify the position and expectations of all parties, at present the lack of enforcement makes them weak instruments that serve to confuse rather than to elucidate.

It is clear that some parents refused to accept that there were any difficulties and may well have ignored indicators that they were likely to lose the care of their baby; nevertheless some felt that social workers had not been sufficiently straight with them about what changes they would need to make to provide a satisfactory standard of care (see Chapter 8). Written agreements have the potential to introduce genuine transparency into the picture; they can also be very empowering for parents, for setting clear criteria for change and ensuring that plans and timescales are in place for its achievement, and can help parents

---

1   One child had two written agreements.

feel included as genuine participants in the decision-making process (see Jones *et al.* 2006). Written agreements could be developed further, but the issue that still needs to be confronted is the extent to which they should be enforced. At present the way in which they are used appears to reflect an underlying ambivalence concerning the extent to which very vulnerable parents can or should be responsible for safeguarding the welfare of their children; the extent to which it is acceptable for them to be dependent on support from the local authority and its partner agencies; and whether their behaviour can or should be monitored, possibly for lengthy periods.

Why was neglect so hard to identify?

The findings add to the wealth of evidence showing that, despite a growing body of knowledge of its adverse impact on early development, children are often left with inadequate support in grossly neglectful homes (see for instance Daniel *et al.* 2011; Farmer and Lutman forthcoming; Wade *et al.* 2011). Twenty of the babies were neglected: three infants, Maria, Paul and Bella, remained with birth parents who forgot to feed them, Bella for so long that she ceased to cry; Ava's siblings had been allowed to lick drugs from a spoon; at the age of three, Wayne was able to demonstrate how to prepare heroin for consumption; and when, at the age of 13 months, Liam was finally placed away from his parents, his care had deteriorated to the extent that he 'had no clean clothes or socks in cold weather, his bedding had been covered with dry vomit for three days, he was being left on the floor with stale food, he had gastroenteritis and he had very bad nappy rash with open sores on his bottom and penis'.

As other studies have also shown, neglect was rarely acted upon unless a crisis occurred, such as a child found alone in the home (see Daniel *et al.* 2011; Farmer and Lutman forthcoming). It seems probable that a constellation of factors contributed to this reluctance to respond to evidence of chronic, long-term exposure to maltreatment. The issues already discussed in this chapter played a major role: for instance, ambivalence over the extent to which parents should be required to shoulder their responsibilities meant that cases were sometimes closed despite ongoing concerns. Similarly, the tendency to regard the preservation of the family and thereby the support of birth parents and the acknowledgement of their rights as primary objectives made it difficult to recognize the level of neglect and its impact on children's wellbeing. However, other factors also came in to play.

First, practitioners occasionally over-identified with birth families to the extent that they became enmeshed in the dynamics of an abusive family. This was identified as an issue for Peter's social worker, who was strongly criticized by the children's guardian on the grounds that she lacked professional objectivity and that 'it is incomprehensible why and how children an people's services continued to be almost passive in the decision-making pro of what action should be taken'.

There is also ample evidence (see Daniel *et al.* 2011) to show that constant exposure can inure social work practitioners to evidence of neglect – a strong argument for close collaboration with health visitors, nursery nurses and teachers, who see a much wider spectrum of the population.

The evidence also suggests that some front-line social work practitioners may have had insufficient knowledge and understanding of normative child development, or of maltreatment and its consequences. All those interviewed for whom data were available were professionally qualified and all but one had more than one year's post-qualifying experience. They had all studied child development as part of their training, but often very superficially, and some could remember little about it. Although they had had extensive post-qualifying training on intimate partner violence, and some had followed courses on substance misuse and parental mental health problems, there was little evidence of any specific training on neglect (or indeed other types of maltreatment) and its impact on early development. This is an important finding given the recent evidence of the impact of neglect on neurophysiological development in early childhood (see Chapter 1). While there are some indications that practitioners were concerned about delayed speech development, there is little evidence that they picked up on the anger and frustration that were becoming of increasing concern to these very young children's parents and carers.

Similarly, the data suggest that, although most social work practitioners had undertaken some training on attachment at pre or post-qualifying level, there were a number of gaps in understanding. In particular, timeframes for developing attachment were variably understood, as was the potential impact of the loss of an attachment figure. May, for instance, was very nearly placed for adoption at the age of 28 months on the grounds that she was securely attached to her (non-abusive) birth mother and that therefore she would be able to attach easily to another carer.

Checks and balances

It must be evident from the above that numerous factors impact on decisions when children are likely to suffer significant harm, and make it particularly difficult to keep their best interests firmly in focus. In particular, difficult decisions to remove children from parental care are 'discordant with a professional sense of duty and therapeutic optimism' (Jones *et al.* 2006, p.286); they go against the grain of concepts of parental rights and responsibilities and value systems held not only by social workers but also by many other in this area. For this reason, it is important to make ufficient checks and balances within the system to ensure e made.

ıan (forthcoming) argue that a second opinion should be ıfficult cases, where maltreatment can easily be overlooked. ıe need for a fresh pair of eyes was particularly evident in cases w... bies had suffered long-term neglect, and practitioners may have become inured to the signs of chronic, corrosive maltreatment.

There was ample evidence of social workers and team leaders jointly discussing case material; in many instances supervision sessions appeared to be more frequent and more usefully employed than, for instance, the Social Work Task Force recently found (Department for Children, Schools and Families 2009a). Decisions about whether to initiate care proceedings were jointly made between social workers and their managers, with the final decision resting with the manager and the local authority solicitor. However, there is little evidence of joint visits to birth families' homes or joint interviews with birth parents in particularly difficult cases.

The study also raises some questions concerning the extent to which team leaders felt able to use their authority to constructively challenge the perceptions of front-line staff. For instance, one felt that, rather than intervening directly, he had to wait until a social worker had moved on before he could reallocate the case to someone who might take proactive action:

> [Social worker] is leaving us soon because she's changing her job and I'm hoping that with, because with these cases where it's the neglect issues, but not chronic neglect, but they're borderline neglect, which keep coming back. It can be quite difficult for workers to maintain direction because I think it does become very muddy and I think what I will do is I will have a change of worker to give a fresh eye to it and I'm hoping that once [social worker] moves then a fresh eye on the case, we can get a new plan together and to try and focus in on the key issues, and to be much more tighter. (Team leader, social care)

Moreover, when managers did use their authority, front-line staff did not necessarily feel bound to accept it. For instance, the social worker disagreed so strongly with her manager's decision to close Ava's case that the next day she re-referred her to the intake team to take a fresh look at the situation. This child suffered from neglect and emotional abuse and was witness to intimate partner violence. She was one of the 12 who were not safeguarded at age three, having by then moved from medium to high risk of harm.

Furthermore, procedures that have been put in place nationally to try to ensure that formal, evidence-based plans are made, with clear objectives and timescales, could occasionally be disregarded by practitioners who did not see their purpose (see also Ward *et al.* 2006).

> Not that we paid any attention to it [care plan]… Well, you just do that because it's expected, it's not a living document that informs anything that we do, or only in the vaguest way. It's very rare for anyone in my experience say, in supervision or in a review to say, well, what is the care plan, what does the care plan say about this? … I think the core assessment is something again, a bit like the care plan, it's done as an activity and it's put by the side and the business carries on. (Social worker)

These points all raise well-known questions concerning the extent to which professional autonomy should give social workers freedom to act independently, and the extent to which they should be bound by the views of managers and policy-makers.

Team managers provided much-needed support, but they were not always, perhaps, sufficiently critical of the perceptions and practices of front-line staff. Further into the process, children's guardians frequently provided a much-needed check, and often challenged decisions made by the local authority that were arguably not in the best interests of the child, successfully fulfilling their role as children's advocates. The most dramatic example was in May's case, where the guardian intervened, preventing four children from being unnecessarily placed for adoption.

May and her siblings came to the attention of children's social care when a neighbour recognized their father as someone who had been convicted of a serious sexual offence against a 13-year-old, 20 years previously. The mother had not been fully aware of the seriousness of the offence, and did not consider her husband to be a danger to his current family. She questioned the ultimatum, laid down by children's social care, that if she did not leave her husband in order to protect her children they would be removed from her care. The social worker was convinced that the children should be placed for adoption and apparently concealed parts of the psychologist's report from the court in order to further this argument.[2] The case was approved by the adoption panel, but then the guardian, along with the parents' barrister, successfully argued that the Placement Order requested by the local authority would be inappropriate because the children were closely bonded with their mother and there were no concerns about her care. The guardian also pointed out that the children were also closely bonded to each other and the local authority was unable to guarantee that the four siblings would remain together in an adoptive placement.

(May: medium risk of harm at identification; low risk, living with birth parent and safeguarded at age three)

There were other, less notable, cases in which guardians fulfilled this role. For instance, in Peter's case the guardian identified the extent to which the social worker had become enmeshed within the family; and in Pippa's case she made it clear that there was no point in delaying decisions by undertaking an additional parenting assessment for a mother who had shown no capacity to change. The ability of children's guardians to act as critical challengers was acknowledged by some judges; for instance:

Social workers can get very close to the families they are dealing with and it can be very difficult to make that sort of decision. I think it's also the case that guardians come with a new eye as well. And sometimes their investigations throw up things that perhaps the social workers haven't seen or thought about as carefully as they might do. And the guardians have been of uniformly high quality, very experienced... (Judge)

---

2   This was the only case where there was apparently a deliberate intention to misinform; in all other cases the participants were striving to act in the interests of the child, although opinions could differ as to where these lay.

Children's guardians were often well qualified, and those we interviewed were generally more experienced than front-line practitioners or team leaders. Their opinions carried considerable weight, and they were particularly valuable in bringing the focus back to the interests of the child.

Formal checks and balances were provided by the joint, inter-agency discussions held at child protection conferences, and legal representation of opposing parties in court proceedings. However, it was the front-line practitioners and the children's guardians who spent time with the families and were most likely to have a detailed view of how parental behaviour was impacting on the welfare of the children.

Conclusion

This chapter has examined the factors that influenced professional decision-making in the children's cases. In particular it has explored how considerations of parental rights, empowerment, fairness and responsibility sometimes made it difficult to focus on the interests of the child, rather than on those of the parent or the family as a whole. Such issues were particularly apparent in the use of assessments and written agreements and in the difficulty of identifying neglect. They are not only of academic interest; as previous chapters have shown, they had a major impact on the outcomes of decisions and on the subsequent welfare of these very young children.

Moreover, some of the questions raised by the management of sample cases, and the professional perspectives that they reveal, are of particular significance in that they closely reflect issues identified by a number of serious case reviews, including the one conducted into the death of Peter Connelly, the child whose maltreatment became a *cause célèbre* in 2008 (see Brandon *et al.* 2008, 2009; Haringey Local Safeguarding Children Board 2010). It will be remembered that almost all the babies in this study were born in the same year as Peter Connelly. Although none of them experienced the same extent of maltreatment as he did, and none experienced the same comprehensive failure of safeguarding systems, nevertheless there are some striking resemblances between the questions raised by his case and those identified by the cases of some of these infants. Issues such as an over-identification with service users and a focus on preserving the family at all costs are raised both by this study and by the Connelly review; confusion over parental responsibility, and the failure to set clear goals and/or to take action if these are not met, are also evident in both, as is the failure to identify or act on neglect, the acceptance of poor parenting standards and the ease with which parents' apparent engagement with services can be mistaken for a genuine desire to change (see Haringey Local Safeguarding Children Board 2010, *passim*). This chapter has tried to shed further light on the factors that can lead to a shift in focus away from taking the child's welfare as the paramount consideration, with the objective of identifying how children at very high risk of harm might be better safeguarded in the future.

Summary points for Chapter 7

- Initially, decisions made by all professionals, including judges, magistrates, psychologists, psychiatrists and children's guardians, as well as social workers, were influenced by a desire to keep families together wherever possible.

- The expectation that children should remain in their birth families was underpinned by views of parents' rights, and concepts of empowerment and fairness.

- This was epitomized in the extensive use made of parenting assessments. Many of these appeared unnecessary, and were a major source of delay. The recommendations from specialist assessments were almost always followed; the majority of these were in favour of babies remaining with birth parents, although over half of these did not lead to children being adequately safeguarded.

- Extensive efforts were made to keep children within their extended families if parents were unable to safeguard them. However, many of the relatives were struggling with similar levels of adversity as the parents. Assessing them further delayed the development of permanence plans.

- Extensive efforts to keep children within the extended family meant that some kinship placements were of poor quality, and many kinship carers would have been disqualified as potential adopters. Some of them had only a tenuous link with the index child.

- Where intimate partner violence or sexual abuse was an issue, rather than keeping the family together, the focus was on excluding the abuser. There was very little evidence of interventions designed to support abusers in changing their behaviour. Many of them must have gone on to abuse another family.

- Most interventions were relatively short, and less intrusive actions were almost always favoured above those that introduced greater levels of coercion. Half the child protection plans were for 32 weeks or less; only two children who had not been permanently separated were still subject to Care Orders by the time they were three.

- Some parents were themselves concerned at the short-term nature of interventions and the lack of subsequent monitoring.

- Although short-term interventions may partly be attributed to a lack of resources, they also reflected concerns that parents should shoulder their responsibilities and not become dependent on services.

- The ambivalent nature of these concerns is evidenced in the use of written agreements. These were frequently used and might have been employed as a means of empowering parents and articulating a shared responsibility. However, the terms were often breached, with few repercussions.

- Both the concerns over dependency and the tendency to take the parents' part contributed to the difficulties in identifying or acting upon severe neglect. Insufficient training on child development and the impact of maltreatment, together with the tendency of social workers to become over-exposed, and therefore desensitized, to neglect, were also factors. There was little evidence of joint visits or interviews that might have provided a second opinion.

- While team leaders appeared to provide effective supervision and support, they did not always appear to adopt a sufficiently critical approach to the perceptions and practices of front-line practitioners.

- Children's guardians provided a valuable counterweight. They appeared to fulfil their role as children's advocates, and often successfully challenged decisions that were arguably not in the best interests of the child.

8

Parents' Perspectives

Introduction

All the professionals interviewed wanted to ensure that the welfare of the infants was properly safeguarded, and their chances of long-term wellbeing improved; the previous chapter has identified a range of factors that made it difficult to realize this objective within these very young children's timeframes. Similarly, all the parents, in their own judgement, wanted to do the best for their children; however, they were often struggling against considerable odds to provide a nurturing home.

Almost all parents in the study were at risk of permanent separation from their infants, and needed professional support to overcome their difficulties. They were often able to relate best to professionals whom they deemed to be on their side, such as drug and alcohol workers, psychologists and health visitors. Support for drug and alcohol addiction was particularly appreciated by those parents who were able to change. Out of the 17 families in which drug or alcohol misuse was cited as a risk factor, five mentioned the specialist services they had received, and all described them in a positive light. All except one of these were families in which positive change was achieved.

However, as we have seen, professionals in adult services in particular could be reluctant to take responsibility for ensuring that children were safeguarded, and did not have the authority to make decisions concerning permanence. Parents also needed at least a working relationship with social workers if they were to understand what changes were necessary to safeguard and promote the welfare of their children. There were, however, a number of barriers to achieving this.

Decisions to require compliance with a child protection plan, to remove children from the care of birth parents or to place children for adoption inescapably indicate that birth parents have been judged and found wanting; we have already seen how far they go against the grain of a professional culture which seeks to reduce discrimination and empower those who are disadvantaged. On the other hand, reports of parents' views of social work interventions demonstrate the extent of loss, shame and sometimes resentment felt by those at the receiving end (see for instance Morgan 2008).

A number of studies have shown how parents' perceptions of extremely difficult social work decisions can impact on both their own ability to come to terms with a painful situation and, ultimately, the subsequent experience of the child. We have already seen that many of the parents in this study had an older child who was going through care or adoption proceedings at the time of the pregnancy and birth of the baby we studied; we know that the finality of permanent separation is often a traumatic experience that engenders intense feelings of bereavement, depression and anger (Neil *et al.* 2010). These feelings are likely to have coloured some of the parents' perceptions of decisions made in respect of the index baby. We also know that parents who are unreconciled to a decision to place for adoption may go on to have (and lose) other children without appreciating the need to change (Neil *et al.* 2010; Ward *et al.* 2006). Those who cannot accept decisions to place children away from home can jeopardize the child's ability to settle (see Sinclair *et al.* 2007). It is understandable that parents who feel unjustly treated will contest care plans, but whatever the strength or weakness of their case, a contested decision can introduce a lengthy period of delay and instability for the child before permanence is attained (see Ward *et al.* 2006).

The purpose of this chapter is to identify those factors which influenced parents' understanding of decision-making, and to explore how they impeded or facilitated working relationships between parents and professionals, particularly social workers. The chapter also demonstrates how some social workers succeeded in getting the best from their relationship with parents regardless of the circumstances, and shows what can be learnt from parents and their experiences. It is evident from what follows that those who had overcome previous adversities, developed some insight into the impact of their behaviour and were now providing a satisfactory home for the index child tended to view children's social care in a more positive light than those who had not, but perceptions were not entirely polarized, and there is much to be learnt from parents' own explanations of what had happened.

It is also important to remember that the views expressed are from the parents and their lived experiences of often extreme adversity. Interviews often took place during those times when emotions were very fragile and parents' views may have been distorted by experiences of powerlessness and loss. We know that some parents had come eventually to understand earlier decisions to remove older siblings; it is possible that others who were angry and resentful at the actions taken to safeguard the babies we studied may, in time, have come to adopt a more balanced view.

Parents' expectations and experiences of adult services

As indicated in previous chapters, many parents were familiar with a wide range of services, designed to support them in overcoming adversities and changing their lifestyles sufficiently to provide nurturing homes for their babies. They particularly valued adult-focused therapeutic support such as that given by drug and alcohol workers, domestic violence workers and community mental health teams (CMHTs). Outside the support offered by children's social care, these types of services also seemed to have the greatest influence in facilitating parental change. Some parents found that their sessions with an adult services worker were able to offer them an insight into their own behaviour and how this affected their parenting. For example, Richard's mother described the changes effected by counselling from a drug and alcohol service:

> I guess that's helped me, because until I started going there [drug and alcohol service counselling] I couldn't see how my childhood affected my motherhood and now I can see quite clearly. Because when I talked about my childhood and then talked about how it went with [older children who had been adopted], I can see a lot of similarities, and if I compare them it's not that different. (Mother of Richard: medium risk of harm at identification; low risk, living with birth parents and safeguarded at age three)

Parents particularly appreciated the way these services focus on adult needs; they valued being able to form a close bond with a particular worker, who they viewed as being *on their side*. Some parents were supported by an adult services worker who advocated on their behalf with children's social care. However, this was not always in the best interests of the child, as some of these workers viewed their role in protecting the parents' rights as taking precedence over their responsibility to safeguard the child (see Chapter 7). This did not go unnoticed by the parents; for instance, Madeleine's father identified a conflict between his drugs worker and his social worker:

> He [drugs worker] was quite understanding and he wrote a good report saying that he had no concerns whatsoever and that me and her [mother] had made great strides, you know, in our struggles, and that we'd put down our medication and that we'd changed our lifestyles totally. And he said that if he thought that she [Madeleine] wasn't being looked after, he'd be the first person to say something… He [drugs worker] and [social worker] do not get on. He's told me he doesn't like her. (Father of Madeleine: medium risk of harm at identification; high risk, living with birth parents but not safeguarded at age three)

The social worker in this case found this particular drugs worker a constant source of irritation: 'I'm incredibly frustrated by them…very unhelpful.'

Some parents came to rely on the support they received from adult services, particularly if they did not have close relationships within their extended family. However, these services were often terminated as soon as parents were regarded as doing well, and they then experienced a sense of loss when the particular worker with whom they had a close bond no longer visited. Jordan's mother recounts being told that she no longer needed to visit the CMHT:

> I went to [CMHT] and they told me they didn't want to see me no more, so I left again. They said you're fine, we won't see you anymore. (*In an aggrieved tone*) I thought: 'Whatever then.' (Mother of Jordan: high risk of harm at identification; high risk, living with birth parents but not safeguarded at age three)

Lily's father expressed his concerns about how support from all agencies, including adult and children's services, would gradually reduce:

> Not many parents get a lot of support like we do. And if you go from a lot of support to hardly any in a certain time, it's going to be a shock to your system. (Father of Lily: medium risk of harm at identification; medium risk, living with birth parents but not safeguarded at age three)

Parents' views of universal and targeted children's services

Universal services, such as those offered by local Sure Start children's centres, mother and toddler groups and self-help groups, were also widely used by the parents. However, they had mixed views about their usefulness. Some parents, mainly those who were able to make and sustain changes, valued the regular support and contact with other people, both parents and professionals, that universal services offered them. They most valued the practical support these services provided, such as help with establishing good routines for the baby, and being given baby equipment. For example, Jaz's mother regularly visited the local children's centre:

> If you need anything for the child she [family support worker from children's centre] would do it for me, like fire gates…she were lovely…she taught me how to do breastfeeding and encouraged me to carry on. (Mother of Jaz: high risk of harm at identification; low risk, living with birth parents and safeguarded at age three)

However, other parents, mainly those who were unable to make and sustain changes, did not engage with universal or targeted services. Their reasons were varied and included not wanting to mix with other parents; feeling they were somehow different from other parents; and the local groups being made up of people of a different ethnic origin from themselves. For instance, Wayne's social worker described why his mother did not wish to engage with universal services:

> She's not confident; she's not trusting of other people. Essentially, we tried to get her to access what you call mainstream services, like mother and toddler groups, Home Start, all the kind of routine things, and she didn't follow through any of them. And that's basically because she's scared of new people, scared of new situations. She worked with us [children's social care] because she had to, and in some ways it was probably more comfortable. Social services might not be something she likes but it's something she's familiar with. (Social worker for Wayne: medium risk of harm at identification; high risk, living with birth parents but not safeguarded at age three)

On the other hand, health visitors were highly regarded by most parents who were more likely to approach them for support and advice, particularly after a case had been closed by children's social care. Their role was regarded as pivotal both by social workers, because they provided an additional layer of monitoring, and by parents, because they were able to offer practical and emotional help and guidance, and work closely with their social worker. For instance, particularly in the early months of his life, Simon's health visitor went to see him and his mother regularly and visited when his social worker could not, to ensure that at least one professional saw him every week. Jordan's mother described how she valued health professionals working closely with children's social care:

> My health visitor helped me out, my midwife helped me out, and my social worker helped me out. I had a lot of support behind me, a lot. They got together in a room, with the housing people, and actually told them I needed a house, that the conditions I was living in were not good enough. They all clubbed together and did it. Which I thought was excellent. (Mother of Jordan: high risk of harm at identification; high risk, living with birth parents but not safeguarded at age three)

Parents' expectations and experiences of social workers

There were, however, a number of factors within the parents' own expectations that hindered the development of a good working relationship with social workers. These largely related to parents' previous experience of social work involvement and their awareness of the weakness of their own position in dealings with professionals. For some parents, these potential barriers were enhanced by feelings of ineffectiveness that were often exacerbated by the situation in which they found themselves, and by misunderstandings that arose from cultural differences.

As we have seen in Chapter 3, a high proportion of parents had extensive earlier experience of children's social care, either from their own childhood or from involvement with older children. Such experiences had often influenced their relationship and ability to work with social workers. These parents tended to be highly mistrustful of children's social care, disappointed that they had not graduated from their involvement and, in more extreme cases, completely unwilling to work with social workers at all. These latter were the highly resistant families who may appear outwardly compliant, but 'who do not engage or cooperate with services to protect children…or demonstrate positive change despite intervention and support from child protection services' (see Fauth *et al.* 2010, p.6).

Cassie's parents, for instance, had both been looked after as children, and her mother had had an older child placed for adoption. Neither of them was willing to co-operate with children's social care, and the father, in particular, was adamant that they could raise Cassie themselves, without professional involvement. By the end of the study they were refusing to comply with the child protection plan or to allow social workers to see the children in their home. The father resented the continuing social work involvement, and was disappointed that he had not been able to move on:

> I've been under social services all my life and I was expecting to have a baby without them, do you know what I mean? I thought this was what the whole point of growing up was all about…I felt really, really disappointed, because they were there, meant to be for help, if I asked for help then they're there for that, but I didn't ask for help at the time, and they just basically poked their noses in. (Father of Cassie: medium risk of harm at identification; high risk, living with birth parents but not safeguarded at age three)

Experiences of abuse in childhood altered parents' ability to form working relationships with social workers, particularly if they believed that children's social care were to blame. Blossom's father had been looked after by the local authority for most of his childhood and had been abused in at least one placement:

> In the sense of I don't fucking like them [social workers], do you know what I mean, don't tell me to love my rapist because I never will…
>
> They ripped everything off me, you know. All they left were the bad things, the anger that they built up over those years you know, the hatred you know, that's the things they gave me, you know what I mean?…
>
> I've been with them people since I was eight years old, I know how to fucking fight them, do you know what I mean? They have never broke me yet and they never will, and I told them that from day one, do you know what I mean, you've fucked up my childhood, but you ain't going to do my daughter's childhood… (Father of Blossom: severe risk of harm at identification; safeguarded through separation at age three)

However, some parents were able to distinguish between negative experiences of children's social care in their childhood, and current experiences with their own children. Jaz's mother recounted her past experiences:

> So it's different when you're a child, social workers don't listen to what you're feeling… They were thinking about me, thinking about my feelings. They're thinking what I need, but they didn't know… But when you're older, they take your feelings into account, they do… (Mother of Jaz: high risk of harm at identification; low risk, living with birth parent and safeguarded at age three)

Past experience of children's social care with older children was also a significant factor in determining how parents would relate to social workers as regards the index child. Past decisions to remove children did not always act as an impediment, for if parents could understand the rationale for interventions, their ability to work with social workers this time around was facilitated. For example, Richard's mother had previously misused alcohol and been engaged in violent relationships. Her two older children had been neglected and physically abused and had witnessed intimate partner violence, as a result of which they had been removed. However, she had been able to learn from her previous refusal to co-operate with children's social care and use that knowledge to help her form a good relationship with her current social worker. She explained:

If I look at how it's going now to how it went years ago, the difference is me and [partner] are co-operating together with them. We're…it's not social services, they're not doing anything really, it's me and [partner]. Because we're co-operating and doing what they want us to, because we want to, not because we have to, that's where we're finding it easier and actually can see where social services are helpful. Whereas before we couldn't see it because we thought we were better than everyone else…we thought…social services were a bunch of, you know, and we didn't want them involved with us. So therefore we just tried to close out what was going on. Whereas now we can see social services haven't changed at all, it's us that have changed, we're making the difference. Social services aren't as bad as everyone seems to think if you co-operate with them and work with them and not think that they're trying to run your life but they're trying to work with you and help you, then they're good, it is, they're actually a good thing to have on board sometimes if you actually need them, whereas before we couldn't see that. So, like I say, it's not social services that have changed their ways, it's us that have changed our ways. (Mother of Richard: medium risk of harm at identification; low risk, living with birth parent and safeguarded at age three)

Not all cases where birth parents were able to form a better relationship with their current social worker resulted in a positive outcome for the child. Wayne's mother compared her current and past experiences:

Interviewer: So what do you think was different about this time and last time?

Mother: Just that everyone, just like everyone was against me, I had the wrong social worker, she wanted to take the baby away from me at the time, if it was left to her, do you know what I mean? This social worker, it was different, gave me a chance, they weren't on me back all the time, he listened to me instead of everybody else, do you know what I mean? Because there was a lot of people against me when I had my first.

(Mother of Wayne: medium risk of harm at identification; high risk, living with birth parent but not safeguarded at age three)

However, although his mother believed she had a good relationship with her social worker, this did not enable her to gain insight into the impact of her continuing substance misuse on Wayne's welfare. He remained likely to suffer significant harm at age three, and is the child who could imitate the use of heroin as described in Chapter 7.

For some parents, reconciliation of past decisions was extremely difficult. In particular, the grief and sense of enduring loss engendered by the removal of an older child tended to impact on the relationship between the birth parent and the social worker; unless parents had gained some insight into the part they had played, such decisions had a negative impact on their subsequent relationship with children's social care.

The unequal partnership between parents and professionals

The principle that, whenever such an approach was consistent with the child's welfare, local authorities should work in partnership with parents was introduced by the Children Act 1989, and has subsequently been reiterated by further legislation and policy (Department for Education and Skills 2007; Department of Health 1989). Concepts of empowerment and partnership are also embedded in social work training and culture (see, for example, Adams et al. 2009; Williams and Churchill 2006). Most parents, however, were well aware that the partnership was an unequal one, and that professionals ultimately had the power to over-ride their wishes if they thought this was in the interests of their children.

Parents were particularly aware of the weakness of their position in formal settings, such as court hearings, review meetings and case conferences, where they might feel at a disadvantage in the face of professionals who were not only more powerful than they, but also likely to be better educated and more skilled at presenting an argument. They sometimes had difficulty in understanding the language used in meetings and were anxious about presenting their own opinions. They also found formal occasions frightening, and felt under intense scrutiny. Martin-Louis' mother explained:

> [About meetings] A bit too formal, I was nervous, bad, I was shaking and didn't want to go and felt sick, they're frightening things to go to, they really were, yes, I didn't like them. But I knew I had to go, so again I got pressure, and if I didn't go then the kids would be put on the at-risk register and who wants that for their kids, well I don't, certainly don't, so felt a bit blackmailed. (Martin-Louis' mother: medium risk of harm at identification; low risk, living with birth parent and safeguarded at age three)

Other parents were at a disadvantage because they felt inferior to the professionals:

> The way they spoke to us in the meeting! You know, like, they could have put it polite. They kept looking down on us, if you know what I mean. (Harry's mother: medium risk of harm at identification; low risk, living with birth parent and safeguarded at age three)

These feelings were amplified when cases came to the attention of the courts. Some parents who had experiences of court proceedings described an intimidating and frightening ordeal that they found difficult to deal with. One parent thought that proceedings were 'a long process' and admitted she 'felt petrified'. Cassie's father gave the following explanation of how daunting the experience could be:

> It was quite scary, it is, it is very scary, do you know what I mean, because your children's life is in the court's hands at the end of the day, and what they say goes, so if they would have said that [baby] was going into social services then I'd got nothing to say about that, do you know what I mean? And it is very scary, from a father's point of view, and his first child as well, it's very, very, very scary. (Cassie's father: medium risk of harm at identification; high risk, living with birth parent but not safeguarded at age three)

Peter's mother expressed her view that the outcome of care proceedings was practically a foregone conclusion, an opinion which may have added to feelings of helplessness. This mother, who had been permanently separated from all her children including Peter, held a particularly negative view which is perhaps understandable in the circumstances. She commented that 'nine times out of ten everyone who goes in that court don't have their kids handed back anyway', and attributed this to the negative outcomes of assessments, alleging 'they always diagnose everyone's got a personality disorder, I've noticed that'. The experience of having her children removed by the court led her to advise others in her position to avoid proceedings under any circumstances: 'Don't let it go to court, just do what the social workers tell you basically.'

Nathan's mother felt similarly powerless when trying to express herself in court. Although she was able to defend her position and felt that sometimes her views were taken into account, she noted that the balance of power was against her:

> I just feel like whatever I say there it doesn't matter, it's like right what they're saying is right, you've just got to sit there and sort of do…I mean they can be all right sometimes, but I find it hard sometimes getting my ideas across and it comes out the wrong

way…that's the way it is, it's like judged. (Nathan's mother: high risk of harm at identification; high risk, living with birth parent but not safeguarded at age three)

However, not all parents felt daunted by the formal settings. Those who had had previous experiences with older children were better prepared, as were parents who had an advocate present who could explain the reports and discussions in a way they could understand. Solicitors also helped parents to feel more comfortable in these settings and therefore to express their views. Oscar's mother described the benefits of an advocate:

Interviewer: And, so, if we go back to your meetings, how able are you to put your views across, do you feel?

Mother: Because I've got an advocate and I've now got a solicitor, my solicitor hasn't been to any meetings yet but I did feel quite able to get my point of view across because of my advocate and, you know, but because there was a lot of people in that room and I felt on the first meeting, that everyone was against me, sort of thing, although they weren't, I was, I didn't like speaking in that group because it was just, you know, too many people.

(Oscar's mother: medium risk of harm at identification; intermediate follow-up group)

Parents expressed concerns that written reports or statements made during meetings were not always accurate or based on sound knowledge. In these circumstances they felt frustrated and disempowered as they believed that they were not being given a fair chance; nor did they feel able to challenge what had been said about them. One birth mother recalled her experiences of a case conference:

But, you know, I'm an intelligent adult and they could have talked to me like an intelligent adult rather than like a criminal, really, that's how I was treated… But the social worker essentially came out to see me two days before the case conference with her report, and she'd never met my daughter. She'd written this report; there were things in it that she claimed I said which I had never said. There were things in it that had been completely misinterpreted of what I'd said. I mean, she actually wrote in the report that in her opinion I didn't have a bond with either of my children, when she'd never even met them. You know, I just, kind of, found it all a bit ridiculous, really, you know, there was no need for it. (Charles' mother: not classified; withdrew after first interview)

Cultural issues

In some circumstances these issues were compounded by cultural differences. These included parents' misunderstanding of maltreatment and social workers' misunderstanding of parents' culture. A small minority of parents were born outside the UK in cultures where there were different thresholds and concepts of abuse and neglect. In these cases it was difficult for social workers to convince parents of the possible consequences of their actions. Yolanda's father, who came from the Middle East, had difficulty in understanding why intimate partner violence was so unacceptable:

> …because the social worker sometimes don't explain, because I don't know this country, she [wife] don't know this country, sometimes explain for us. The baby very important in this country, problems, problems always very important in this country, worry about family have baby, yes, explain for us sometimes… (Yolanda's father: medium risk of harm at identification; low risk, living with birth parents and safeguarded at age three)

Perceptions of abuse also differed depending on the culture of the social worker. One team leader, for example, who had qualified in Eastern Europe, pointed out that she had had to make several conceptual changes:

> I also had to readjust all, you know, a lot of things like concept, like risk and neglect and, you know, emotional abuse because what is, what constitutes abuse here doesn't in [country]. (Team leader, children's social care)

In addition, parents also felt that some professionals were insensitive to their culture and this impacted on their ability to form a successful working relationship. For example, one birth mother from Russia described a meeting with social workers in which they had appeared insensitive:

> I started disputing them calling my husband of 12 years a boyfriend and then it escalated into further things and they said well you know you shouldn't be uptight about these things because this is England, and I said, well, the way I was brought up I don't have children out of wedlock. So please don't call my husband a boyfriend, we have been married for 12 years. So they said this is not Russia, this is England. People don't have to get married, they could just have babies with whoever they like. None of us are married to the fathers of our children, ha ha! And the ladies are in their forties and because they were mocking me it came out in the wrong way. Well I am sorry, but I am not English. I wouldn't

do that, I wouldn't sleep around…and then things went from bad to worse. (Noah's mother: high risk of harm at identification; low risk, living with birth parents and safeguarded at age three)

Factors which influenced the relationship between social workers and parents

A number of factors could facilitate or inhibit the development of a constructive relationship between parents and social workers. Positive factors included the ability to listen and to appear sensitive to parents' feelings, and honesty and openness about parents' problems and their potential consequences. Negative factors included frequent changes of social worker and disregard of parents' timescales and commitments. In order to overcome the barriers identified above, and develop a viable working relationship with parents, social workers had to be particularly sensitive to their vulnerability.

Sensitivity and the ability to listen

There is considerable evidence that professionals who are prepared to listen to their point of view are highly valued by service users (see for instance Morgan 2008; Skuse and Ward 2003). Parents in the current study emphasized the importance of social workers listening as a key catalyst in forming and maintaining good working relationships. It was important that they felt that they were not being judged and that their views were being considered. Parents were more likely to respect social workers who took the time to listen and consider their views; these parents were then more likely to take on board advice and engage well with services that were offered.

Parents also considered it important for social workers to take the time to explain decisions. Those whose social workers did not do this were either left confused or relied on explanations from other professionals:

> And it was only until she [children's guardian] took the time, I think she was here for about three hours the one day explaining the ins and outs of what they can do and what they can't do, even with an Interim Care Order. And it was only through her advice and the time she took with me that I agreed to one… Like I say, I've had more help and support from people like the children's guardian, you know…none, none, there's been no support, no advice or anything from social services. Surely it should have been their job to come out and talk to me about an Interim Care Order, not the children's guardian. (May's mother: medium risk of harm at identification; low risk, living with birth parent and safeguarded at age three)

Some parents were concerned that the confidential nature of their involvement with children's social care was not always adequately respected. For example, one parent was unhappy that postal correspondence was marked with a large 'Child Protection' stamp, a particular worry as her postman was a neighbour. Another was annoyed that when her social worker had asked for directions, she had told the neighbours her occupation.

Changes of social worker

Frequent changes of social worker are known to have a detrimental impact on service delivery (Cleaver *et al.* 2008; Skuse and Ward 2003). In the current study it was evident that they hindered parents' ability to work in partnership. Parents expressed frustration that they were retelling their story time and time again, and they felt that because of this the case was not progressing as effectively as it should. Their ability to trust and engage with services appeared to be facilitated if they were able to relate consistently to the same social worker. For example, Harry's parents explained their differing experiences of having several social workers compared with a sustained period without a change:

> *Mother:* Oh, every time someone came to the house, it was someone different. Every time, until I went into hospital, weren't it?

> *Father:* Yeah, then [social worker] said I'll see you through this one.

> *Mother:* And I said to [social worker] I don't want a different social worker every time. Can you get me one person, and I'll deal with that one person? We got [social worker], we were lucky to get [social worker].

> (Harry's mother and father: medium risk of harm at identification; low risk, living with birth parents and safeguarded at age three)

For this family, a period of continuity appeared to be one of the factors that facilitated positive change. Four older children had been removed previously and the couple had a history of non-engagement that continued until after Harry was born. However, they began to engage when they were able to establish a constructive relationship with a worker who held case responsibility for an extended period; the relationship continued beyond case closure.

Several changes of social worker could lead to confusion and uncertainty; Janis' mother recounted her experiences over the previous two years:

> Well, at the moment I don't really know who my social worker is…I was seeing [social worker one], then she left, erm, and then I crossed over to [social worker two] and I was under [social worker

> three] and then [social worker four]; then I was with a lady called
> [social worker five] who I've not met… Now I don't know if I'm
> still with [social worker five] or…I think there's some talk about
> [social worker five] on maternity leave…or something, but I've
> never met her. (Janis' mother: severe risk of harm at identification;
> severe risk, living with birth parent but not safeguarded at age
> three)

The reader will remember that Janis suffered neglect and emotional abuse
throughout the study period. The lack of continuity undoubtedly contributed
to the failure on the part of children's social care to appreciate the extent or
level of his maltreatment.

Other parents felt that numerous changes had impacted on their ability to
trust social workers; May's mother, for instance, had had eight different social
workers over the previous two years:

> Because I've had eight social workers, how do they expect you to
> build a relationship with them if you've had eight social workers?
> And half the time you wasn't told you was having a new social
> worker: they just used to turn up. (May's mother: medium risk
> of harm at identification; low risk, living with birth parent and
> safeguarded at age three)

However, some parents welcomed a change of social worker, believing that
they would be given a second chance, that the new social worker would
view their case less critically, and that this would lead to different outcomes.
Occasionally the change reinvigorated the parent/social worker relationship,
and improved their engagement with services. A change could be particularly
valuable if a previous social worker had presided over the removal of an older
child. Richard's mother was in this situation, and was able to relate better to
the new social worker, partly because by then she had overcome her previous
adversities:

> I think I was also lucky because you hear of some people that
> haven't got very nice social workers, you know, they've done it all
> by the book, they haven't got any children, and unfortunately the
> last time round we…that's the social worker we had, she hadn't
> no children, she hadn't experienced things hands on. (Richard's
> mother: medium risk of harm at identification; low risk, living
> with birth parent and safeguarded at age three)

Straight talking

Although parents were aware that social workers had the power to remove children in order to safeguard their welfare, they were nevertheless not always prepared for this to happen in reality. Placing children away from home, particularly against the wishes of their parents, is one of the most difficult actions for social workers to perform. Parents had much to say about how social workers might approach coercive and unwelcome interventions with greater sensitivity.

It is no surprise that parents who experienced permanent separation from their children felt anguish and heartache at the actions taken by children's social care. It is important to understand their perceptions as and when these actions were being taken, and identify what might have helped them in their understanding and in their ability to recognize the extent to which their children were likely to suffer harm.

Parents were overwhelmingly insistent that social workers should have been honest about the reality that children would be removed if they did not make sufficient changes. They said they wanted to be held accountable for their actions and know what the consequences of their behaviour would be. Social workers who told 'black as black', did not 'beat around the bush' and had the ability to 'break bad news' were able to build better relationships with parents and improve their insight into their problem behaviour and the possibility that their child would be separated from them.

Parents who did not feel that they were being told the absolute truth had difficulties understanding what to change in their behaviour, and what the consequences would be if they failed to do so. They felt as though they were being told what they wanted to hear rather than the truth. Those social workers who were honest about the strong possibility that they would remove children were considered nicer, easier to work with and more trustworthy.

One birth mother, who had one child removed at six months old and then his younger sibling removed when she was two, following an unsuccessful rehabilitation attempt, explained her reaction to the removal of her second child:

> They let me feel I were doing all right. And it's like telling parents that they shouldn't have done, like concerns, why didn't they tell me about concerns? If they had big concerns like they said they had, why didn't they tell me about them, stuff like that? But they never told me. If they don't tell me something, how can I do it? (Stephen and Erin's mother: severe/high risk of harm at identification; safeguarded through separation at age three)

Social workers' openness was therefore fundamental to the formation of working relationships with parents, particularly when these very complex, difficult decisions were being made. Richard's mother explained how she valued her new social worker's honesty regarding the threat of permanent separation:

> She [social worker] did turn round to us and she did say, 'If ever you put a foot out of line, it'll be me taking this baby from you.' There was no, no beating around the bush. And that's what we like about her, she's basically been an open and shut case, whereas the people we've had dealings with before were two-faced, we found, which is why we found it hard to trust. (Richard's mother: medium risk of harm at identification; low risk, living with birth parents and safeguarded at age three)

A small number of parents also wanted decisions to remove their children to be taken more promptly than was sometimes the case, as they felt that prolonging the process was cruel both to them and to their children: 'They just dragged it on, and dragged it on.'

Olivia's father also wanted more decisive action when older children were removed:

> The first one didn't like breaking bad news, and I said he shouldn't really be doing the job. Yeah, he didn't like saying that she [partner] wasn't going to get [child's older sibling] back. He said she [partner] would have [child's older sibling] back at Christmas, he said, so that's giving someone false hope. But the next, like, two [social workers] we had were really on the ball, they said, 'There's no chance,' and I found that more respectful than being deceived all the time...I mean, if people aren't there to break bad news, they shouldn't be doing the job... 'Cos that is a tough job, and I mean decisions have to get made, on the spur of the moment, you can't just linger people along and get their hopes up. (Olivia's father: medium risk of harm at identification; low risk, living with birth parent and safeguarded at age three)

Timing

The emotional impact of section 47 enquiries was rarely explicitly acknowledged by professionals. As we noted in Chapter 2, 32 of the babies in the follow-up groups were identified before birth: assessment during pregnancy was a particularly sensitive issue and had a potentially detrimental impact upon parents' attachment to their unborn or newborn baby. A small number of parents outlined how the timing of the assessment and the intervention had affected them. Their experiences need to be understood within a context in which, as we have seen (Chapters 4 and 7), initial plans made by social care could be altered following a child protection conference, a specialist assessment or a court ruling.

There was one case in which a pre-birth assessment was purposely postponed in recognition that the stress of children's social care involvement risked exacerbating a mother's health condition. In general, however, less sensitivity appeared to be shown. One mother described her reluctance to make preparations for her baby's birth because she was uncertain whether or not she would be allowed to keep her child. Such fears and anxieties were informed by past experiences. Social workers rarely regarded referrals made during a pregnancy as urgent because, although plans could be made, few actions could be taken until after the baby's birth; however, the length of time before an assessment was made left a small number of parents in limbo awaiting decisions about whether or not their child would be immediately removed. For example, one family indicated that children's social care had been first notified of the pregnancy five months before a social worker was allocated. In another case, a support worker ('not a proper social worker') visited in the early stages of the pregnancy but then no action was taken until two months before the birth. Late intervention or changes in plan were criticized. These included cases in which families had expected social workers to make an assessment, as well as those where their involvement came as a total shock.

> They didn't even do the pre-birth assessment, they didn't tell us that I was able to keep [baby's name] until a week before. (Ava's mother: medium risk of harm at identification; high risk, living with birth mother but not safeguarded at age three)

> It was like last minute thing as well. They came in two weeks before she was meant to give birth which made her ill on the last week, so she was like one week late. (Cassie's father: medium risk of harm at identification; high risk, living with birth parent but not safeguarded at age three)

A small number of parents expressed concerns about how cases were managed around the time of their child's birth. This study has found no evidence that young children are being separated from their parents without due cause, as is sometimes alleged (see Alderson *et al.* 2008; Hemming 2007). However, there was evidence that the timing of the intervention, at an emotive point in the parents' lives, could compound the distress and fear that birth parents experience when faced with the possibility of a child being placed away from home. According to the parents, the timing of some interventions was particularly clumsy. For instance, Madeleine's father was not asked if he would agree to the new baby being accommodated by the local authority until his wife was in labour:

> I've gone into this room here and I've seen a bloke sat there… says 'I'm a social worker, I want to know if you'll [sign] a form, saying [baby] can go into care'…I said, 'No way, fuck that'… The social worker said, 'Erm, well you've messed things up now.' (Madeleine's father: medium risk of harm at identification; high risk, living with birth parent but not safeguarded at age three)

Isla's mother recounted that:

> Social services phoned up on that day wanting to take [child] there and then. Which broke my heart, said you can't do that, just given birth. Please don't take her, don't take her away. (Isla's mother: severe risk of harm at identification; safeguarded through separation at age three)

In cases where a legal order was thought necessary to safeguard vulnerable babies from harm, local authorities instigated family court proceedings. This meant that, alongside childbirth, the fear or reality of a baby's removal and/or caring for them, some parents were also having to cope with the added stress of attending court.

> I had to go to court three times because they kept adjourning it and it was annoying, because I couldn't sleep or anything…I missed out on quite a lot of things, first feed, first bath…it just killed me, do you know what I mean? (Cassie's father: medium risk of harm at identification; high risk, living with birth parent but not safeguarded at age three)

At this time of heightened emotion, practitioners were particularly likely to be perceived as having acted unprofessionally or insensitively. For instance, Peter's mother alleged that a midwife had told her 'You're the one whose child's going into foster care'. At this stage she had not been told that this was the plan for her baby, and in the event, Peter was allowed home, supported by daily visits from the health visitor or social worker. Another mother explained that she had not attended a court hearing, as she was caring for the baby. She had been expecting a Supervision Order to be granted. Instead, the police arrived to take her baby and toddler into foster care. Her distress was compounded because she apparently did not receive any information about the carers or contact arrangements over the weekend.

We do not know how much truth there was in some of the allegations made, but the actions taken by these professionals were bitterly resented. Such experiences, although by no means universal, are likely to jeopardize future partnership working with parents.

Parents' perspectives on social work support

Those elements of social work support that most strongly facilitated the establishment of successful working relationships with parents included practical help; the perception that support was offered on a voluntary basis; and ongoing and consistent support.

First, parents greatly appreciated any practical help that was given. They most valued assistance with funding for nursery places to give them 'time off', or to go to court, to attend child protection conferences, or to visit other children; finance for furnishing homes and baby equipment; and help with applying for benefits and housing.

Second, parents did not want to feel as though support was being forced upon them; their engagement with services seemed to work better if they perceived their attendance as voluntary. Brendan's mother, who was experiencing post-natal depression, explained:

> Well, she did listen and she advised me of a group that was going…
> where single parents go. Some of them may have suffered from
> post-natal depression or some of them are just single parents. Just
> want to meet other mums rather than having to sit at home kind
> of thing. (Brendan's mother: medium risk of harm at identification;
> low risk, living with birth parent and safeguarded at age three)

Her experience is in contrast to that of Ranjit's mother, who felt that support was being forced upon her and that she was under scrutiny. After two years of intense intervention her child was removed:

> Do you know if I didn't go to [name of support group], they just
> turn round and say come on, you've got to do this, and do that?
> Oh, it's a nightmare. (Ranjit's mother: medium risk of harm at
> identification; safeguarded through separation at age three)

Effective relationships appeared to be better established when intervention was ongoing. We have already seen (Chapters 5 and 7) that services were quickly withdrawn where parents showed evidence of progress. Some of these parents expressed concerns that their case was not open for long enough and that it had been abruptly closed with no continuing supervision. At least six of them indicated that they had valued the ongoing support and supervision that children's social care offered, and two of them expressed their hope that it would continue. They were also worried that if and when it did stop they would revert back to their old lifestyles, and consequently cause harm to their children. At least two parents went as far as to request that the child protection plan be extended for longer than was deemed necessary by professionals because of this fear:

> I didn't want it to go downhill and, plus, I didn't want to (…) take him off [the child protection plan]…sat down and discuss, just sat down and discuss having to keep him on it…keep him on anyway. If he were going to come off it, I wouldn't be happy because I didn't want to, I had to break away, I don't know, can't explain how I wanted it. I do need the support but I do, I did want him in a way, it's so, it works two ways…I wanted to prove (…) from six months, another three months to look after my son because anything could happen in three months. (Jaz's mother: high risk of harm at identification; low risk, living with birth parent and safeguarded at age three)

Furthermore, Connor's father disputed the wisdom of ever ending the child protection plan:

> *Interviewer:* So, what would you like to have happened differently, if you like, in terms of social services input?
>
> *Father:* I'd have liked them to have kept him on the at-risk register. Because even though I don't want to think it, I do feel as though [partner] will hurt him again at some point, whether it be emotional or physical.
>
> (Connor's father: medium risk of harm at identification; withdrew after first interview)

Other parents, who appeared to have overcome their problems, nevertheless expected children's social care to check up on them occasionally to make sure that they had been able to maintain the changes they had made. For instance, Martin-Louis' mother, who had experienced intimate partner violence, recounted her surprise that children's social care had closed the case with no ongoing supervision:

They've never said might just come and see you, or we will come and see you in a year's time, do you know what I mean, they've just left it, they was all concerned at that time, and because the meeting was all closed up and done on the last one and they were happy with everything that was in place, it just seemed a bit of an abrupt end. (Martin-Louis' mother: medium risk of harm at identification; low risk, living with birth parent and safeguarded at age three)

This same mother, in a later interview, remained concerned that children's social care had had no further involvement since closing the case two years previously:

I think, well hang on a minute, they've signed me off and all done, but two years down the line who's to say [violent ex-partner] wouldn't move back in here again, they wouldn't know, it could all blow up and happen again and they wouldn't know, they'd be none the wiser. I can't understand why they signed me off, but then they don't come back after like two, three, five years. Are you with me? (Martin-Louis' mother: medium risk of harm at identification; low risk, living with birth parent and safeguarded at age three)

Other parents were also shocked that children's social care did not visit to monitor them following case closure, and at least two parents were surprised that they were not supervised more frequently whilst their cases were open. These parents argued that social workers were unaware of what might or might not be occurring within their homes.

Some of those who had experienced intense intervention, particularly over prolonged periods, felt a sense of loss when their cases were closed. They missed the regular contact they had with their social worker: 'I'm going to miss her [social worker] coming and talking. She's been right helpful' (Harry's mother).

It is important to note that parents who were unwilling or unable to change tended to resent ongoing social care involvement. It was largely those who succeeded in overcoming their problems who valued ongoing support, and the feeling that somebody was there for them if and when they needed it. Where these parents felt ready to move on, they did so with an appreciation of the support they had received. After three years of children's social care involvement, Lily's father concluded:

All that help has been nice when it's been there, but there's a time where every parent who's got social services and they've done good, need to spread out on their own, and bring up their child. (Lily's father: medium risk of harm at identification; medium risk and not safeguarded at age three)[1]

Conclusion

As the reader will recall, the parents in the study were faced with a wide range of difficulties that affected their ability to safeguard their children adequately. Nevertheless, as we have seen in this chapter, they all claimed to want the best for them and, in their view, did whatever they could to make this possible. Whether or not their efforts were successful in safeguarding the child was influenced, to at least some extent, by the support given by health visitors, drug and alcohol workers, psychologists, domestic violence workers and practitioners from a range of partner agencies, but primarily with their relationships with social workers. These relationships were intricate and influenced by various factors including, perhaps most prominently, parents' own insight into the impact of destructive behaviour patterns on their children; their previous experience of social care involvement; and their preconceptions of how social workers operate. Some parents were able to overcome negative experiences from the past and engineer a successful working relationship, while others were not.

Another barrier to successful working relationships was the perceived imbalance of power between parents and social workers, as parents were well aware that they were unequal partners. This made its presence felt most acutely in formal settings, where parents' feelings of inferiority through being less well educated and articulate were exacerbated by the intense scrutiny to which they were subjected. For some, this resulted in perceptions of disempowerment, and ultimately left them feeling disenfranchised.

However, there were also positive messages, and these indicate how relationships between parents and social care agencies can be improved. Social workers who were thought to be candid, sensitive and able to listen received positive feedback from parents. It is also important to note that parents who were able to forge positive working relationships valued ongoing support and supervision.

---

1   This child was classified as at medium, rather than low, risk of harm at age three because her mother had an ongoing mental health condition which intermittently caused concern.

Summary points for Chapter 8

- Parents were often able to relate best to professionals, such as substance misuse workers, whom they considered to be on their side.

- Parents who succeeded in making substantial changes appreciated the support they received.

- A successful working relationship with social workers was an important element in achieving change; however, there were a number of barriers to developing this.

- Some parents who had negative past experiences of children's social care involvement found it difficult to form effective working relationships for the index child, but others were able to set the past aside and successfully work with social workers this time around.

- Parents were well aware of the unequal relationship between themselves and social workers and other professionals.

- Parents felt intimidated and frightened in formal settings, particularly during court proceedings, where the weakness of their position became all too apparent.

- Parents were most positive about social workers who were frank and open with them about the chances that children would be removed, and who were able to break bad news honestly. They also valued social workers who were sensitive and able to listen.

- Some parents felt that the timing of interventions was flawed, and thought their own feelings were not recognized by social workers who undertook case planning. There were particular concerns that professionals were insensitive to their emotions around the time of the baby's birth.

- Some parents thought that interventions were too short, and would have appreciated more long-term involvement. Those who had successfully overcome major adversities were surprised when there was no attempt to check whether they had succeeded in sustaining these changes.

9

Summary, Key Findings and Their Implications for Policy and Practice

Introduction

This book explores the difficult decisions that professionals face when attempting to safeguard babies and very young children from abuse and neglect. The evidence it examines comes from a research study that traced the decisions made and their consequences for a sample of 57 infants identified as suffering or likely to suffer significant harm before their first birthdays; 43 of them were traced until they were three. The early chapters have described the children and their birth parents, and identified those risk and protective factors that made maltreatment or its recurrence more, or less, likely. Later chapters have then traced the different pathways the children followed. They have also explored how children's experiences were shaped by decisions made by those professionals who referred them to children's social care, by social workers and their managers, by child protection conferences and the courts, and by those who were asked to provide expert advice and assessment. Parents played a major part in the decision-making process, for not only were they involved in planning, but also their capacity to change – or their apparent willingness to do so – was a key determinant of the actions taken by professionals. Parents' views and understanding of professional interventions and their own actions have been explored, as have the perspectives of professionals, and the rationale for their decisions. Finally, the outcomes for both parents and children have been considered: evidence concerning which parents were able to overcome adverse behaviour patterns has been presented, as has evidence concerning the impact of continuing abuse and neglect on the subsequent development of some of the children. This last chapter draws together the key findings from the study and considers their implications for policy and practice.

Summary

As a result of difficulties in gaining access and in recruitment, the findings are based on evidence from a very small sample of children: there is some data on 57 children, but much of the study focuses on the 43 who were followed from birth until their third birthdays. Moreover, the sample is skewed towards infants who were particularly likely to suffer significant harm. Both the small size of the sample and the bias indicate that findings should be treated as exploratory, and they should be tested out with a much larger group of children in similar circumstances before they can be regarded as definitive.

The babies were suffering, or likely to suffer, significant harm resulting from their parents' multiple problems. These included constellations of risk factors such as mental health problems, drug and alcohol misuse, intimate partner violence and experience of childhood abuse. Known protective factors such as the presence of a supportive partner or extended family were often absent. The majority of infants came from families who were already known to children's social care through their involvement with older siblings. At least 20 mothers and an unknown number of fathers had already been separated from at least one, and usually more than one, older child before the birth of the baby. Such separations were often very recent and a continuing source of grief. Many of the mothers were contesting care or adoption proceedings for older children while they were pregnant with the index child.

At the start of the study, the babies were allocated to one of four groups, classified according to evidence of parental risk and protective factors, and their apparent capacity to change; 19 infants were at severe or high risk of suffering harm and 24 at medium or low risk. Only those parents with babies in the low or medium risk of harm groups had shown some capacity to change.

By the time they were three, 28 children were living with a birth parent and 15 were permanently placed away from home. However, not all were adequately safeguarded. Sixteen children were now living with birth parents who had succeeded in overcoming their problems, who had protective factors in place and who had shown the capacity to sustain the necessary changes; all these were now classified as at low risk of harm. Fifteen children were now separated; however, at least two were in unsatisfactory placements, some other placements were showing signs of strain and two were in temporary care pending permanent placements. A further 12 children were living with birth parents at the age of three, but there had been little evidence of positive change and these children were now at medium, high or severe risk of being harmed. The level of risk had increased over the study period for some children in this latter group.

The most common form of maltreatment was neglect, although this was often compounded with witnessing intimate partner violence. However, whilst the risk of maltreatment was realized in many cases, and 12 (28%) of these very young children continued to experience abuse or neglect or were only sporadically safeguarded throughout the study period, there was no evidence that 19 (44%) of them had ever been maltreated by the time they were three.

At the start of the study parents' problems had already impacted on some children. Alcohol and substance misuse during pregnancy had meant that almost a third of the infants were at risk of foetal alcohol spectrum disorders and/or neonatal abstinence syndrome (NAS), although there is little recorded evidence of them showing any symptoms.

However, by their third birthdays over half the children who did not have a recognized medical condition were showing signs of substantial behavioural difficulties and/or developmental delay (16/28: 57%): aggression and speech problems were prominent. At least four of these infants were regarded as so aggressive as to be a danger to other children – Ranjit required one-to-one care at nursery, Liam had attacked the family dog, Dabir had tried to harm his kin carer's newborn grandchild and Bella was not taken to the park for fear that she would hurt another child. Developmental and behavioural difficulties were more evident amongst children who had experienced some form of maltreatment, often whilst professionals waited fruitlessly for parents to change. These were children who, at the end of the study, either remained living at home amidst ongoing concerns, or were permanently separated from their parents after experiencing lengthy episodes of maltreatment and/or instability. Some of these infants had experienced the double jeopardy of late separation from abusive birth families followed by the disruption of a close attachment with an interim carer when they entered an adoptive placement. The aggression, frustration and delayed speech displayed by some children as they reached their third birthdays were likely to cause specific and possibly long-standing problems as they entered school. This issue is currently being explored in a subsequent study (see Ward, Brown and Maskell-Graham forthcoming).

Key findings with implications for policy

A number of findings from this study have obvious implications for the development of policy and practice. Before considering those areas which need further development, it is important to note that in many cases decision-making was of high quality, showed evidence of extreme care and was based on hard evidence. For example, 11 of the 12 infants classified independently by the research team as at severe risk of harm at identification had been permanently separated by the age of three; all but one of those children who had originally been classified as at medium or low risk of harm were still living with a birth parent at the end of the study. The study provides no evidence to support criticisms that decisions made by professionals are arbitrary or taken without careful thought.

However, the study does raise a number of issues that need to be addressed or further explored. These are outlined below.

Inter-agency issues

The study raises a number of questions about inter-agency working. There was evidence of considerable tension between professionals in adult and children's services. Those whose role was to support adults tended to give insufficient attention to the potential impact of problems such as parental substance misuse on children's current welfare and long-term life chances. Some parents received mixed messages, on the one hand being told by substance misuse workers or mental health professionals that they were making good progress, while at the same time social workers, concerned at continuing neglect or abuse, were preparing to remove children. Tensions between the services resulted in poor communication and sometimes refusal to share information that was necessary to make decisions concerning children's safety. Social workers were also concerned that some other professionals still refused to share responsibility for safeguarding children and left it to them to confront parents with the implications of adverse behaviour patterns. We know that there have been improvements in inter-agency collaboration (Laming 2009). However, this is clearly an area that needs continuing development.

Social work education

The findings reveal a number of gaps in social work knowledge and understanding. Although many of the infants were exposed to alcohol or substance misuse and intimate partner violence *in utero*, and to neglect and maltreatment in their first few months of life, core assessments gave only limited attention to their developmental needs or to the potential consequences of adverse early experiences for their long-term life chances.

Interviews with social workers revealed that child development had only been a small part of pre-qualifying training, often quickly forgotten. Lack of understanding of infant attachments and their implications or insufficient knowledge about the impact of abuse or neglect on children's long-term development was evident in the case files and interviews, and clearly needs to be addressed through qualifying training and continuing professional development.

Delay

Research on the development of the brain, the regulation of emotions and emerging attachment behaviour in early childhood provides substantial evidence of a need for urgency, both in removing children from abusive and neglectful family situations and in placing them permanently. However, the findings show little understanding of the need to avoid delay. Very few infants were swiftly removed from abusive parents, and less than half of those separated were permanently placed by their first birthdays. There were no formal paediatric assessments to find out whether children's development was being compromised by their experiences. All professionals involved in decision-making for these very young and vulnerable children need to be more fully aware of the importance of taking swift and decisive action so as not to jeopardize their life chances.

The main causes of delay were the almost universal expectation that children would be able to remain with their birth parents; the extensive use of parenting assessments; and the fallibility of expert opinions.

Focus on birth parents to the exclusion of the child

Almost all professional decision-makers did everything they could to keep families together and to ensure that parents were fairly treated and given every opportunity to prove they could look after a child. Decisions were informed by concepts of rights and empowerment as well as by research evidence. Excessive attention to the need to be fair could mean that important information concerning parents' previous histories might not be taken into account in making decisions about their capacity to look after a new baby. Occasionally social workers were placed in the confusing position of arranging for the adoption of one child at the same time as they were supporting the mother in caring for a new baby. In the drive to ensure that parents' rights were properly respected, the baby's needs could be overlooked both by children's social care and the courts. This was particularly true for the many infants who suffered long-term, chronic neglect while professionals waited for parents to overcome their difficulties and develop the capacity to meet a child's needs. A number of these were younger siblings of children who had already been removed. Acknowledging that some parents may not be able to overcome their difficulties sufficiently within a child's timeframe goes against the grain for all involved: there needs to be more open discussion concerning how this issue should be confronted.

The extensive use made of parenting assessments was a major cause of delay. These were undertaken repeatedly for some parents, in an effort to provide evidence of progress, sometimes when there had been only a very short space of time since the previous assessment. Some parents had their parenting capacity assessed for the index child within months of having an older child placed for adoption; they might also be assessed regardless of the evidence of severe and enduring risk factors.

The majority of parenting assessments were undertaken by specialists, and their opinions were widely respected; the recommendations were followed in all specialist assessments for which data were available. Two thirds of these assessments recommended that the infant should remain with birth parents; but over half of these recommendations proved untenable, in that eventually these children had to be removed. The older the children were, the less the chance of a successful parenting assessment, but these continued to be a major source of delayed decision-making. The use made of such assessments and their value should be further explored and weighed against the delays they cause.

Kinship placements

Where separation became inevitable, extensive efforts were made to place the babies within the extended family. Although placing children with relatives and friends can be very beneficial, research evidence concerning the value of this type of placement when compared with those provided by unrelated carers is inconclusive. Ours was a particularly high risk sample, and many of the infant's relatives had extensive difficulties themselves. As with birth parents, professionals made extensive efforts to assess relatives, sometimes in the face of strong contra-indications of their ability to care for a child. This was a further cause of delay. Some children were placed with relatives who had extensive histories of offending, or whose own children had had very poor outcomes. Others were placed with distant relatives who were virtually unknown to themselves or their parents. Kinship carers often received minimal support, particularly after special guardianship had been awarded. A number of these placements were nearing breakdown by the end of the study. These findings raise questions concerning the limitations of kinship care and the extent of both financial and emotional support needed to ensure the stability of these placements.

Parents who changed sufficiently to care for the child

Fourteen parents (or sets of parents) succeeded in making and sustaining substantial changes that enabled them to safeguard their children adequately, at least until they were three. The findings demonstrate a number of factors that appeared to distinguish those parents who successfully changed from those who did not. Parents who overcame their difficulties were less likely to have experienced abuse (particularly sexual abuse) in their own childhoods, to be more likely to have been subject to intimate partner violence or to have formed a relationship with an adult who posed a danger to children – but to have been able to initiate an end to such relationships. Further defining factors were their ability to come to terms with the removal of older children and acknowledge that their behaviour may have played a part in such decisions and their ability not so much to engage with services as to make use of the support they offered in overcoming their problems. A number of these parents had also had a defining moment when they realized that they would need to take substantial action if they were to meet the new baby's needs.

Findings concerning the timing of parental change are of particular importance. First, it was extremely rare for parents who had shown no capacity for change at the beginning of the study to have succeeded in overcoming their difficulties by the time the index child was three. Most parents had already begun the process of change before the birth of the baby – many of them before conception. All but one of those parents who succeeded in overcoming their difficulties did so before the baby was six months old; those who overcame substance misuse did so before (or in one case as soon as) the baby was born. The one parent who did not fit this timeframe was an exceptional case, where the risk of harm posed by a partner had taken several years to emerge. A major difficulty for practitioners was that many other parents made a small amount of progress; however, unless major change had occurred by the time the baby was six months old, this proved unsustainable despite the extensive provision of services.

Long-term monitoring

The findings raise questions about whether, and for how long, parents who have successfully changed should continue to be monitored. If parents had made significant improvements their cases were often quickly closed. Some parents were surprised that they were not followed for longer, arguing that it was in the children's interests for them to be checked up on at routine intervals, in order to ensure that progress was sustained. Many of them had overcome extensive difficulties and were, for the first time, looking after a child after others had been permanently removed. Some consideration needs to be given to the extent to which their progress should be monitored and continuing support offered.

Many parents whose cases were closed had been simply left with a contact number and told to telephone children's social care if they ran into further difficulties. This was an unrealistic expectation: the removal of the index child had often been a very real possibility at some stage, and no one was going to risk it happening by admitting to social workers that they were running into difficulties. Some parents did, however, seek help from health visitors in dealing with children's behavioural problems. Exploring how health visitors might be better integrated into the monitoring of such cases might be advisable.

Parental responsibility and its limits

A number of findings indicate some ambivalence concerning the extent to which very vulnerable parents should be dependent on children's social care. The professionals' objective appeared to be to ensure that they took greater responsibility for their children. Wherever possible the least intrusive intervention was offered, and for the minimum duration necessary. Cases were closed at the earliest opportunity. However, some parents had entrenched difficulties, and efforts to encourage them to take more responsibility could rebound on the child, an example being the withdrawal of a nursery place if a parent did not pay. In some cases it may be necessary to accept that, if children are to be adequately safeguarded while remaining with birth parents, long-term, extensive support may be required.

However, such support needs to be properly focused, with clear aims and objectives, and consequences if it is not appropriately used. Written contracts appeared to be a useful means of clarifying the expectations both of social workers and birth parents, and can empower parents through including them in decision-making. They could be developed further, although at present they are often broken with no repercussions, and their value is thereby diminished.

Violent men

The study raises some questions concerning the effectiveness of policy and practice towards families where violence is an issue. Many perpetrators of intimate partner violence apparently saw little need to change their behaviour, but there appeared to be very little support available for those who did (see also Barlow *et al.* 2008). Policies to offer few services except for support to the victim in excluding the abuser may simply result in perpetrators moving on to abuse another family.

Parents' views

The study collected a wealth of data concerning birth parents' perspectives: much of what they say corroborates the findings of other studies (see for instance Neil *et al.* 2010), and demonstrates a genuine need for agencies to listen to the views of service users. Birth parents' relationships with social workers were often influenced by past experience; perceived injustices had long-term consequences. The birth of a child was a time of heightened emotion: practitioners who failed to appreciate the need for additional sensitivity during this period were particularly resented. However, some social workers were highly valued, particularly by those parents who succeeded in overcoming their difficulties. As well as sensitivity and the ability to listen, birth parents strongly appreciated a 'straight talking' social worker who was upfront and honest about the threat that their children would be removed. Practitioners who found it difficult to break bad news or who encouraged parents to be over-optimistic about their progress were not so highly valued.

Thresholds of significant harm

As many other studies have found, neglect was particularly difficult to identify; practitioners sometimes became inured to the evidence, and too accepting of low standards of parenting (see for instance Farmer and Lutman forthcoming).

Within this context, the study raises considerable questions concerning the threshold used by children's social care and the courts to determine significant harm, particularly where neglect and/or emotional abuse are the key issues. None of the infants died, though two or three were left in extremely dangerous situations. However, the welfare of several was seriously compromised, quite probably on a long-term basis. Some of these very young children lived with parents who forgot to feed them, or who left them alone over prolonged periods: Liam was left to forage for food in the waste bin; Ava's siblings were allowed to taste illicit drugs from a spoon. If the welfare of the child is indeed the paramount consideration, then we need to ask much more stringent questions concerning what constitutes acceptable – and unacceptable – levels of parenting in a civilized society.

Conclusion: recommendations

The evidence from this study, discussed above, suggests that the following recommendations should be considered.

Recommendations for policy

Findings concerning those factors that may distinguish between parents who are able to change from those who are not, together with the evidence of the timescales for change are particularly valuable. We recommend that they are first tested out with a larger database and then that those which prove to be robust are used to develop guidelines for both the courts and children's social care concerning which children can be adequately safeguarded with birth families and which are more likely to require permanent separation.

We recommend that the use of expert assessments of parenting capacity be evaluated and guidelines developed concerning appropriate timing and purpose. Delays are often incurred by assessing carers who are not able to provide a suitable home: guidelines concerning those factors which render such carers immediately ineligible (e.g. a recent conviction for a violent offence; substance misuse; very poor outcomes for their own children) should be established.

Delays risk disadvantaging young children twice over, first by leaving them too long in abusive situations, and second by separating them from interim carers to whom they have become attached. We would recommend that existing guidelines for both children's services and the courts be revisited and the extent to which they take account of this timeframe be evaluated.

Recommendations for service development
SPECIALIST INTERVENTIONS
While there is an obvious need to develop effective interventions to help improve parenting capacity, much more attention needs to be given to addressing the needs of children. Particular attention should be given to developing, implementing and evaluating programmes designed to enrich the experiences of neglected children and to address issues such as delayed speech and language development and aggressive behaviour that are likely to impact on the stability of placements and jeopardize children's chances of making progress at school. Evidence-based programmes that might address the needs of these very vulnerable children and their birth parents, such as Family Nurse Partnerships, Parents Under Pressure and interaction guidance, are now being introduced in the UK (see Davies and Ward 2011), though none were offered to the families in this study. They should be made more widely available.

At present there is only limited evidence of how intimate partner violence might be prevented, either in terms of supporting the victims or in enabling perpetrators to overcome their adverse behaviour patterns (see Barlow *et al.* 2008). Effective programmes need to be designed, evaluated and made more widely available. These should both include preventive programmes in schools aimed at encouraging young people to understand the causes of intimate partner violence, and specialist programmes designed for perpetrators as well as for victims.

HEALTH VISITORS
We recommend that consideration be given to the role of health visitors in monitoring and offering support to families who are thought to have overcome adverse behaviour patterns that had previously jeopardized their children's safety and welfare.

Recommendations for education and training
Attachment, child development and the impact of maltreatment and neglect on children's subsequent life chances should be a core module of education and training for all those who intend to work with children in need and their families. This should be a requirement at undergraduate as well as at post-qualifying level. Knowledge and understanding are continually advancing

in this field. This subject should also be a core element of continuing professional development.

Training on the impact of delay on infants' subsequent life chances and the need for urgency in such cases should also be a core component of education and continuing professional development for all those likely to be involved in decision-making in this area. As well as practitioners in children's social care, this should also include those working in adult social care, health, education and the family justice system.

Recommendations for practice

Utilizing a simple methodology based on solid research evidence concerning risk and protective factors in families where there are concerns about abuse and neglect has proved to be a useful means of identifying which children are at greatest risk of suffering future harm, and could provide a valuable practice tool for social workers.

Consideration should be given as to why there are so few repercussions when written agreements between children's social care and its service users are broken. Their potential value as a formal means of clarifying expectations should be further developed but within the context of a contract that has more than nominal status.

Procedures should be put in place to ensure that the courts and those who undertake specialist assessments are informed of the long-term outcomes of their decisions and recommendations in terms of children's welfare.

Discussions need to be held between the judiciary, directors of children's services and local authority solicitors concerning acceptable levels of parenting and how the definition of significant harm is operationalized, particularly in terms of the likely consequences for children's long-term wellbeing.

Our final recommendation concerns the parents and children in this study. The findings are greatly enriched by the extensive interviews with birth parents. Without their views there would have been far less understanding of those factors that might or might not contribute to positive change and improved safeguarding of children. Ascertaining the views of users is now a fundamental principle in the development of policy and practice. We would recommend that consideration be given as to how such consultation can be further developed and utilized.

Appendix 1

Aims, Methodology and Issues Concerning Recruitment and Retention of the Sample

Aims and objectives

The aim of this study was to trace the decision-making process influencing the life pathways of a sample of very young children who were identified as being at high risk of significant harm before their first birthdays in order to improve the understanding of how such decisions are reached and their consequences.

The specific objectives were:

1. to explore how, and at what point, the decision between providing family support services or placements is made; to explore the extent to which certain factors such as assessments of parents' capacity to address difficulties in family functioning, and the likely availability of support services, influence such decisions

2. to examine what role various participants have in the decision-making process, and how differences in professional opinion are reconciled; to explore whose views have the greatest influence

3. to explore how far birth parents feel involved in the decision-making process; to examine how far certain interventions support or inhibit partnership working

4. to assess the extent to which certain decisions influence children's life pathways and promote or inhibit opportunities for satisfactory outcomes

5. to discover whether children with similar needs become looked after in some authorities but remain at home with family support services in others, and to identify the reasons for these variations.

Study design

In order to answer these questions a prospective longitudinal study was designed. The plan was to recruit a sample of very young children who had been identified as suffering, or likely to suffer, significant harm before their first birthdays, and to trace the decisions made about their care and the impact these had on their subsequent experiences and life chances from birth until at least their second birthday. Data would be collected from information held on children's social care case files and records held by health visitors; case-specific interviews would be held with birth parents, foster carers and adoptive parents where appropriate, social workers, social work team leaders, health visitors and children's guardians; towards the end of the study more general interviews would also be held with senior managers, local authority solicitors, judges and magistrates in order to gather information that would provide a context to facilitate understanding of the infants' experience.

In the event, the research team experienced exceptional difficulties in recruiting the sample and in accessing case file data and arranging interviews with some professionals. As a result a number of modifications had to be made to the original plan.

Ethical approval and informed consent

The study focused on an exceptionally vulnerable, hard-to-reach population. Particular care had to be taken to ensure that the research processes had received appropriate ethical approval, that informed consent was given to all interviews and that the limits of confidentiality were understood by all participants. Ethical approval was sought from (and given by) the following: Loughborough University Ethics Committee; research governance liaison officers in all participating local authorities; the Ministry of Justice; the Central Office for Research Ethics Committees (COREC); and the Children and Family Court Advisory and Support Service (CAFCASS). Throughout the study careful attention was given to following ethical requirements: consent forms gave parents the choice of agreeing or refusing access separately to different data sources including children's case files; no interviews were conducted without informed consent; and participants were made aware of: their right to withdraw at any time, arrangements to ensure that what they said would remain confidential, and the limitations of confidentiality.

Recruitment process

Informed consent from birth parents was necessary before any child could be recruited to the sample and case files scrutinized or interviews arranged. Administrators in the participating authorities posted promotional materials and consent forms to all parents who met the criteria for selection. Leaflets and posters to publicize the study were also circulated to family centres, GPs and baby clinics. A CD audio version of the leaflet was also made available for those with lower levels of literacy. Following each interview, parents and carers were given a £20 gift voucher for a shop of their choice, as both an incentive to participate and to thank them for their time.

Selection of local authorities and sample criteria

Ten local authorities participated in the study. Authorities were selected on the basis that they undertook a relatively high proportion of core assessments, so as to maximize the likelihood that they would have sufficient numbers of very young children suffering, or likely to suffer, significant harm to meet the sample quota. National returns on numbers of core assessments undertaken within the preceding year and ages of children looked after or placed on the child protection register (the subject of a child protection plan) were used to inform the initial selection of authorities. The children's statistical returns (Department for Education and Skills 2005, Department of Health 2005a) were also used to identify authorities showing variations in their relative spend on care/accommodation and family support services, in the proportion of their looked after population who were aged under one at the start of a care episode, and in their rates of adoption. These criteria were chosen to facilitate exploration of different practices within and between authorities and analysis of their impact upon decision-making and outcomes.

Sample recruitment

Criteria for selection were that, before their first birthday, the infant had been the subject of a core assessment or section 47 enquiry.

The statistical data demonstrated that all the authorities could each identify at least 50 children who met these criteria. However, despite heavy investment in the recruitment process and the design of accessible materials, only around 4 per cent of families meeting the sample criteria returned a reply slip indicating a willingness to find out more about the research. The rate of uptake was similar in all the authorities.

Overall, 84 families responded to the request to participate in the study, and of these, 57 (68%) took part in at least the first stage. Of those that did not take part, three declined to participate following telephone contact from the research team and three did not meet the sample criteria. The remaining 21 families could not be contacted as the details they provided were incomplete or had changed: for example, digits were missing from telephone numbers, house numbers were not included in addresses, and some respondents had given temporary addresses such as hostels and friends' or partners' homes. Although attempts to locate families by using the Electoral Register were made, many of them were not registered. The research team did not have permission to contact social workers until parents had given informed consent following the initial contact, with the result that more accurate addresses and telephone numbers could not be accessed from this source at this stage.

Our experience of working with the families who did participate over the course of the study show that they frequently changed mobile telephone numbers, rarely had landline numbers, and often moved in and out of temporary accommodation. Where possible we collected details of a relative or close friend who could be contacted should their own details change, and this was of particular importance later in the study when cases were more likely to be closed to children's social care. However, this only proved successful in maintaining contact with a small number of families, as many of the parents did not have a trusted relative or close friend with whom they stayed in contact. Some parents 'dipped' in and out of taking part in this study over the three years. They were more likely to take part when events in their own lives were settled than when they were volatile. For example, one mother was available to be interviewed when her violent partner had moved out or was in prison, but unsurprisingly unavailable when he was living with her. Another mother, who withdrew from the study following a miscarriage, contacted the research team

Table A1.1 Study sample by geographical location and local authority type (full sample: n=57)

Local authority	Authority type	Number of cases in the sample
1	Metropolitan	3
2	Unitary	3
3	Shire	6
4	Shire	8
5	Metropolitan	11
6	Shire	2
7	Metropolitan	11
8	Shire	4
9	Unitary	6
10	Unitary	3
	Total cases	**57**

again two years later and was reintroduced. The longitudinal design of this study allowed for considerable flexibility, but it was evident that a great degree of understanding and respect is also required when conducting research with such a high risk population.

Table A1.1 provides details of the type of authorities represented and the number of children each contributed to the sample. The authorities covered a wide geographical spread that included five of the nine English geographical regions. Children were not recruited from Inner and Outer London boroughs as these were considered to have insufficient numbers to easily meet the sample quota.

Methods

Children's social care case file and interview data on life experiences, reasons for referral and evidence of need were collected at the point the babies were recruited to the sample. Case file information was traced back to the infant's birth (or pre-birth where applicable). Semi-structured interviews were held with social workers, team managers, birth parents, and carers if the babies were accommodated away from their birth parents, as near as possible to the point of identification. The Home Observation for the Measurement of the Environment for Infants and Toddlers (IT-HOME Inventory) was used in interviews with carers (including birth parents) to give an indication of areas of strength and/or weakness in the child's environment (Cox and Walker 2001). The method employs direct observation in the home alongside an interview with the main caregiver (Caldwell and Bradley 2003). However, these scores proved to be misleading and to contradict the evidence from other data sources (see Appendix 2); consequently they were not included in the analysis.

Follow-up quantitative and qualitative data were collected as near as possible to the children's first, second and third birthdays, to monitor changes in needs, circumstances, care plans, domiciles and placements. Case file data were complemented with extensive interviews with birth parents and with key professionals involved in the decision-making process. Where applicable, foster carers and adoptive carers were also interviewed and additional interviews were also completed with children's guardians in the final year of data collection, when most of the sample were aged three. During this period non-case-specific interviews were also held with senior managers and solicitors in local authorities, judges and magistrates. It proved impossible to access health visitors on a one-to-one basis, and their proposed interviews were replaced with six focus groups.

Altogether 49 children's social care case files were scrutinized and interviews held with birth parents for 56 cases and carers for 12 cases. Interviews were held with social workers in 44 cases and with team leaders in

41 cases. More than one interview with social workers occurred in 25 cases and with team leaders in 21 cases. In total 73 interviews with social workers and 61 interviews with team leaders were carried out over the duration of the study. In addition, nine children's guardians were interviewed. On a non-case-specific level, interviews were also held with ten senior managers, four judges, six magistrates and ten local authority solicitors.

Quantitative data were analysed in SPSS.15. The software package NVivo8 was used to manage the qualitative data. Interview data were analysed thematically both by case and by professional group. Using NVivo8 for the analysis of interview data allowed for transparency between the two members of the research team who coded the data. In order to ensure inter-rater reliability these two researchers worked independently and then reviewed each other's codings. They also met daily to discuss discrepancies or differing perspectives so that these could be resolved throughout the process of analysis.

Final sample

The final sample comprised 57 babies, the majority of whom were recruited between October 2006 and October 2007. All had undergone a core assessment or section 47 enquiry before their first birthday; many of the assessments were undertaken before they were born. Although funding was made available to trace the infants until they were two, access difficulties were such that the majority became three before data collection was complete. In order to retain such a hard-to-reach sample for possible future research, wherever possible case file data were traced and birth parents interviewed until the child was three.

As was inevitable with a sample of this nature there was some attrition: six parents withdrew after initial interviews and refused access to their children's case files. Some case file data were collected for 49 children; although parental consent to view case files was granted for two other children, several attempts over the course of the study to gain access proved unsuccessful. Two more parents actively withdrew following the initial stages of data collection, one family moved out of the study area, and three children were not yet three at the time of writing. The sample therefore includes **43** children who were followed from birth to age three; **eight** whose parents gave consent to view files and interview professionals but could not be followed for the full three years; and **six** children whose parents withdrew after the first interview.

The study was dependent to a large extent on the active participation of birth parents and other primary carers, 33 of whom continued to be interviewed at regular intervals until their child was three. Table A1.2 shows the size of the sample following attrition at each stage of the study. It will be seen that by the time of the children's second birthdays a relatively stable group had been established.

Table A1.2 Attrition of primary carers (full sample: n=57)

Time point	Number of children	Percentage*
At identification (up to age 1 year)	57	100
At second birthday	35	61
At third birthday	33	58

* Percentages are rounded figures.

Limitations

The sample provided a wealth of data, much of which is valuable in answering the research questions. However, our original plans to recruit a large sample of at least a hundred children did not come to fruition, with the result that while there are ample qualitative data, the quantitative database is relatively limited. For example, the current numbers are too small in most instances for formal probability tests to be viable or appropriate where comparisons are made; in particular it has not been possible to compare practice between the authorities involved. However, the extensive qualitative database has enabled us to identify indicators whose validity should be tested out at a later stage with a more extensive quantitative dataset. We know that only about 4 per cent of children who met the eligibility criteria were included in the current sample; at a later stage it would be valuable to work with a number of local authorities to explore how far the findings from this study can be replicated in a wider population of children with similar profiles.

There are numerous reasons why, in spite of intensive efforts from the research team and substantial support from senior managers in the local authorities, such a small sample of children could be identified. Obviously one factor was the focus on an exceptionally hard-to-reach group of parents, many of whom laboured under multiple adversities which made their participation at best precarious. It is not surprising that only a small proportion responded to the invitation to participate, and a few were lost along the way.

However, the research process also raised other issues which materially affected the size of the sample and the data that could be accessed. Recruitment of local authorities began at about the time the *Research Governance Framework for Health and Social Care* (Department of Health 2005b) was first implemented. Some of the difficulties encountered by the research team undoubtedly reflected the teething problems of introducing new procedures (see Boddy and Oliver 2010; Munro 2008) and this needs to be taken into account in assessing our experiences.

The authorities were justifiably concerned to protect the interests of both parents and children in this study – and families where very young children are considered to be suffering, or likely to suffer, significant harm are a particularly vulnerable group. All participating authorities decided that, in an area of this sensitivity, the research team could only approach parents who had actively opted in to the study. We know that opt-in arrangements produce much lower response rates than opt-out procedures – although it is rare for research participants to object to the latter (see Munro, Holmes and Ward 2005). Many of this very vulnerable group would not have been sufficiently proactive or organized to respond to the invitation and were consequently lost to the study – one reason for the small sample size. Moreover, even when parents had formally given written consent for the research team to collect information from case files, access was frequently queried by local authority staff. Protracted negotiations over access to documents lasted for over two years in some cases; some case files had been archived by the time the research team were able to look at them – and the staff who held the archive sometimes required a new set of permissions before data collection could proceed. Access to information became markedly more difficult following the intense media coverage that surrounded the death of Peter Connelly. Although the necessary ethical approvals and consent from birth parents were obtained, it proved impossible to arrange interviews with health visitors or access to their case files – all planned for this period – and these had to be abandoned. Focus group discussions with health visitors provided a substitute source of information.

Sample bias

All the babies fitted the study criteria, and were therefore suffering, or likely to suffer, significant harm, a point later confirmed by the data. Cleaver and Walker with Meadows (2004) audited 2248 referrals to children's social care and found that 38.5 per cent (866) progressed to an initial assessment and 3 per cent (68) to a core assessment. The relatively low proportion of cases in which a core assessment is undertaken is likely to indicate a high level of need. Nevertheless, the sample is only comprised of infants fitting the criterion *whose parents gave their informed consent* to participation. Only certain parents will have volunteered to take part – the interview data suggests that these were most likely to be parents with very positive or very negative perceptions of children's social care, and that those whose experience was less polarized were less likely to come forward.

In recognition of the potential for sample bias, anonymous summary data from management information systems were collected from local authorities to allow for some assessment of how far the sample cases reflected the profile of the wider population who met the criteria, but whose parents did not participate. Data were received from four local authorities, providing summary information on 639 children. Table A1.3 shows the similarities and differences between the sample children and this wider population.

Table A1.3 Similarities and differences between sample and wider population of children who met eligibility criteria in four local authorities (full sample: n=57)

	Eligible population			Sample group	
	Frequency	%*	Range	Frequency	%*
Male	342	54	51–60	36	63
White British	429	67	61–89	35	69
Referred pre-birth	152[1]	43	19–50	32	65
CPR Neglect[2]	59[3]	50	36–75	13	62
CA NFA[4]	194	54	30–57	3	6
CA S17 services[5]	229	46	43–70	32	71
Looked after before first birthday	132[6]	22	17–26	25	51
Looked after S20	396[7]	57	55–59	6	46
Looked after legal action to protect child	30	43	41–45	7	54

* Percentages are rounded figures.

1 Data from three authorities.
2 Child Protection Register under category of neglect.
3 Data from three authorities.
4 No further action following core assessment.
5 Services under the Children Act 1989, s.17, following core assessment.
6 Data from three authorities.
7 Data from two authorities.

Comparing the study sample with the eligible population

The eligible population from the four local authorities was used to calculate expected values for the variables shown in Table A1.3 for the sample of infants in the study. Pearson's Chi Square was used to test for differences between observed and expected values and these are shown in Table A1.4. The study sample had significantly more infants than expected who were referred before birth (p<0.01), who received section 17 services after core assessment (p<0.05) and who became looked after before their first birthday (p<0.001); there were also significantly fewer infants who received no further action following core assessment (CA NFA) (p<0.001).

Table A1.4 A comparison of the sample and eligible population using Pearson's Chi Square (full sample: n=57)

Sample attributes	Pearson's Chi Square	Significance
Male/Female	2.128	ns
White British/Other ethnicity	0.072	ns
Referred pre-birth/Referred after birth	8.722	p<0.01
CPR Neglect[1]/Other	1.276	ns
CA NFA[2]/Other outcome	27.821	p<0.001
CA S17 services[3]/Other outcome	5.627	p<0.05
Looked after before first birthday/Not looked after before first birthday	21.418	p<0.001
Looked after S20/Looked after legal action to protect child	0.569	ns

1 Child Protection Register under category of neglect.
2 No further action following core assessment.
3 Services under the Children Act 1989, s.17, following core assessment.

Conclusion

There were many difficulties in undertaking this study. Nevertheless, a sample of 57 infants was obtained, 43 of whom were traced from birth or pre-birth to age three. These babies were statistically more likely to be at higher risk of significant harm than the population eligible for selection. It seems likely that those birth parents who chose to take part either had very positive stories to tell and were proud of them, or were resentful of children's social care involvement with their family and wanted to express their anger and frustration to a listening ear.

Appendix 2

Issues Concerning the Scores from the IT-HOME Inventory

Overall, at least one IT-HOME Inventory was completed with the parents/carers of 36 (36/57: 63%) children, and more than one with 24 of them. All the researchers undertook a specific half-day training course before completing the IT-HOME. For the first three months of data collection assessments were also undertaken jointly, by two researchers working independently and then comparing scores. Following the induction period, the majority of IT-HOME assessments were completed by one researcher, although internal checks continued to show strong inter-rater reliability on the few occasions that other researchers were used. However, analysis of these assessments raised a number of issues which prevented us from including the findings in this report.

The total IT-HOME score is comprised of separate scores from the following subscales: responsivity, acceptance, organization, learning materials, involvement and variety. The scoring methodology offers two ways of identifying concerns: through analysis of the total score, and scores of individual subscales. If a total score is more than five points below the median then the home environment 'should be considered suspect'. Similarly, if a score in any subscale is two or three points below the median, 'a flag' is raised highlighting a possible cause for concern (Caldwell and Bradley 2003). This could indicate an environment that may pose a risk to some aspect of the child's development.

The overall IT-HOME scores for the sample are counter-intuitive. Of the 27 infants who were living with their parent/s when the IT-HOME Inventory was completed, only ten were scored at two points below the median within the subscales and only one was given a total score of more than five below the median. When the initial IT-HOME was completed, the majority of the children who were living with their parents were experiencing risk factors known to be associated with maltreatment (see Jones *et al.* 2006), such as exposure to extensive substance misuse in their household or witnessing intimate partner violence, and all but one was thought to be suffering or likely to suffer significant harm. The parents of seven of these infants showed no evidence of the capacity to overcome these adversities during the three years of the study, yet the IT-HOME scores only indicated concerns for four of these parents, and only on the subscales of involvement, variety and organization.

For example, the IT-HOME scores did not highlight any concerns in the case of Madeleine. Her parents both had a history of substance misuse, and her father had previously had two children placed for adoption on grounds of neglect. There were concerns about his anger issues, and intimate partner violence was considered to be a risk factor. At referral there were also concerns about the family's poor housing conditions and the harassment to which they were subject from neighbours. Although the parents were considered to be able to cope and keep their substance misuse under control for much of the time, the situation deteriorated when they were under stress. By the time Madeleine was three another baby had been born and the substance misuse was getting out of hand. There were concerns about there being 'more people in the house than the parents were admitting to' and the mother was reportedly prostituting herself to pay for drugs.

Within the subscales IT-HOME did highlight weaknesses in the home environment for ten children. All of these children had parents who were displaying risk factors that had not been addressed and four were showing no capacity to overcome them. The specific areas where the subscales indicated weaknesses included: variety (two children); involvement (three children); learning materials (one child); responsivity (two children); and combinations of learning materials, organization and involvement (two children). However, the subscales did not show weaknesses in the home environment in more than three subscales for any child, and for the majority (8/10) they only identified one area where there might be concerns. Moreover, the IT-HOME scores did not draw attention to weaknesses in the area of acceptance for any child, and raised concerns in the area of organization for only one child, in what, on other criteria, were often very disorganized and rejecting households.

An example is that of Erin. The main concern for this child was the neglect and emotional abuse she suffered as a result of her mother's inability to prioritize her needs. Her mother invited drug users into their home and had numerous late night parties where the police were called. Erin was also left in the care of drug users. However, the IT-HOME only highlighted areas of weakness to Erin's environment within the subscale of variety. When Erin was two, she was permanently removed from her mother's care due to the neglect and emotional abuse she had experienced.

Based on the IT-HOME scores alone, it could be argued that a nurturing home environment was provided for most infants in this study. However, evidence regarding risk factors, the occurrence of maltreatment and the prevalence of emotional and behavioural difficulties as the babies grew older suggests otherwise. While subscale scores highlight some areas of weakness in the environment of a minority of children, the total IT-HOME scores are above the threshold for concern in all but one case. The research team therefore concluded that for some reason the IT-HOME scores in this study were misleading and they were not utilized in the analysis. Further analysis will seek to explore why these scores were so inconsistent with other data, and whether these findings have implications for practice (see Brown and Ward forthcoming (a)).

References

Adams, R., Dominelli, L. and Payne, M. (2009) *Critical Practice in Social Work*. London: Palgrave Macmillan.

Advisory Council on the Misuse of Drugs (2003) *Hidden Harm: Responding to the Needs of Problem Drug Users*. Edinburgh: Scottish Executive.

Alderson, A., Leapman, B. and Harper, T. (2008) 'System taking hundreds of babies for adoption.' *Daily Telegraph*, 19 April.

Aldgate, J. (2006) 'Children, Development and Ecology.' In J. Aldgate, D. Jones, W. Rose and C. Jeffery (eds) *The Developing World of the Child*. London: Jessica Kingsley Publishers.

Aldgate, J. and Bradley, M. (1999) *Supporting Families Through Short-Term Fostering (Studies in Evaluating the Children Act 1989)*. London: The Stationery Office.

Allen, G. (2011) *Early Intervention: The Next Steps. An Independent Report*. London: The Cabinet Office.

Appleton, J.V. (1996) 'Working with vulnerable families: A health visiting perspective.' *Journal of Advanced Nursing 23*, 5, 912–918.

Barlow, J., Jarrett, P., Mockford, C., McIntosh, E., Davis, H. and Stewart-Brown, S. (2007) 'Role of home visiting in improving parenting and health in families at risk of abuse and neglect: Results of a multicentre randomised controlled trial and economic evaluation.' *Archives of Disease in Childhood: Education and Practice Edition 92*, 3, 229–233.

Barlow, J., Kirkpatrick, S., Stewart-Brown, S. and Davis, H. (2005) 'Hard-to-reach or out-of-reach? Reasons why women refuse to take part in early interventions.' *Children and Society 19*, 3, 199–210.

Barlow, J. and Schrader McMillan, A. (2010) *Safeguarding Children from Emotional Maltreatment: What Works?* London: Jessica Kingsley Publishers.

Barlow, J., Schrader McMillan, A., Smith, M., Ghate, D. and Barnes, J. (2008) *Health-Led Parenting Interventions in Pregnancy and Early Years*. Research Report DCSF-RWO70. London: Department for Children, Schools and Families.

Barlow, J. with Scott, J. (2010) *Safeguarding in the 21st Century: Where to Now?* London: Research in Practice.

Barlow, J. and Underdown, A. (2008) 'Attachment and Infant Development.' In C. Jackson, K. Hill and P. Lavis (eds) *Child and Adolescent Mental Health Today: A Handbook*. Brighton: Pavilion Publishing/Mental Health Foundation.

Barnard, M. (2007) *Drug Addiction and Families*. London: Jessica Kingsley Publishers.

Berridge, D. and Cleaver, H. (1987) *Foster Home Breakdown*. Oxford: Blackwell.

Biehal, N., Ellison, S., Baker, C. and Sinclair, I. (2010) *Belonging and Permanence: Outcomes in Long-Term Foster Care and Adoption*. London: British Association for Adoption and Fostering.

Biehal, N. and Parry, E. (2010) *Maltreatment and Allegations of Maltreatment in Foster Care: A Review of the Evidence*. York: Social Policy Research Unit, University of York.

Boddy, J. and Oliver, C. (2010) *Research Governance in Children's Services: Scoping to Inform the Development of Guidance. Final Report*. London: Department for Children, Schools and Families.

Brandon, M., Bailey, S., Belderson, P., Gardner, R. *et al.* (2009) *Understanding Serious Case Reviews and their Impact. A Biennial Analysis of Serious Case Reviews 2005–7.* DCSF-RR129. London: Department for Children, Schools and Families.

Brandon, M., Belderson, P., Warren, C., Howe, D. *et al.* (2008) *Analysing Child Deaths and Serious Injury through Abuse and Neglect: What Can We Learn? A Biennial Analysis of Serious Case Reviews 2003–5.* DCSF-RR023. London: Department for Children, Schools and Families.

Brandon, M., Howe, A., Dagley, V., Salter, C. and Warren, C. (2006) 'What appears to be helping or hindering practitioners in implementing the Common Assessment Framework and Lead Professional Working?' *Child Abuse Review Special Edition: Integrated Services for Children 15,* 396–413.

Brandon, M., Sidebotham, P., Ellis, C., Bailey, S. and Belderson, P. (2011) *Child and Family Practitioners' Understanding of Child Development: Lessons Learnt from a Small Sample of Serious Case Reviews.* London: Department for Education.

Brooks-Gunn, J., Klebanov, P.K. and Liaw, F. (1995) 'The learning, physical, and emotional environment of the home in the context of poverty: The Infant Health and Development Program.' *Children and Youth Services Review 17,* 251–276.

Brown, R. and Ward, H. (forthcoming (a)) *Issues Raised in Using the IT-HOME Inventory in a Research Setting.* Loughborough: Centre for Child and Family Research, Loughborough University.

Brown, R. and Ward, H. (forthcoming (b)) *Dependable, Disengaged or Dangerous: The Role of Fathers in Decision-Making for Infants Suffering, or Likely to Suffer, Significant Harm.* Loughborough: Centre for Child and Family Research, Loughborough University.

Caldwell, B.M. and Bradley, R.H. (2003) *Home Observation for Measurement of the Environment: Administration Manual.* Little Rock, Ark: University of Arkansas.

Chisholm, K., Carter, M.C., Ames, E.W. and Morison, S.J. (1995) 'Attachment security and indiscriminately friendly behavior in children adopted from Romanian orphanages.' *Development and Psychopathology 7,* 283–294.

Chugani, D.C., Muzik, O., Behan, M., Rothermel, R. *et al.* (2001) 'Developmental changes in brain serotonin synthesis capacity in autistic and nonautistic children.' *Annals of Neurology 45,* 3, 287–295.

Cleaver, H., Nicholson, D., Tarr, S. and Cleaver, D. (2007) *Child Protection, Domestic Violence and Parental Substance Misuse.* London: Jessica Kingsley Publishers.

Cleaver, H., Unell, I. and Aldgate, J. (2011) *Children's Needs – Parenting Capacity: The Impact of Parental Mental Illness, Learning Disability, Substance Misuse, and Domestic Violence on Children's Safety and Development* (2nd Edition). London: The Stationery Office.

Cleaver, H. and Walker, S. with Meadows, P. (2004) *Assessing Children's Needs and Circumstances: The Impact of the Assessment Framework.* London: Jessica Kingsley Publishers.

Cleaver, H., Walker, S., Scott, J., Cleaver, D. *et al.* (2008) *The Integrated Children's System: Enhancing Social Work and Inter-Agency Practice.* London: Jessica Kingsley Publishers.

Coleman, R. and Cassell, D. (1995) 'Parents who Misuse Drugs and Alcohol.' In P. Reder and C. Lucey (eds) *Assessment of Parenting: Psychiatric and Psychological Contributions.* London: Routledge.

Connell-Carrick, K. (2003) 'A critical review of the empirical literature: Identifying correlates of child neglect.' *Child and Adolescent Social Work Journal 20,* 5, 389–425.

Coram Family (2011) Unpublished, personal communication.

Courtney, M.E. and Needell, B. (1997) 'Outcomes of kinship care: Lessons from California.' In R.P. Barth, J.D. Berrick and N. Gilber (eds) *Child Welfare Research Review II.* Columbia, New York: University Press.

Cox, T. and Walker, S. (2001) *The HOME Inventory.* Brighton: Pavilion Publishing.

Currie, J. and Widom, C.S. (2010) 'Long-term consequences of child abuse and neglect on adult economic wellbeing.' *Child Maltreatment 15*, 2, 111–120.

Daniel, B. (2006) 'Early Childhood: Zero to Four Years.' In J. Aldgate, D. Jones, W. Rose and C. Jeffrey (eds) *The Developing World of the Child.* London: Jessica Kingsley Publishers.

Daniel, B., Taylor, J. and Scott, J. (2010) 'Recognition of neglect and early response: Overview of a systematic review of the literature.' *Child and Family Social Work 15*, 2, 248–257.

Daniel, B., Taylor, J. and Scott, J. (2011) *Noticing and Helping the Neglected Child: Evidence-Based Practice for Assessment and Intervention.* London: Jessica Kingsley Publishers.

Darker, I., Ward, H. and Caulfield, L.S. (2008) 'An analysis of offending in young people looked after by local authorities.' *Youth Justice 8*, 134–148.

Davies, C. and Ward, H. (2011) *Safeguarding Children Across Services: Messages from Research on Identifying and Responding to Child Maltreatment.* London: Jessica Kingsley Publishers.

Department for Children, Schools and Families (2009a) *Building a Safe Confident Future: The Final Report of the Social Work Task Force.* London: Department for Children, Schools and Families.

Department for Children, Schools and Families (2009b) *Referrals, Assessments and Children and Young People who are the Subject of a Child Protection Plan, England – Year Ending 31 March 2009.* Available at www.education.gov.uk/rsgateway/DB/SFR/s00873/index.shtml, accessed on 12 October 2011.

Department for Education (2010a) *Children in Need in England, including their Characteristics and Further Information on Children who were the Subject of a Child Protection Plan (2009–2010 Children in Need Census, Final).* London: Department for Education.

Department for Education (2010b) *Referrals, Assessments and Children who were the Subject of a Child Protection Plan (Children in Need Census, Provisional) – Year Ending 31 March 2010.* London: Department for Education.

Department for Education (2011a) *Characteristics of Children in Need in England, 2010–2011, Final.* London: Department for Education.

Department for Education (2011b) *Children Looked After by Local Authorities in England (including adoption and care leavers) - year ending 31 March 2011.* London: Department for Education.

Department for Education and Skills (2003) (Cm 5860) *Every Child Matters.* London: The Stationery Office.

Department for Education and Skills (2005) *Children Looked After by Local Authorities Year Ending 31 March 2004.* London: Department for Education and Skills.

Department for Education and Skills (2007) (Cm 7137) *Care Matters: Time for Change.* London: The Stationery Office.

Department of Health (1989) *An Introduction to the Children Act 1989.* London: HMSO.

Department of Health (1995) *Child Protection: Messages from Research.* London: The Stationery Office.

Department of Health (2000) *Protecting Children, Supporting Parents: A Consultation Document on the Physical Punishment of Children.* London: Department of Health.

Department of Health (2005a) *Personal Social Services Expenditure and Unit Costs (England) 2003–2004.* London: Department of Health.

Department of Health (2005b) *Research Governance Framework for Health and Social Care* (2nd Edition). London: Department of Health.

Department of Health, Department for Education and Employment and the Home Office (2000) *Framework for the Assessment of Children in Need and their Families.* London: The Stationery Office.

Falcov, A. (2002) 'Addressing Family Needs when a Parent is Mentally Ill.' In H. Ward and W. Rose (eds) *Approaches to Needs Assessment in Children's Services*. London: Jessica Kingsley Publishers.

Farmer, E. and Dance, C. with Beecham, J., Bonin, E. and Ouwejan, D. (2010) *An Investigation of Linking and Matching in Adoption – Briefing Paper*. London: Department for Education.

Farmer, E. and Lutman, E. (forthcoming) *Working Effectively with Neglected Children and their Families: Understanding their Experiences and Long-Term Outcomes*. London: Jessica Kingsley Publishers.

Farmer, E. and Moyers, S. (2008) *Fostering Effective Family and Friends Placements*. London: Jessica Kingsley Publishers.

Farmer, E. and Pollock, S. (1998) *Sexually Abused and Abusing Children in Substitute Care. Living Away from Home: Studies in Residential Care*. Chichester: Wiley.

Fauth, R., Jelicic, H., Hart, D., Burton, S. and Shemmings, D. (2010) *Effective Practice to Protect Children Living in 'Highly Resistant' Families*. London: C4EO.

Featherstone, B., Fraser, C., Lindley, B. and Ashley, C. (2010) *Fathers Matter: Resources for Social Work Educators*. London: Family Rights Group.

Forrester, D. (2008) 'Is the care system failing children?' *The Political Quarterly 79*, 2, 206–211.

Gerhardt, S. (2004) *Why Love Matters: How Affection Shapes the Baby's Brain*. London: Routledge.

Gilbert, R., Kemp, A., Thoburn, J., Sidebotham, P. *et al.* (2009) 'Child maltreatment 2: Recognising and responding to child maltreatment.' *Lancet 10*, 373, 167–180.

Glaser, D. (2002) 'Emotional abuse and neglect (psychological maltreatment): A conceptual framework.' *Child Abuse and Neglect 26*, 6/7, 697–714.

Gunnar, M.R., Morison, S.J., Chisholm, K. and Schuder, J. (2001) 'Salivary cortisol levels in children adopted from Romanian orphanages.' *Development and Psychopathology 12*, 611–628.

Hannon, C., Wood, C. and Bazalgette, L. (2010) *In Loco Parentis: To Deliver the Best for Looked After Children, the State must be a Confident Parent*. London: DEMOS.

Hardiker, P., Exton, K. and Barker, M. (1991) *Policies and Practices in Preventative Childcare*. Aldershot: Avebury.

Haringey Local Safeguarding Children Board (2010) *Serious Case Review: Child A. March 2009*. London: Department for Education.

Harwin, J. and Forrester, D. (2002) *Parental Substance Misuse and Child Welfare: A Study of Social Work with Families in which Parents Misuse Drugs or Alcohol*. London: Interim Report for the Nuffield Foundation.

Harwin, J., Ryan, M., Tunnard, J., Pokhrel, S. *et al.* (2011) *The Family Drug and Alcohol Court (FDAC) Evaluation Project: Final Report*. London: Nuffield Foundation and the Home Office.

Haugaard, J.J., Wojslawowicz, J.C. and Palmer, M. (1999) 'Outcomes in adolescent and older child adoptions.' *Adoption Quarterly 3*, 61–69.

Hearn, J., Poso, T., Smith, C., White, S. and Korpinen, J. (2004) 'What is child protection? Historical and methodological issues in comparative research on *lastensuojelu*/child protection.' *International Journal of Social Welfare 13*, 28–41.

Hemming, J. (2007) 'Expert witnesses: Case for the prosecution.' *Times Higher Education Supplement*. 29 June. Available at www.timeshighereducation.co.uk/story.asp?sectioncode=26&storycode=209518, accessed on 22 September 2011.

Hibbard, R.A. and Desch, L.W. (2007) 'Maltreatment of children with disabilities.' *Pediatrics 119*, 5, 1018–1025.

Hilpern, K. (2008) 'Unfit to be a mother?' *The Guardian*, 15 January.

Hindley, N., Ramchandani, P.G. and Jones, D.P.H. (2006) 'Risk factors for recurrence of maltreatment: A systematic review.' *Archives of Disease in Childhood 91*, 9, 744–752.

HM Government (2010) *Working Together to Safeguard Children: A Guide to Inter-Agency Working to Safeguard and Promote the Welfare of Children.* Nottingham: Department for Children, Schools and Families.

HM Government (2011) *No Health without Mental Health: A Cross-Government Mental Health Strategy for People of All Ages.* London: Department of Health.

Hogan, D. (1998) 'Annotation: The psychological development and welfare of children of opiate and cocaine users – review and research needs.' *Journal of Child Psychology and Psychiatry 39*, 609–619.

Holmes, L., Munro, E.R. and Soper, J. (2010) *Calculating the Cost and Capacity Implications for Local Authorities Implementing the Laming (2009) Recommendations.* London: Local Government Association.

Home Office (2002) *Statistics on Women and the Criminal Justice System.* London: Home Office.

House of Commons Children, Schools and Families Committee (2009) *Looked-After Children: Third Report of Session 2008–09.* London: The Stationery Office.

Howard, J., Beckwith, L., Espinosa, M. and Tyler, R. (1995) 'Development of infants born to cocaine-abusing women: Biological/maternal influences.' *Neurotoxicology and Teratology 17*, 4, 403–411.

Howe, D. (1998) *Patterns of Adoption: Nature, Nurture and Psychosocial Development.* Oxford: Blackwell Science.

Howe, D. (2005) *Child Abuse and Neglect: Attachment, Development and Intervention.* Basingstoke: Palgrave Macmillan.

Hughes, M., Church, J. and Zealey, L. (eds) (2009) *Social Trends 2009.* London: Palgrave Macmillan.

Humphreys, C. and Stanley, N. (eds) (2006) *Domestic Violence and Child Protection.* London: Jessica Kingsley Publishers.

Hunt, J., Waterhouse, S. and Lutman, E. (2008) *Keeping them in the Family: Children Placed in Kinship Care Through Care Proceedings.* London: BAAF.

Irish, L., Kobayashi, I. and Delahanty, D.L. (2009) 'Long-term physical health consequences of childhood sexual abuse: A meta-analytic review.' *Journal of Pediatric Psychology 35*, 5, 450–461.

Iwaniec, D. (1995) *The Emotionally Abused and Neglected Child.* Chichester: Wiley.

Jackson, S. and Thomas, N. (1999) *On the Move Again? What Works in Creating Stability for Looked After Children.* Essex: Barnardo's.

Jones, D. (1991) 'The Effectiveness of Intervention and the Significant Harm Criteria.' In M. Adcock, R. White and A. Hollows (eds) *Significant Harm.* Croydon: Significant Publications.

Jones, D. (1998) 'The Effectiveness of Intervention.' In M. Adcock and R. White (eds) *Significant Harm: Its Management and Outcome* (2nd Edition). Croydon: Significant Publications.

Jones, D. (2008) 'Child Maltreatment.' In M. Rutter, D. Bishop, D. Pine, S. Scott *et al.* (eds) *Rutter's Child and Adolescent Psychiatry.* Oxford: Blackwell.

Jones, D. (2009) 'Assessment of Parenting.' In J. Howarth (ed.) *The Child's World: The Comprehensive Guide to Assessing Children in Need* (2nd Edition). London: Jessica Kingsley Publishers.

Jones, D., Hindley, N. and Ramchandani, P. (2006) 'Making Plans: Assessment, Intervention and Evaluating Outcomes.' In J. Aldgate, D. Jones and C. Jeffery (eds) *The Developing World of the Child.* London: Jessica Kingsley Publishers.

Klee, H., Jackson, M. and Lewis, S. (2002) *Drug Misuse and Motherhood.* London: Routledge.

Kroll, B. and Taylor, B. (2003) *Parental Substance Misuse and Child Welfare.* London: Jessica Kingsley Publishers.

Laming, Lord (2003) (Cm 5730) *The Victoria Climbié Inquiry: Report of an Inquiry by Lord Laming.* London: The Stationery Office.

Laming, Lord (2009) (HC 330) *The Protection of Children in England: A Progress Report.* London: The Stationery Office.

Law Society (2010) *Good Practice in Child Care Cases: A Guide for Solicitors Acting in Public Law Children Act Proceedings* (2nd Edition). London: The Law Society.

Leslie, B. (2005) 'Housing Issues in Child Welfare: A Practice Response with Service and Policy Implications.' In J. Scott and H. Ward (eds) *Safeguarding and Promoting the Wellbeing of Children, Families and Communities.* London: Jessica Kingsley Publishers.

Lewis, M., Feiring, C., McGuffoy, C. and Jaskir, J. (1984) 'Predicting psychopathology in six year olds from early social relations.' *Child Development 55,* 123–136.

Lloyd-Selby, M. (2008) 'When it comes to adoption, the rights of the child are foremost.' *The Guardian.* 24 January.

Lord Chancellor's Department (2002) *Scoping Study on Delay in Children Act Cases.* London: The Stationery Office.

MacMillan, H.L., Wathen, C.N., Barlow, J., Fergusson, D.M. *et al.* (2009) 'Child maltreatment 3: Interventions to prevent child maltreatment and associated impairment.' *The Lancet 373,* 9659, 250–266.

Maguire, S., Mann, M.K., Sibert, J. and Kemp, A. (2005) 'Are there patterns of bruising in childhood which are diagnostic or suggestive of abuse? A systematic review.' *Archive of Diseases in Childhood 90,* 2, 182–186.

Malinosky-Rummell, R. and Hansen, D.J. (1993) 'Long term consequences of childhood physical abuse.' *Psychological Bulletin 114,* 68–79.

Marks, K. (2009) *Lost Paradise: From Mutiny on the Bounty to a Modern-Day Legacy of Sexual Mayhem. The Dark Secrets of Pitcairn Island Revealed.* New York: Free Press.

Masson, J., Pearce, J., Bader, K., Joyner, O., Marsden, J. and Westlake, D. (2008) *Care Profiling Study: Research Summary 1.* London: Ministry of Justice.

McBurnett, K., Lahey, B.B., Rathouz, P.J. and Loeber, R. (2000) 'Low salivary cortisol and persistent aggression in boys referred for disruptive behavior.' *Archives of General Psychiatry 57,* 38–43.

McConnell, D. and Llewellyn, G. (2002) 'Stereotypes, parents with intellectual disability and child protection.' *Journal of Social Welfare and Family Law 24,* 3, 297–317.

Moe, V. and Slinning, K. (2003) 'Parental drug exposure and the conceptualisations of long-term effects.' *Scandinavian Journal of Psychology 43,* 41–47.

Monck, E., Reynolds, J. and Wigfall, V. (2003) *The Role of Concurrent Planning: Making Permanent Placements for Young Children.* London: BAAF.

Montgomery, P., Gardner, F. and Bjornstad, G. (2009) *Systematic Reviews of Interventions following Physical Abuse: Helping Practitioners and Expert Witnesses Improve the Outcomes of Child Abuse.* London: Department for Children, Schools and Families.

Morgan, R. (2008) *Children's Care Monitor 2008: Children's Views on How Care is Doing. A Report by the Children's Rights Director.* London: OFSTED.

Munro, E. (2011) (Cm 8062) *The Munro Review of Child Protection: Final Report. A Child-Centred System.* London: Department for Education.

Munro, E.R. (2008) 'Research governance, ethics and access: A case study illustrating the new challenges facing social researchers.' *International Journal of Social Research Methodology 11,* 5, 429–439.

Munro, E.R., Brown, R., Sempik, J. and Ward, H. (2011) *Scoping Review to Draw Together Data on Child Injury and Safeguarding and to Compare the Position of England and the UK with that in Other Countries: Report to Department for Education.* London: Department for Education.

Munro, E.R., Holmes, L. and Ward, H. (2005) 'Researching vulnerable groups: Ethical issues and the effective conduct of research in local authorities.' *British Journal of Social Work 35,* 1023–1038.

Murphy, M. and Ingram, S. (2008) *Residential Care and Substance Misuse: Exploring the Relationship.* Outcome-Network.org. Available at www.outcome-network.org/paper/44:residential_care_and_substance_misuse_exploring_the_relationship, accessed on 22 September 2011.

Neil, E. (2000) 'The reasons why young children are placed for adoption: Findings from a recently placed sample and a discussion of implications for subsequent identity development.' *Child and Family Social Work 5,* 4, 303–316.

Neil, E. (2007) 'Coming to terms with the loss of a child: The feelings of birth parents and grandparents about adoption and post-adoption contact.' *Adoption Quarterly 10,* 1. Available at www.tandfonline.com/toc/wado20/10/1, accessed on 12 October 2011.

Neil, E., Cossar, J., Lorgelly, P. and Young, J. (2010) *Helping Birth Families: Services, Costs and Outcomes.* London: British Association for Adoption and Fostering (BAAF).

Newcomb, M.D. and Felix-Ortiz, M. (1992) 'Multiple protective and risk factors for drug use and abuse: Cross-sectional and prospective findings.' *Journal of Personality and Social Psychology 63,* 280–296.

Newton, R.R., Litrownik, A.J. and Landsverk, J.A. (2000) 'Children and youth in foster care: Disentangling the relationship between problem behaviors and number of placements.' *Child Abuse and Neglect 24,* 1363–1374.

Noll, J.G., Trickett, P.K., Harris, W.W. and Putnam, T.W. (2009) 'The cumulative burden borne by offspring whose mothers were sexually abused as children: Descriptive results from a multigenerational study.' *Journal of Interpersonal Violence 24,* 3, 424–449.

Norgrove, D. (2011) *Family Justice Review: Final Report.* London: Ministry of Justice, the Department for Education and the Welsh Government.

Office of the Tánaiste (1997) *Report of the Task Force on Violence Against Women.* Dublin: Stationery Office.

O'Hagan, K. (2006) *Identifying Emotional and Psychological Abuse: A Guide for Childcare Professionals.* Berkshire: Open University Press.

Parton, N. (2006) *Safeguarding Childhood: Early Intervention and Surveillance in a Late Modern Society.* Basingstoke: Palgrave Macmillan.

Peters, J. (2005) 'True ambivalence: Child welfare workers' thoughts, feelings, and beliefs about kinship foster care.' *Children and Youth Services Review 27,* 6, 595–614.

President of the Family Division (2008) *The Public Law Outline.* London: President's Office. Available at www.judiciary.gov.uk/NR/rdonlyres/A61353A8-AD84-491F-9614-5A95F1A90837/0/public_law_outline.pdf, accessed on 22 September 2011.

Putallaz, M., Costanzo, P.R., Grimes, C.L. and Lipton, D. (1998) 'Intergenerational continuities and their influences on children's social development.' *Social Development 7,* 389–427.

Radford, L., Corral, S., Bradley, C., Fisher, H. *et al.* (2011) *The Maltreatment and Victimisation of Children in the UK: NSPCC Report on a National Survey of Young People's, Young Adults' and Caregivers' Experiences.* London: NSPCC.

Rushton, A. (2003) 'A scoping and scanning review of research on the adoption of children placed from public care.' *Clinical Child Psychology and Psychiatry 9,* 1, 89–106.

Rutter, M. (2000) 'Children in substitute care: Some conceptual considerations and research implications.' *Children and Youth Services Review 22,* 685–703.

Rutter, M. and Rutter, M. (1993) *Developing Minds: Challenge and Continuity Across the Lifespan.* Harmondsworth, Middlesex: Penguin Books; New York: Basic Books.

Ryan, M. (2000) *Working with Fathers.* Abingdon: Radcliffe.

Schore, A. (2003) *Affect Dysregulation and Disorder of the Self.* New York: Norton.

Schore, A. (2010) 'Relational Trauma and the Developing Right Brain: The Neurobiology of Broken Attachment Bonds.' In T. Baradon (ed.) *Relational Trauma in Infancy: Psychoanalytic, Attachment and Neuropsychological Contributions to Parent–Infant Psychotherapy.* New York: Routledge.

Selwyn, J., Quinton, D., Harris, P., Wijedasa, D., Nawaz, S. and Wood, M. (2010) *Pathways to Permanence for Black, Asian and Mixed Ethnicity Children.* London: British Association for Adoption and Fostering (BAAF).

Selwyn, J.T., Sturgess, W., Quinton, D.L. and Baxter, C. (2006) *Costs and Outcomes of Non-Infant Adoptions.* London: British Association for Adoption and Fostering (BAAF).

Sergeant, H. (2006) *Handle with Care.* London: Centre for Policy Studies.

Sinclair, I., Baker, C., Lee, J. and Gibbs, I. (2007) *The Pursuit of Permanence: A Study of the English Child Care System.* London: Jessica Kingsley Publishers.

Sinclair, I. and Gibbs, I. (1998) *Children's Homes: A Study in Diversity.* London: Wiley.

Skuse, T. and Ward, H. (2003) *Outcomes for Looked After Children: Children's Views, the Importance of Listening. An Interim Report to the Department of Health.* Loughborough: Centre for Child and Family Research, Loughborough University.

Smith, D. and Brodzinsky, D.M. (2002) 'Coping with birthparent loss in adopted children.' *Journal of Child Psychology and Psychiatry 43,* 213–223.

Stanley, N., Cleaver, H. and Hart, D. (2009) 'The Impact of Domestic Violence, Parental Mental Health Problems, Substance Misuse and Learning Difficulties on Parenting Capacity.' In J. Howarth (ed.) *The Child's World* (2nd Edition). London: Jessica Kingsley Publishers.

Stein, M. and Munro, E.R. (eds) (2008) *Young People's Transitions from Care to Adulthood: International Research and Practice.* London: Jessica Kingsley Publishers.

Stein, M., Ward, H. and Courtney, M. (eds) (2011) Special Issue on Young People's Transitions from Care to Adulthood. *Children and Youth Services Review 33,* 12, 2409–2540.

Sullivan, P. and Knutson, J. (2000) 'Maltreatment and disabilities: A population-based epidemiological study.' *Child Abuse and Neglect 24,* 10, 1257–1273.

Tannenbaum, L. and Forehand, R. (1994) 'Maternal depressive mood: The role of the father in preventing adolescent problem behaviours.' *Behaviour Research and Therapy 32,* 321–325.

Thoburn, J. (2002) *Adoption and Permanence for Children who Cannot Live Safely with Birth Parents or Relatives.* Quality Protects Research Briefing 5. London: Department of Health/Making Research Count/Research in Practice.

Thoburn, J. (2005) 'Stability through Adoption for Children in Care.' In N. Axford, V. Berry, M. Little and L. Morpeth (eds) *Forty Years of Research, Policy and Practice: A Festschrift for Roger Bullock.* Chichester: Wiley.

Thomas, C. (forthcoming) *Overview of the Findings from the Adoption Research Initiative.* London: British Association for Adoption and Fostering (BAAF).

Tompsett, H., Ashworth, M., Atkins, C., Bell, L. *et al.* (2009) *The Child, the Family and the GP: Tensions and Conflicts of Interest in Safeguarding Children.* London: Department for Children, Schools and Families.

Totsika, V. and Sylva, K. (2004) 'The Home Observation for Measurement of the Environment revisited.' *Child and Adolescent Mental Health 9,* 1, 25–35.

Tunnard, J. (2002) *Parental Problem Drinking and its Impact on Children.* Dartington: Research in Practice.

Van den Dries, L., Juffer, F., Van IJzendoorn, M.H. and Bakermans-Kranenburg, M.J. (2009) 'Fostering security? A meta-analysis of attachment in adopted children.' *Children and Youth Services Review 31,* 410–421.

Van IJzendoorn, M.H., Schuengel, C. and Bakermans-Kranenburg, M.J. (1999) 'Disorganized attachment in early childhood: Meta-analysis of precursors, concomitants, and sequelae.' *Development and Psychopathology 11,* 225–249.

Velleman, R. (1993) *Alcohol and the Family.* London: Institute of Alcohol Studies.

Wade, J., Biehal, N., Clayden, J. and Stein, M. (1998) *Going Missing: Young People Absent from Care.* Chichester: Wiley.

Wade, J., Biehal, N., Farrelly, N. and Sinclair, I. (2011) *Caring for Abused and Neglected Children: Making the Right Decisions for Reunification or Long-Term Care.* London: Jessica Kingsley Publishers.

Wade, J., Dixon, J. and Richards, A. (2010) *Special Guardianship in Practice.* London: British Association for Adoption and Fostering (BAAF).

Wand, G.S., McCaul, M.E., Gotjen, D., Reynolds, J. and Lee, S. (2001) 'Confirmation that offspring from families with alcohol-dependent individuals have greater hypothalamic-pituitary-adrenal axis activation induced by naloxone compared with offspring without a family history of alcohol dependence.' *Alcoholism: Clinical and Experimental Research 25,* 1134–1139.

Ward, H. (2009) 'Patterns of instability. Moves within the English care system: Their reasons, contexts and consequences.' *Child and Youth Services Review 31,* 1113–1118.

Ward, H. (forthcoming) *Separating Families: How the Origins of Current Child Welfare Policy and Practice can be Traced to the Nineteenth Century Child Rescue Movement.* London: Jessica Kingsley Publishers.

Ward, H., Brown, R.C. and Maskell-Graham, D. (forthcoming) *Young Children Suffering, or Likely to Suffer, Significant Harm: Experiences on Entering Education.* Loughborough: Centre for Child and Family Research, Loughborough University.

Ward, H., Holmes, L., Munro, E., Moyers, S. and Poursanidou, K. (2004) *Safeguarding Children: A Scoping Study of Research in Three Areas. Report to the Department for Education and Skills.* Loughborough: Centre for Child and Family Research, Loughborough University.

Ward, H., Holmes, L. and Soper, J. (2008) *Costs and Consequences of Placing Children in Care.* London: Jessica Kingsley Publishers.

Ward, H. and Munro, E. (2010) 'Very Young Children in Care in England: Issues for Foster Care.' In E. Fernandez and R. Barth (eds) *How Does Foster Care Work? International Evidence of Outcomes.* London: Jessica Kingsley Publishers.

Ward, H., Munro, E.R. and Dearden, C. (2006) *Babies and Young Children in Care: Life Pathways, Decision-Making and Practice.* London: Jessica Kingsley Publishers.

Ward, H. and Peel, M. (2002) 'An Inter-Agency Approach to Needs Assessment.' In H. Ward and W. Rose (eds) *Approaches to Needs Assessment in Children's Services.* London: Jessica Kingsley Publishers.

Ward, H., Skuse, T. and Munro, E.R. (2005) 'The best of times, the worst of times: Young people's views of care and accommodation.' *Adoption and Fostering 29,* 1, 8–17.

Waylen, A., Stallard, N. and Stewart-Brown, S. (2008) 'Parenting and health in mid-childhood: A longitudinal study.' *European Journal of Public Health 18,* 3, 300–305.

Williams, F. and Churchill, H. (2006) *Empowering Parents in Sure Start Local Programmes.* London: Department for Children, Schools and Families.

List of Cases

K & T v. *Finland* (App no 25702/94) ECHR 16 July 2001; 2 FLR 673.

R (on the application of L and others) v. *Manchester City Council*; R *(on the application of R and another)* v. *Same* [2001] EWHC Admin 707, CO/3954/2000, CO/965/2001.

Subject Index

Page numbers in *italics* refer to tables.

adoption
  delayed 113–14
  developmental issues 21–2
  legal perspectives 150–1, 156–7
  outcomes 23–6, 27–8
  see also placement away from home
Adoption and Chidren Act 2002 30
Adoption Orders 108, 109
Adoption Research Initiative 31
adult services 180–1
age
  at identification 39
  three, position of children at 95–7
alcohol and drug misuse, parental 15, 55–6
  development of insight 134–5
  during pregnancy 19, 41, 55, 79
  and housing 62
  insufficient change 125–6
  sufficient change, timing of 136
  support workers
    information sharing 154
    parents' perspective 180–1
    referral from 78–80
assessments
  core/section 47 enquiries 83–90
    information collected 84–5
    initial and 11–12, 76–7
    outcomes 85–92

reasons for 83–4
local authority *vs* independent 152
specialist/expert 155–9
  and delay 160–3, 206–7
  psychological 135
  reliability of recommendations 159–60
attachment 18–21, 108–9
  alcohol and drug misuse 56

behavioural/emotional difficulties 20, 139–44
brain and emotional development 18–23

Care Orders 105, 165–6
care proceedings 150–3, 156–7, 158–9, 187–8
checks and balances 171–5
Children Act 1989 15–16, 28–9, 90, 150, 151, 157, 165
  see also assessments, core/ section 47 enquiries
Children Act 2004 29
children (study sample)
  characteristics 38–41
  evidence of maltreatment 41–6
  types and experience of abuse 46–8
children's services 181–2
Climbié, Victoria 29
complex cases 46, 59–60
Connelly, Peter 29, 152, 175
core assessments *see* assessments, core/ section 47 enquiries
cortisol levels 19, 20
cultural issues/ethnicity 38, 65, 189–90

decision-making 14–17, 97–8
  inter-agency working 85–6
  timing 99
  types 98
delay 206
  assessments and 160–3, 206–7
  developmental 139–44
  later separations 110–14
developmental issues 18–23
  delayed 139–44
  health, disabilities and 40–1
  insufficient parental change 142–4
  sufficient parental change 144
disabilities 40–1
double jeopardy: late separations 110–14

education and training 205, 211–12
emotional abuse 20–1, 45
Emotional Abuse and Neglect Checklist 155
emotional development *see* developmental issues
empowerment, parents' rights and 150–2, 206, 209
ethnicity/cultural issues 38, 65, 189–90
European Court of Human Rights judgements 151
expert assessments *see* assessments, specialist/ expert
extended family *see* kinship care
external and internal risk factors 125–9

236

Author Index